ANOTHER WORLD IS POSSIBLE

GEOFF MULGAN

Another World Is Possible

How to Reignite Social and Political Imagination

HURST & COMPANY, LONDON

First published in the United Kingdom in 2022 by
C. Hurst & Co. (Publishers) Ltd.,
New Wing, Somerset House, Strand, London, WC2R 1LA
© Geoff Mulgan, 2022
All rights reserved.

A Cataloguing-in-Publication data record for this book
is available from the British Library.

ISBN: 9781787386914

This book is printed using paper from registered sustainable
and managed sources.

www.hurstpublishers.com

Printed in Great Britain by Bell and Bain Ltd, Glasgow

CONTENTS

v

CONTENTS

INTRODUCTION

This is a book about imagination. Its focus isn't imagination in the arts or sciences, or the imaginative worlds of fiction and poetry. Instead, it's about how we might imagine a better society, one with less unhappiness, poverty, violence and ecological harm, as a first step to making it happen.

Many now fear the future, visualised more readily in the dark terms of apocalypse than as a place of hope. Horizons have shrunk. Novelists and filmmakers seem far more at home with dystopias than with the possibility that the world might get better. The institutions that once fuelled our shared imagination have, for different reasons, given up, leaving public intellectual culture recycling old ideas, while much of politics has drifted into nostalgia.

Yet this is a time when we desperately need more creativity to cope with the multiple crises swirling around us—crises of trust, climate, equality and much more. Old attitudes and ideas simply aren't adequate to help us navigate what lies ahead. And pervasive gloom about the future risks being self-fulfilling.

This book aims to help reverse these trends. It looks at the lessons to be learned from past attempts to imagine utopias, advocate ideas or create model communities, as well as what we can take from their successes and failures. It shows the many methods that can be used to imagine and then to turn dreams into reality, with sufficient humility to learn along the way.

At the heart of the book is a way of understanding the codes that lie behind complex patterns of social change. Once we grasp these, we can more easily reimagine and redesign the social world around us—from schools, workplaces and neighbourhoods to social media, healthcare and democracy—cultivating the skill of looking at things not only in terms of what they are, but also what they *could* be.

The book focuses on a simple question: how could we become better at imagining the society in which we might like to live a generation or two from now? It draws on literature from the social sciences, the arts, philosophy and history, but also on a lifetime's involvement in making ideas real—working top down in the heart of government; working bottom up with hundreds of social entrepreneurs and innovators; and working in digital technology during a period when it was being used to transform so many fields. It is designed to be an antidote to fatalism—to remind us that other worlds are possible.

The imaginary crisis

Over the last two centuries, many looked ahead to the future and expected that at some point, humanity would reach a more perfect steady state, a promised land, a world of peace, prosperity and kindness. Yet today, however far into the future our imaginations stretch, we are more likely to believe that the road will be paved with disasters, cycles rather than progress, and downfalls more than improvements.

This suspicion may well be justified. However, a piece of family history makes me sceptical of such apparently rational pessimism. A cousin of mine, John Mulgan, was a well-known writer in 1930s New Zealand and author of the iconic book *Man Alone*, set amidst the political conflict of the Great Depression. During the Second World War, after fighting in the Battle of El Alamein, he was sent to Greece and put in charge of coordinating the resistance against the Nazis in one region. There he was awarded the Military Cross. Then, aged thirty-three, just as the war came to an end, John killed himself with a morphine overdose in Cairo, apparently disillusioned and pessimistic about the world's prospects (partly because the British were restoring the discredited Greek monarchy). At that time, the future seemed unbearably bleak.

Yet I was brought up to see 1945 as one of the great years of hope, when much of Europe and Asia was liberated from oppression and when Britain began to create a welfare state. From this story, I therefore conclude that our personal sense of pessimism or optimism about the future will likely never be accurate. We may be inclined to hope when we should despair, and we may despair when in retrospect we should have been hopeful. On balance, we should always choose hope over fear. We may be wrong, but at least hope is productive (and there are worse things in life than disappointment).

This thought came to me early in 2020, as I found myself talking to a group of teenage eco-activists. They came from all over the world, from Canada to Morocco, Sweden to Korea. All had been involved in what had become the extraordinary worldwide movement of school strikes for the climate. They'd spent the previous months travelling to each other's countries, sleeping on floors and talking passionately into the night. They were eloquent and impressive.

When I was a teenager, I was quite like them: furiously active in political campaigns of all kinds. I couldn't bear the unfairness I saw all around me, the complacency and smug satisfaction of the rich and powerful. I took for granted that I could, somehow, be part of fixing what was wrong, even if then I had only the dimmest idea of how to do it.

But whereas the activism I'd been raised on was fuelled by hope, what struck me most about these young people was their profound pessimism. They wanted humanity to avert disaster, but, despite politicians announcing Green Deals of many kinds, they had little hope that their societies could become much better.

Their gloominess got under my skin, and I started having similar conversations with people from different backgrounds and in different parts of the world, asking them to describe a plausible, desirable society thirty or forty years in the future. I found that people had no trouble imagining catastrophes, from the extinction of the human race to domination by robots or the triumph of demagogues. But they too found it hard to imagine positive alternatives; it was almost impossible to conceive of their own children living in a better world, for example one with far lower incidence of mental illness, or in which poverty really had been eliminated.

I've found a strikingly similar pattern among political leaders, academics, NGO workers, businesspeople and young high-fliers, and not just in Europe and North America. Young people that I met in Africa were generally quite optimistic, but here too, despite burgeoning science-fiction scenes, dynamic hubs of digital innovation and lively political magazines, there was little debate about ideas that the rest of the world might want to copy in the future. Even in China, a country with good reason to believe it might dominate the twenty-first century economically, culturally and politically, I came upon a surprising dearth of creative imagination. Among the young people I spoke to, the same patterns reoccurred: there was a willingness to talk about technological futures; a deep anxiety about existential collapse; and an almost complete incapacity to describe how their society might evolve in the years to come.[1]

When I asked many leading thinkers what methods they used to fuel their imagination, few could offer a coherent answer, and whole disciplines, like economics, seemed to lack any means of thinking a generation or two into the future. This prompted me to review many of the hundreds of books published each year on society, economics and politics. While many offer a striking diagnosis, most offer little in the way of prescription, which is usually left to a final chapter. I was also struck by another pattern: that the world's most visible public intellectuals today more often revive or reassert old ideas, rather than generating new ones. The result is that old zombie orthodoxies survive far longer than they should.

Politics echoes this. The 2020 US presidential election was not just a battle between two septuagenarians. It was also a battle in which neither even attempted to set out an ambitious programme for the future.[2]

I'm convinced that we're suffering from an 'imaginary crisis'. By this, I don't mean that the various crises around us aren't real, but rather that there's a deep malaise affecting our capacity for imagination, whether social or political. We can more easily imagine the end of the world than a better future. The places that once were sources of exciting new ideas—universities, think tanks and political parties—for the most part no longer produce them. A sullen depression has swept over elites, commentators and much of the public, and you're more likely to get a hearing if you try to explain why progress is so difficult, or why decay, collapse and decline are likely, than if you attempt the opposite.

Some of the most motivated activists have become convinced that truly apocalyptic disaster lies ahead, a collapse of not just ecological systems but also societies. A fascinating open letter from one of the founders of the Extinction Rebellion movement exemplifies this. Climate change, Roger Hallam wrote, 'means the slaughter of young men and the rape of young women on a global scale ... 6 or more billion people will have been killed through mental illness, starvation or slaughtered in wars. ... If you don't feel the terror and horror of what is to come, then you soon will, and then you will feel the rage, the hatred, and then despair.'[3]

Hallam may have a point, but in his desire to spark urgent action, he risks paralysing it. All my experience tells me that such a level of fatalism isn't realistic; we can, up to a point, design and choose the society we wish to live in. Besides, there have been few moments in history when we have needed creativity more—to work out how to get to net zero carbon emissions and avert climate change; how to cope with ageing populations; how to reverse deep inequalities; and how to ensure that our lives are enriched, not harmed, by new technologies. We need creativity to do the long overdue work of redefining the social contracts that any society depends on—not least the freedoms and responsibilities of companies, banks, tech giants and others whose power and wealth have exploded in recent years.

I've seen so many ideas move from being impossible to becoming everyday realities that I find fatalism hard to stomach. Gay marriage; carbon markets; governments committed to happiness as a more important goal than GDP; cities where the people, and even children, make decisions about public spending; global corporate minimum taxes... these are just a few examples. In my own career, too, I've seen the pattern repeatedly. I helped oversee some of the UK's first carbon reduction strategies in the early 2000s; for all their inadequacies, these helped to cut the country's greenhouse gas emissions by 2020 to nearly 50 per cent below 1990 levels and to boost renewables to nearly half of all electricity production—against all expectations.[4] I was involved in projects that largely eliminated street homelessness, halved the rates of teenage pregnancy and sharply cut child poverty—again, against expectations. I've been closely involved in growing global fields of social innovation and the theory and practice of collective intelligence, working with hundreds of people to solve and transcend pressing problems. Throughout my career, I've learned that with the right mix of determination, focus and patience, change is possible. World-weary realism often turns out to be extraordinarily unrealistic.

This matters because many signs point to ours being a time of profound transition. It could be a transition away from an era in which power has been monopolised by white, rich, educated men (and, in other parts of the world, by rich, educated, Brahmin or Han men, or men from a few ruling families in the Middle East or Latin America) towards a world where decision-making is more truly democratic. It could be a transition away from a high-waste, high-consumption economy towards a radically different, sustainable pathway. Such shifts could permanently change our world for the better.

But nothing is guaranteed. History can get stuck and can go into reverse. Powerful interests will do whatever they can to resist, divert, confuse or disrupt trends that they find threatening.

Imagination is one of the weapons with which to confront them—imagination that is compelling, rigorous and thought through. Extinction Rebellion put the point well (and more positively than the letter I just quoted): 'We need to rewild our imagination. We must learn how to dream again, and we have to learn that together.'

But how? To find the answers, I went on a journey of exploration. I wanted to find out what we could learn from the past. Did the most useful ideas come fully formed or half-formed? From the lived experiments of new towns and communes or from philosophers and theorists? How did the world translate these dreams and visions into the reality of daily life? What role do the arts play? Was the poet Percy Bysshe Shelley right to believe that poets are the unacknowledged legislators of the world, or the artist Joseph Beuys right to claim, 'Only art is capable of dismantling the repressive effects of a senile social system that continues to totter along the deathline'?[5] What is the contribution of fiction? And how can the social sciences not only interpret the present and past but also shape the future?

In this book I share what I found. Although imagination is messy and fragmentary, I've found many patterns that we can make use of. I highlight that all novel inventions extend, invert or combine existing ideas; imagination is never a tabula rasa. Instead, our minds play with what's around us, building on already familiar concepts, and we can choose to do this more systematically.

I show that we can distinguish what I call 'thick' imagination from 'thin' imagination. Thin imagination is vague and partial, whereas thick imagination combines ideas, philosophy, programmes and detailed implementation. Most influential ideas achieve their impact by becoming thick in this sense, as well as through repetition.

I argue that we can distinguish imaginaries that feed off the frontiers of thought—in art, science and ideas—from imaginaries that look backward, and I suggest that the most powerful of all are dialectical, going both with and against the grain of powerful trends in political economy and technology. Indeed, it is this ability to grasp and challenge at the same time, to sense directions of change while simultaneously trying to shift and shape them, that makes imagination both most useful and most exciting.

The methods I describe are ones we can use to explore our own possible futures and utopias, as well as those of our families, communities, towns, cities and nations, or indeed of our planet. They are methods that should be widely understood because to be fully human is to be aware not just of where we have come from, but also of where we might be going.

I reach some surprising conclusions. It's better to prefer incompleteness over completeness; capacious imagination instead of futures that are too specific or neat; and experimentation and exploration over visions and blueprints. I'm sceptical of overly coherent utopias or the belief that societies follow simple logics.

Instead, I see the work of imagination (and the life of real societies) as a bricolage of diverse elements.

I argue that we need to learn how to combine creativity with depth of knowledge, which means mobilising academic disciplines and universities as well as activists. I show that although imagination is part of our nature, it also needs to be worked at. So, I advocate new roles for museums and galleries, suggesting how they could showcase alternative futures just as they tell us about our past. I make the case for universities to play a much more active role in thinking ahead, through what I call 'exploratory social science'. I argue for teaching politicians how to better grasp and shape the future and decry the odd assumption (in the West at least) that being a politician is the only serious professional role that requires no formal training or preparation.

I also address the odd paradoxes of social imagination, as well as the psychological challenge of working in this area. We can imagine almost anything, but only a tiny fraction of what we imagine can become real. There is no easy way to verify how much change is possible. Hard-nosed realists may be right much of the time, but then, periodically, they become dramatically wrong. Wild-eyed visionaries may be wrong much of the time, but occasionally they become dramatically right. Only in retrospect is it possible to judge which ideas were crazy and which were wise, and it is only through working on the world, pushing, prodding and testing its plasticity, that we begin to discover which other worlds are possible.

I also explore the links between imagination and consciousness. Even though it is extraordinarily hard to predict how consciousness might develop in the future, any picture of progress in society and politics has to involve some progress in how we think and feel: an escape from illusions and delusions, attachments and symbols that no longer serve us well, towards some deeper and more accurate truths. Much of what we count as progress has been a progress in consciousness of just this kind—progress in our knowledge of the cosmos and its life forms, progress in how we understand race, gender, sexuality, nature and much more— rather than just a progress in material technology and machines. This is very easy to see in retrospect, but it's much harder to see clearly in advance. Despite the many wrongs committed in past attempts to change human nature, this kind of progress is surely what we should aspire to, to rein in the bad and reinforce the good of our natures rather than seeing them as immutable.

I hope that the journey taken in this book will inspire readers to see—and act—in a different way. Its essential message is simple. As the late David Graeber put it, 'the ultimate, hidden truth of the world is that it is something that we make and could just as easily make differently'.[6] An architect looking at an empty plot can't help but envisage the buildings that they could build there. A garden designer looking at a wasteland can't help but imagine a future in which flowers bask in the sunshine or an orchard sways gently in the breeze. I hope to encourage something similar in my readers, so that they look at any social arrangement and see not just what it *is* but also what it *could be*.

Navigating the book

Each chapter of the book offers a perspective on imagination, and each is quite self-contained.

In Chapter 1, I describe the current position. I ask if there has been a decline of imagination and, if so, why it might have happened, whether this links to broader trends, and whether it matters.

Next, in Chapter 2, I introduce some of the key ideas: the nature of imagination; the role of social imagination in daily life; and how imagination shapes both the present and the future.

Chapter 3 offers a history of social and political imagination, exploring the past role of utopias, new concepts, prefigurative communities, simulations and fictions and how these tilled the soil and planted the seeds of ideas that came to life later.

Chapter 4 draws some initial conclusions about the patterns: the role of explorers relative to visionaries; the dialectics of imagination; and the relationship of thick imagination to thin imagination.

I then turn in Chapter 5 to the many methods that can be used to amplify or quicken imagination—the tools that can be used to spark creative thinking; techniques from design and fiction; the role played by institutions; and approaches that involve large numbers of people in imagining together.

In Chapter 6 (and its continuation in Appendix 2), I show how we might think about the specifics of imagination in the next few decades, with ideas that may be relevant to the future of fields like healthcare, democracy and the economy. How could we reimagine everyday institutions—the public beach, park or library; the workings of a parliament; and systems of property ownership, taxation or the family? Could other countries adapt elements of China's social credit system to cope with cutting carbon? Could the law help to encourage truth-telling in digital media?

Chapters 7 and 8 make sense of the journeys that ideas take. Where do they come from? Where do they go?

Next, in Chapters 9 and 10, I look at the limits of imagination—just how much freedom any society has to choose its destiny—and at the ethics of imagination, which so often can be a force for evil as well as good.

In Chapter 11, I turn to politics, since social imagination is both the fuel for political change and strongly influenced by political dynamics. I show some of the main candidates for shaping thought in the decades ahead: more assertive and authoritarian techno-nationalism; deep green thinking; a revived globalism; and hybrids that combine apparently opposite elements.

Chapter 12 focuses on the role of government and on the idea of future government as shared intelligence. I argue that any plausible imagination of the future has to include a place for government (though there is a long-standing, and perpetually disappointed, current of thought that has wished for utopia without government).

Chapter 13 turns to consciousness. Can we imagine a society better able to imagine and shape its own future? I look at the evolution of consciousness, then at wisdom as part of future imagination, arguing why we should aspire to creating a wiser society, not just a richer, greener or healthier one.

Chapter 14 looks at time. How should we think about the relationship between time and imagination? Is it possible to grasp the likely rhythms of change or are we condemned to timeless ways of imagining, rather like our dreams where past, present and future bump into each other without any clear patterns?

Chapter 15 examines the role of the arts. Can they spark imagination? Can they describe a future society? Or are they better understood as prompts, offering commentary and criticism and bearing witness to present wrongs?

Finally, in Chapter 16, I turn to who in our society is responsible for the health of our collective imagination. Is this a role equivalent to that of the artist, the composer or the architect? And, if so, is it best held by people working in universities? By think tanks? Political parties? Private clubs? Social movements?

By the end of the book, I hope to have convinced you both that there is a problem and that there are solutions. Hopefully, you may also find new ways in which you can play a role in this renewal, awakening a muscle that has too often fallen out of use. In the words of speculative fiction writer Ursula Le Guin: 'As great scientists have said and as all children know, it is above all by the imagination that we achieve perception, and compassion, and hope.'[7]

1

THE PRESENT

IMAGINATION STALLED

Losing our imagination

For most of the last two centuries, it was reasonable and realistic to expect that life would get better. By most measures, humanity advanced at a pace never seen before: life expectancy, prosperity, mobility, education and indices of freedom all shot upwards at exponential rates. They brought with them costs, including exponential rises in CO_2 emissions and environmental damage, but for most people, there was progress in the things that matter—security, welfare and health—and good reason to believe that this progress would continue.

Now the picture is less clear. Germans talk about the phenomenon of *das Verschwinden der Zukunft*, the disappearance of the future, and a widening gulf between what people hope for and what they think is likely to happen. A sizeable majority of the world's population (more than three in five) now believe the world is getting worse. Many polls and surveys show the young in the grip of a pervasive pessimism, particularly about whether democracy is the best way to govern a society or whether the environment can be saved. One survey of four Western countries found widespread expectations that humanity would be wiped out and that our way of life would not survive. Large majorities of parents expect their children to be worse off than them, by a margin of 80 per cent to 15 per cent in France, 76 per cent to 15 per cent in Japan, 61 per cent to 19 per cent in Italy, and 57 per cent to 33 per cent in the traditionally optimistic United States. In the United Kingdom, at the start of the century, only 12 per cent expected their children to be poorer than them. Now, 45 per cent do.

Even green activism can be double-edged. One survey found that although younger people are often thought to be the ones most engaged and active on climate issues, they were more likely than older generations to say there's 'no point' in changing their behaviour to tackle climate change because it won't make any difference.[1]

Some parts of the world have escaped these pessimistic trends. A few countries, like Poland, which had a miserable time in the nineteenth and twentieth centuries, remain optimistic about the twenty-first. But even in places where there's more optimism, there are fewer signs of social imagination than in the past. We'll later look at China, which has no shortage of energy and hope, yet surprisingly few ideas or dreams to share with the world, certainly by comparison with Mao's time (outside China, few teenagers carry pictures of Xi Jinping).[2] Africa too has good reason to be optimistic about the decades ahead, and its young, exploding population tends to be more positive about the future, specifically about the potential of technology (though in South Africa there is still a pessimistic majority). Again, though, there are few equivalents to the confident ideas that were promoted in the past, like the philosophies of Ujamaa in 1960s East Africa or Ubuntu a few decades later.

These trends can be found in many places. Fascinating recent research surveying the patterns of sentiment in all books published in English, German and Spanish over the last 150 years (as gathered on Google) showed symptoms of a collective depression, on a scale greater than during the world wars, in recent decades. The authors wrote of an upsurge of 'cognitive distortions' since around 2000, leading them to comment that 'large populations are increasingly stressed by pervasive cultural, economic, and social changes. The rising prevalence of depression and anxiety in recent decades seems to align with our observations'.[3]

The science-fiction writer William Gibson suggested that in his lifetime, the future 'has been a cult, if not a religion', but that this has waned.[4] Future fatigue has set in instead.[5] The Brazilian polymath Roberto Unger put the problem starkly: we suffer from a dictatorship of no alternatives.

This closing down of imagination has occurred across the political spectrum. The political left was once built on confidence in the advance of human potential towards equality. Programmes that were often first thought impossible proved repeatedly to be achievable—from universal suffrage and universal healthcare to equal rights for women, gay marriage and carbon taxes. Now, however, the road ahead for the left seems blocked. The overwhelming threat of climate change has amplified the sense that global capitalism is out of control or that the best we can hope for is to avert catastrophe. Many people admire what countries like Denmark or New Zealand do, but there are no longer big role models in the way that China or Cuba were once thought to prefigure a socialist future. Instead, the terrible failures of Marxism-Leninism fatally undermined confidence in grand social projects. Generations of intellectuals have turned away from the future, dispirited at best, cynical at worst.

For liberals, the challenge is different. In the nineteenth century, liberalism was founded on a belief in inexorable progress towards ever greater freedom and prosperity. But by the late twentieth century, its imagination had run out. Having apparently defeated their great enemy, international communism, liberals hoped that history had essentially come to an end as the rest of the world came to adopt the norms of rich liberal democracies. Unfortunately, there was no account of how democracy itself might evolve, or what might come after capitalism: all liberalism could promise was that the rest of the world might catch up with the West. Meanwhile, the promises of steady progress simply didn't materialise for millions, whose incomes stagnated and whose work became more precarious. In a nutshell, the liberal globalisers overpromised and under-delivered. As a result, many returned to older attachments of nation, religion or region, or followed new leaders who echoed their angry sense of being outsiders. In response, liberalism found itself troubled and mute, its greatest thinkers having little to say about the new social divides or about how science and technology were transforming the world both for better and worse. Liberals are now facing a world where the trends are moving against them; by one measure, the share of global GDP coming from what Freedom House called 'free' societies is set to fall from 86 per cent in 2000 to 60 per cent in 2050.[6]

Conservatives, meanwhile, tended to be suspicious of imagination in the past. They were defenders of the status quo, of deference and hierarchy, and of the tried and tested. Castles in the air or built on sand were derided as dangerous fantasies. But for a few decades, conservatism switched. The right of politics, during the 1970s and after, embraced an optimistic account of ever greater freedom and wealth, fuelled first by the liberalisation of domestic markets and then by globalisation. Conservatism's leading thinkers became the standard-bearers for the belief that ideas can transform the world for the better, switching places with an ever more cautious, defensive and pessimistic left. Margaret

Thatcher once said that economics was the means, but the aim was to change the soul. Some adopted the utopian ideas of neo-liberalism (a much misused and abused term), which promised an ideal economy largely free from the state. Radicalism became a badge of honour at least for some conservatives,[7] who saw themselves as the vanguard of a new movement to disrupt and sweep away outmoded structures and assumptions.

By the early years of this century, however, that movement too had run out of steam, disheartened by policy failures. Conservatives reverted to their more traditional pessimism about progress, centred around declining morals and social decay; the familiar safe havens of nation, religion and family; and battlegrounds like those over culture and 'political correctness'. Nostalgia became a safer bet than an uncertain future of sunlit uplands, and of course, for those whose politics is founded on nostalgia, there is no need for imagination.

Meanwhile, both left and right have come together to see technology in much darker terms than in the recent past. Rather than bringing liberation, it is more likely to be seen as the source of surveillance and manipulation, fake news and malign behaviours.

The German sociologist Andreas Reckwitz has described this as a switch from positive to negative politics. Positive politics emphasises the openness and possibility of the future. Negative politics emphasises risk and harms. It is defensive, sceptical and nostalgic, convinced that the best years lie in the past.[8]

The result is that precious few people in politics can articulate in any detail a world in the not-too-distant future in which society is better. There are policies, soundbites and vague aspirations to 'level up' or 'build back better', but nothing remotely close to reaching the level of ambition of the past.

The most radical movements in the US want a greener American version of what Scandinavia has had for decades—not to transcend it. China offers much of the world a route to material development, but little vision of what might come later. Europe, now ageing and shrinking fast in its share of the world population, has lost confidence in itself as a model, buffeted by a decade or more of aggressive populist politics.

Stunted imagination, slowing creativity

For a hint of what's gone wrong, take a look at the fictional country Wakanda in the Marvel Studios movie *Black Panther*. What's shown—uniquely for Hollywood—is a confident, prosperous and high-tech African society, untarnished by colonialism. But there's a striking mismatch between Wakanda's technological prowess and its political backwardness. Wakanda is portrayed as an isolationist nation, a hereditary monarchy that selects leaders through hand-to-hand combat. There's no hint of how its society could be run in ways we might admire or want to copy. *Black Panther* is a well-made and exciting film, but it reveals, unwittingly, just how stunted our social imagination has become.[9]

At first glance, this is surprising. Thanks to digital technology, we can all become film directors, musicians and game-makers. Mass creativity is possible as never before. But this isn't quite the imaginative golden age it should be. Instead, powerful forces seem to be stunting creativity and promoting conformism, complacency, institutional inertia and a fear of being too different.

Research suggests that there has been a decline in imagination in recent years. Analysing data from the Torrance test for creativity, which has been run in the US since the mid-1960s, Kyung Hee Kim concluded that, although various measures of originality and creativity had risen in tandem with intelligence in earlier decades, they have either fallen or remained static since 1990, even as intelligence has continued rising.[10] As she put it, 'the results indicate creative thinking is declining over time among

Americans of all ages, especially in kindergarten through third grade. The decline is steady and persistent'.[11]

There are many possible reasons for this decline: education that has become more rigid and focused on exams; TV; obesity and bad diets. Social media also plays a part, creating echo chambers where people talk only to others just like them, which dampens curiosity and openness.[12] What social scientists call 'assortative mating'—with urban professionals forming relationships almost exclusively with other urban professionals—is on the rise. Again, this means less social mixing and fewer of the chance meetings and combinations that are so vital for creativity.

Other studies have shown a steady decline in the productivity and creativity of research. In other words, it's simply become harder to find new ideas, as if we were depleting a fixed resource, like the seams of coal beneath the surface of the earth,[13] with ever fewer new ideas emerging for each dollar or euro invested. This was the argument of a paper by John van Reenen and others, which asked if 'ideas are getting harder to find' and answered that they were.[14] Ben Jones has shown through detailed studies that the age of Nobel Prize winners has risen and the size of teams involved in science has grown; he suggests that the growing 'burden of knowledge' makes it necessary to spend much more time getting on top of developments in one's field and digesting them before it's possible to make new breakthroughs.[15] Studies show that the age at which academics publish their first solo-authored article in a top journal rose from thirty to thirty-five between 1950 and 2013 for mathematicians and between 1970 and 2014 for economists.[16]

There is no definitive way to measure creativity, or how much our era really is experiencing rapid change compared to, say, the 1880s, when the telephone, the car and electricity all transformed societies alongside universal education, public health and early welfare states, or compared to periods of global war.[17] And there is nothing new about fears that growth has stalled for good. Alvin Hansen's influential 1938 book *Full Recovery or Stagnation?*, for example, warned that growth, population growth and technological innovation might have been exhausted, but he turned out to be quite wrong.

But there are plenty of signals that at least some fields of creative dynamism have slowed down: Disney remaking old cartoons shot-for-shot as live-action movies; baby boomer rock stars on permanent tour; Hollywood franchises churning out ever more reruns of proven box office successes (all of the top ten grossing films in the US in 2019 were sequels, prequels or live-action remakes); a new US president who first ran for office in the 1980s. Countries that used to define themselves through creating bold new institutions no longer do so—there are no recent equivalents to the NHS or the BBC in Britain; no equivalents of NASA or DARPA in the US. In much of academic life, too, you are more likely to succeed by slightly tweaking an established idea than creating a novel one.[18]

All of these are symptoms of a shift from innovation to recycling. Perhaps we shouldn't be surprised that no novels, films, works of visual art or pieces of music of the past few decades can plausibly claim to have changed the world. Many have warned or criticised, from blockbusters like *Wall-E* and *Avatar* to documentaries like *The Social Dilemma*. But none have imagined a better future.

Dynamic technology vs sluggish social imagination

Recognising this doesn't mean ignoring or disparaging the extraordinary advances being made in fields like artificial intelligence and synthetic biology. Indeed, imagination is alive and well in relation to technology: a future is being built where manufactured goods will mainly be grown rather than made, where wars may be settled in a matter of seconds thanks to AI, or where long-standing hopes for the colonisation of space may start to be realised.

Technology has repeatedly expanded the space of possibility for societies. The widespread use of cars made possible suburbs, supermarkets and much more. The internet transformed everything from the daily life of diaspora communities to dating. Access to large quantities of data makes it possible to spot, pre-empt or prevent risks and problems, with profound implications for medicine, policing and education.[19]

Biology has been a wellspring of imagination, feeding off present possibilities like CRISPR-9 and forcing us to imagine worlds where evolution can be accelerated and humans can be programmed and enhanced, with prosthetic devices and neural implants amplifying our vision, memory, touch and smell and enabling us to be in many places at once. Robotics has been just as fertile a source of imagination—robots for sex, companionship and housework complement the many robots at work in factories and warehouses. Blockchain technologies, too, have prompted creative thinking about different, non-hierarchical ways of organising societies, property and monies without the state, carried along with a tsunami of hype about the revolutionary potential of distributed ledgers.[20] DAOs, decentralised autonomous organisations, which are defined by transparent rules in a computer and record all their financial and governance decisions on a blockchain decentralised ledger, are at least an interesting idea, even if their practical applications have been problematic.

The problem is the gulf between this restless, fascinating technological imagination and the much more limited imagination that exists in relation to so much else. It's not that alternative futures are absent.[21] It's just that the scientific side of imagination is far more prominent, far better funded and inevitably far less sensitive to the precariousness of life in general or the much greater precariousness experienced by some groups,[22] in an era in which half the world's population live on under $2.50 a day, nearly a billion go to sleep hungry each night and a similar number lack access to safe drinking water.

California embodies this extraordinary imbalance in imagination.[23] Thousands of homeless people live in makeshift shelters on the streets of San Francisco, many struggling with mental health problems. Yet this terrible social failure[24] sits alongside huge investment in technological progress: start-ups, venture capital funds, and sci-fi writers exploring the coming world of AI and virtual reality.

Indeed, because of this imbalance, Silicon Valley has struggled to understand itself. It's been a very successful frontier in terms of technology but not in terms of social thought. For decades its leaders, such as Bill Gates,[25] promoted a vision of an imminent world of amplified enlightenment and freedom. But none showed much insight in relation to the effects or pathologies of the digital world they were building—whether manipulation of compulsive behaviours, the spread of fake news or the undermining of democracy. Now the high-tech liberators of the last decades of the twentieth century are cast instead as malign predators, devoid of any moral compass or the intellectual capacity to understand the technologies for which they are responsible. Many thinkers have fleshed out the critique, but it was a comedian, Sacha Baron Cohen, who gave perhaps the most coherent denunciation of Facebook as the 'greatest propaganda machine in history' and excoriated its founder Mark Zuckerberg, showing that the digital giant's products were encouraging addictive behaviours and amplifying the worst, not the best, aspects of human nature.

A bigger pattern that I will come back to contributes to this imbalance. This is the common error of 'materiality bias'. Our minds find it easier to grasp visible things, and so we usually exaggerate their influence, whereas the invisible things are underestimated. Kings, emperors and the wealthy believed that their glory was best captured in palaces, monuments and statues, and today's futurology focuses much more on stuff and hardware than on changing values, rights or laws, even though these generally affect life even more than the physical.

If you are asked to imagine a future city, you are bound to think of its transport, its buildings or its public spaces, not the invisible patterns that may explain much more about its character. The discipline of imagining physical things can be extremely creative, and today's architects are at the forefront of thinking through how to live entwined with nature, with zero waste and natural heating and cooling systems. But how we think, plan and design reveals the materiality bias, as what's invisible is downplayed or ignored.

The bias can be seen in the kind of speculation, both dark and light, prompted by the recent surge of artificial intelligence—about a future world saturated by smart technologies, many of which will be hard to comprehend, let alone call to account. Here, too, it's easier to focus on the physical manifestations of AI: cities based on driverless cars and facial recognition surveillance, rather than the opaque workings of algorithms. In the same way, it's easier to discuss how we might enhance humanity with prosthetic devices that amplify our senses than it is to imagine how our minds might work differently.

Technology has sparked vivid imaginaries of how life might be in the future, but these tell us little about how we might think or feel. Its enthusiasms tend to elicit a parallel scepticism, which asks: how might we avoid becoming enslaved by the robots? How should we regulate them? How do we stop deep inequalities between the rich, who will be enhanced and made beautiful, and the poor, who will have to make do with old-fashioned bodies?

This imbalance between well-funded technological imagination and thin social imagination, amplified by materiality biases, explains many of the pathologies of recent years. The internet is a striking example. Over the last forty years, it has become part of almost every aspect of life—from relationships to banking, entertainment to democracy. Its spread is one of the great facts of contemporary life. During its early years, there was a flood of utopian, Panglossian accounts of how it would transform the world for the better, flattening hierarchies and opening up democracy. Wishful thinking was ubiquitous. There were also mirror critiques emphasising its dystopian potential, but it was rare for these to offer alternative actions or options. Indeed, there were very few useful designs suggesting how we might amplify the virtues of the internet and contain its likely vices.

Vast sums were spent on designs for click-through advertising, compelling behavioural nudges through firms like Facebook, and for using the internet for surveillance by national governments. But even when strong evidence emerged that the internet might be having damaging effects on social relationships (notably the evidence in the US by the mid-2000s that the proportion of people who couldn't count on anyone in a crisis had sharply risen at the very time the internet had spread), there were few attempts to respond.[26] Serious philanthropic spending on topics like fake news and 'echo chamber effects' only began in earnest in the second half of the 2010s, after the election of Donald Trump and more than twenty years after the launch of the web. It took just as long for serious work to be done on the powerful trends towards monopoly and manipulation of public opinion and democracy, including the strength of misinformation relative to truth.

The same imbalance can be found in many other fields: decades of work on smart cities largely ignored an understanding of the social dynamics of cities. This meant that although the parts of the smart city that dealt with physical things worked, those that involved humans generally didn't or were rejected.

I suspect historians will be baffled as to why so little attention was paid to these issues before they became such visible problems, or by the remarkable lack of institutions working seriously on issues where technology and society intersect.

Germany invented the idea that you can't have a healthy future unless you've come to terms with the past (summed up in the unwieldy word *Vergangenheitsbewältigung*). After 1945, Germans put huge efforts into confronting their history openly and honestly. But we need this concept's mirror too. In our own lives, it's hard to be happy if we have nothing to look forward to. The same is true of societies: a healthy present depends on a shared view of how tomorrow could be better than today.

That we've lost this ability to picture the way ahead is sometimes hard to see, which is why I call it an imaginary crisis. We may be experiencing a collective version of what's sometimes called the Dunning-Kruger effect. This is the effect—obvious on reflection—that we never have the perspective from which to judge our own ability to think. Dunning and Kruger showed that without what they called 'self-awareness of meta-cognition', people cannot actively evaluate their competence or incompetence in different kinds of thought. We simply lack the tools to judge ourselves or to know how bad we are, short of doing specific tests and exams (and even in a field like driving in which there are tests, a large majority believe themselves to be above average). Dunning called this effect 'the anosognosia of everyday life', referring to a neurological condition in which a disabled person either denies or seems unaware of their disability. He stated: 'If you're incompetent, you can't know you're incompetent ... The skills you need to produce a right answer are exactly the skills you need to recognize what a right answer is.'

Just this may be happening with social imagination. It's hard to spot the falling away of this capacity because we lack the skills with which to make such a judgement. So the world stumbles forward, putting up with half-baked and hare-brained ideas and struggling to distinguish them from the good ones.

ANOTHER WORLD IS POSSIBLE

Do we need imagination?

Does this matter? Does it matter if social imagination has been displaced by other types of imagination? Is imagination good in itself, or can it do harm, even diverting our attention away from practical thinking and problem-solving?

For much of the world, social imagination can seem like a luxury, the blue-sky dreaming of people living easy lives. What most people aspire to is what others already have: prosperity, security, peace and freedom, not some vague utopia. In the development world, the talk has long been of 'getting to Denmark'; if you don't have the things Denmark takes for granted, that is plenty to aspire to. If your life is dominated by a negative, its removal has to be the priority: removing oppression, exploitation, discrimination, precariousness, deficient rights or the threat of war. Catching up is the aspiration, not jumping forward to an uncertain goal.

Because of this, much of politics and political imagination rightly focuses on the removal of negatives and on getting to someone else's normality. This leads to a politics of resistance— challenging and resisting the multiple ways in which power works to oppress or constrain. But from a global standpoint, this is not enough. Collectively, we also need pictures of societal futures that go beyond today's status quo. They complement but do not replace the necessary work of activism that fights against the injustices of the present. We also need new answers to new problems—the vulnerabilities caused by a more connected world, or by potentially lethal artificial intelligence weapons. And, for the world as a whole, psychological well-being depends on a map of the future, as well as maps of the present and past.

A bigger reason is that a stunted social imagination undermines our ability to adapt. Any society benefits from having a wide menu of possibilities to consider. A general feature of evolution is that diversity in the genetic pool of a species makes that species more resilient in the face of environmental change. We now know very well how dangerous it can be for agriculture to become a monoculture—more vulnerable to pests and less adaptable to climate change. In the same way, societies that become too specialised, or too optimised in a particular way, are likely to struggle when conditions change. That is just as true if they seem to be doing well, since history never stands still. In this sense, imagination is functional rather than a luxury. It generates possibilities and keeps them alive.

The motivation to explore seems to be deeply embedded in some people, presumably because in earlier stages of our evolution, we needed some to be willing to find new places to live and try out new foods to eat while others stayed home. The theorist of organisations James G. March described this as the balance between exploiting and exploring: exploiting what we already have or exploring for something new. Getting the balance right is a fundamental challenge for every organisation or society. Too much exploitation leads to stagnation; too much exploration leads to failure and instability. But in fast-changing environments, the optimal balance is likely to shift towards more exploration.[27]

The argument I make in this book is that although many fields have struck a good balance between the two—including science, business and medicine, all of which invest heavily in discovery and innovation—in the social and political fields we do far too little systematic exploration. Yet the sheer scale of the challenges we are likely to face over the next few decades makes it implausible that the status quo will be adequate, or that it will be enough just to exploit our existing stock of concepts and ideas. Instead, we will probably need very radical reform and innovation to cope with climate change (and the required transformation in lifestyles, values and economic organisation); rapid ageing; deep patterns of inequality; and ubiquitous smart technology. Each of these alone would put huge strains on our social institutions. Add them together and it's clear that we need a rapid boost in our capacity to imagine and design better social arrangements.[28]

These are all reasons we should—collectively—care about our shared imagination and whether it is healthy or sick. In personal life, the shrinking of one's future horizons is a kind of illness, associated with poor physical and mental health. It can happen because of stress and poverty, and it is also associated with reduced IQ. Being under pressure literally makes people less intelligent than they are otherwise, often fuelling a vicious spiral of bad decisions that make matters worse and that in turn generate more stress.

There is strong evidence that hope is good for us, and if imagination helps us to hope, then we should worry if it is blocked. One of the most influential accounts of this link was provided by psychiatrist Viktor Frankl in his study of concentration camp survivors. He found that whether prisoners survived depended on whether they had hope for the future. If they lost that faith, or hope, their mental and physical health tended to decline: 'It is a peculiarity of man,' he wrote, 'that he can only live by looking to the future.'[29] Historian Fred Polak was much influenced by this work and studied how images of the future had changed over the last few thousand years. His conclusion echoed Frankl's, but at a larger scale: 'As long as a society's image of the future is positive and flourishing, the flower of culture is in full blossom. Once the image of the future begins to decay and lose its vitality, however, the culture cannot long survive.'[30]

These are broad-brush generalisations; some people can cope with even apparently hopeless situations. But if we become too fixated on what can go wrong, we may stop working to avert disaster. Some may decide only to seek instant gratification rather than long-term goals, which seem pointless. What's more, if we see reason to distrust the world as a whole, we may also be more likely to drift into cynicism and apathy towards more everyday institutions. Psychologist Joanna Macy suggests that people's responses to concerns about global catastrophes are to 'go silent, go numb' rather than protest or retaliate; this 'numbing of the psyche' creates an impoverished emotional and sensory life. Energy expended suppressing despair is 'diverted from more creative uses, depleting resilience and imagination.'[31]

Social science has repeatedly found that young people with little expectation of a better future act in risky ways—driving fast and carelessly, committing crimes with a high likelihood of getting caught, carrying knives—rather than seeing their life as a project worthy of investment, or choosing to make sacrifices now for a payback in the future. Again, this is a pathology at the individual level which has equivalents at the level of the community or the society.[32] If we lose faith in the future, we are likely to do less to make a better future happen. In this way, fatalism can, indeed, become fate.

2

WHAT IS IMAGINATION?

In this chapter, I look at what imagination is and the influence it has on our daily lives. As I'll show, our past, present and future are all, to some extent, imagined. They exist as maps of varying degrees of precision that guide our decisions and actions.

Pictures and maps

The word 'imagine' derives from the word 'image'. To imagine means picturing something to yourself, summoning to your mind things that may or may not exist, though they are strongly influenced by memory (indeed, neuroscience has suggested that impairment of memory also impairs imagination).[1] When we imagine, we literally picture something;[2] most imagined worlds have a visual aspect to them, with mental images at their core, even if these are hazy.[3] Ian McGilchrist put well the vital importance of visual thinking: 'most forms of imagination, ... or of innovation, intuitive problem solving, spiritual thinking or artistic creativity require us to transcend language ... [and] in evolutionary terms, thought, including concept formation, clearly predates language.'[4]

It is very much part of our nature that at night our brains invent dream-worlds, which sometimes resemble those of our waking hours and sometimes are wildly different. Our ancestors imagined all-powerful gods and monstrous demons, elaborate heavens and torturous hells. Our hopes and fears now are different—from promotions at work to new loves, cancers to climate disasters. But like our ancestors, we can create in the theatre of our minds, with scripts, sets, actors and scenes that we can shape and steer and then share. It's this ability that allows us, some of the time, to peer into the future and imagine how our lives, our families and our communities could be different. Whenever two or more people share time together, they start to create a shared imaginary, references that describe their own past, present and sometimes future.

Recent advances in neuroscience suggest that much of the brain uses reference frames of this kind. Many of these are purely visual while others are visual in a more metaphorical sense. The overtly visual ones help us to move around, telling us where we are or need to be, the cones of the neocortex providing a grid which literally maps the physical world and guides us through it. Something very similar appears to happen with our acquisition and development of language and knowledge. We place new pieces of knowledge in relation to others, analogous to how we map physical space.[5]

This theory of the brain has many implications for imagination. It suggests that it is more than a metaphor when we talk about constructing maps of our past, our relationships in the present or our possible routes to the future. It also helps to explain why it is so much easier to absorb a new idea if it is a neighbour to a familiar idea or has similar dimensions to something we already know. The more novel the idea is, the more we need to play with it and reshape it so as to grow reference frames in our brain. It's only through repetition that it becomes part of us by becoming part of our map of the world, and so it is with new ideas—feminism, human rights, a circular economy—that are only absorbed over long periods of time.[6] Lightbulb moments of sudden illumination are very much the exception.

Everyday fictions

That we are more at home among familiar ideas is very apparent, though these ideas are so normalised that we often fail to see them as products of human imagination at all. Much of daily life depends on our ability to believe in things that are, essentially, fictions. As philosopher John Searle points out:

> there is an element of imagination in the existence of private property, marriage, and government because in each case we have to treat something as something that it is not intrinsically. ... children very early on acquire a capacity to do this double level of thinking that is characteristic of the creation and maintenance of institutional reality. Small children can say to each other, 'Okay, I'll be Adam, you be Eve, and we'll let this block be the apple.'[7]

All of these 'necessary fictions' have been created. The joint-stock company was one such fiction; monarchy is another (to this day, the British government is called 'Her Majesty's Government' and its finance ministry is 'Her Majesty's Treasury'). Money is a fiction too; in fact, it has become even more fictional as we've moved from coins and notes to numbers on screens and cryptocurrencies. These creations provide the maps of day-to-day life, and crucially, these maps are shared; indeed, if they were not shared, they wouldn't work. The maps allow us to act as if these fictions have some inner essence, rather than simply being pragmatic constructions.

Similar fictions also help us to make sense of a shared past. Benedict Anderson rightly described nations as 'imagined communities'. They have boundaries and resources but are also held together by selective memories of great battles and heroes—and the equally careful forgetting of uncomfortable facts—woven into useful myths that provide a simplified map of the past into which we can insert ourselves, a reference frame that can be empowering but that can equally become a trap.

A mark of political maturity is the ability to see such constructs for what they are, while recognising the more fundamental values they try to express—justice, for example, or care—and the useful role they play in daily life. By contrast, a mark of political immaturity, and worse, is treating these fictions as facts and endowing them (the nation, the constitution, the party) with cosmic or spiritual meaning.

The ability to accept these fictions makes everyday life possible through conformism and suggestion. But a related ability enables us to reimagine the same institutions or rules; once we can recognise them as being useful fictions, it becomes easier to rethink, adjust, extend or invert them. That ability can enable us to think about a future welfare state that can take both loneliness and physical disability seriously, or an education system that serves the middle-aged and the elderly as well as the young, or a parliament that lets the public take part in its debates. It is this capacity that opens up the possibility that everyone on the planet be given a fixed quota of carbon emissions; or that they have rights to neuro-enhancements, so that these aren't just the preserve of the rich; or that new rules be created to stop autonomous weapons.

This attitude gives us 'possibility perception', the ability to look at the things around us—a park, a primary school, a town hall or a shopping centre—and see not just what they are but also what they could become. We do this all the time with our children, our homes and our gardens. But we do it much less often with our social institutions. Try, for example, to imagine your great-grandchildren visiting a doctor or a town centre, or taking part in an election a century from now. Perhaps your mind searches for helpful images from science fiction, or from today's technologies, or from your own experience, before arriving at an unstable, unsteady picture that won't quite come into focus. Most of us struggle.

This is because future imagination involves two distinct steps, each of which is difficult. The first step involves questioning or rejecting the present, resisting its claim to be natural. The second step means constructing a plausible alternative, moving between an awareness of limits and a search for transcendence of those same limits. Both of these steps are difficult for orthodox social science, which defaults to a view of present arrangements as the only ones possible, or else to rigid ideas about successive stages of evolution that are presented as immutable laws. Yet it is only through imagination that we can think about the future and break free from these intellectual prisons, usually by imagining one step at a time: how to extend, add to, subtract from or graft something new onto the institutions, laws and norms around us, in what is sometimes called the 'adjacent possible'.

Doing this helps us shape the future, but it also enhances our understanding of the present. It does so in ways precisely comparable to the effects of historical knowledge, which shows us the fairly arbitrary choices with which our reality was made. By reminding us of the malleability of the world, it also reminds us of our freedom; as the Lithuanian philosopher Leonidas Donskis put it, it is a form of 'liquid evil' to believe that there are no alternatives.[8]

But, as with our understanding of history, for imagination to be useful it also has to respect constraints: humanity's dependence on a narrow band of soil and air, as well as the limits of our contexts, cultures and past decisions. Indeed, this is where wisdom comes in, to temper and guide imagination, sensitive to the particularities of time and place.

Imagining beyond ourselves and the present

Our ability to think ahead overlaps with our ability to grasp the lives and feelings of others. This shared capacity for empathy has played a vital role in social change. The movement to abolish slavery was energised by novels, first-hand accounts and public talks which transformed an abstract idea into something very human.[9] Frederick Douglass, a former slave, for example, toured Britain for nearly two years in the mid-nineteenth century, vividly showing that the battle against slavery was still underway. Fifty years later, African-American sociologist W.E.B. Du Bois asked white people to understand the 'double consciousness' of black people in the US, who lived with both their own consciousness and that of the society around them, a 'sense of always looking at one's self through the eyes of others'[10] that was both a curse and a blessing, since it provided heightened awareness.

There are many ways to cultivate deeper empathy. Special suits can give an able-bodied young person a sense of what it's like to be disabled or old, a bodily empathy that's often more compelling than cognitive empathy. TV, film and poetry, too, can open up empathic imagination, helping us to see the world through other eyes. The expansion of our awareness of others and their experiences through empathy can help us to more clearly see just how much our own lives are shaped by luck and the lottery of life—who our parents are, and what nation or time period we are born in—rather than our achievements being explained by our own talents.[11] Arguably, this ability to widen and enrich empathic imagination, to understand that what you see and how you live depends on where you stand, is essential to any meaningful sense of progress.[12] The Zapatista movement in Mexico is an interesting recent example, promoting the idea of aspiring towards 'a world where many worlds fit', a nice description of a more capacious and tolerant society.[13]

WHAT IS IMAGINATION?

One reason we struggle to look into the future with any clarity is the very power of imagination in the present. We are so good at buying into the shared fictions of daily life that we tend to see social phenomena as more solid and natural than they really are. Marxist philosophers describe this as 'reification': we see markets, governments and families as objects, facts of the world, rather than as constructs. What are, in reality, social relationships take on the appearance of being things.

Most people seek confirmation from others and will easily believe that others believe in a social norm even if they doubt the norm themselves—a phenomenon labelled as 'pluralistic ignorance', familiar to us in the fable of the emperor's new clothes. This tends to be a conservative force, reinforcing the mental inertia that John Stuart Mill called the 'deep slumber of a decided opinion'. It contributes to excessive deference to the powerful—whether presidents and prime ministers, or the equivalent near-worship of CEOs and billionaire entrepreneurs. Such people may have genuinely admirable qualities of intellect and creativity. But as the great French writer Alexis de Tocqueville put it, there is 'no more inveterate habit of man than to recognise superior wisdom in his oppressor'.

This simple idea was later developed by Marxist philosophers into the theory of false consciousness, which argues that people systematically adopt ideologies that ensure their oppression, believing, for example, in the divine right of kings or the inevitability of market forces. Although much criticised (mainly for its implication that people are stupid), the theory of false consciousness remains all too plausible, and one of its implications is that we tend to underestimate how much can change, whether for better or worse. This is one way in which imagination can restrict us at the same time as having the potential to free us.

Challenging our everyday, conformist imagination with a more open, expansive imagination is vital to creativity. Letting your mind wander; travelling to new places; meeting people from very different backgrounds; drinking alcohol and taking psychedelic drugs—all are ways of disarming our inner police and allowing us to think in fresh ways. All are necessary steps to dial back the conformism of present imagination and awaken imagination of the future. As George Orwell put it, 'we know only that the imagination, like certain wild animals, will not breed in captivity.'[14]

Innovation depends on loosening of this kind, lubricated by clubs and bars, unprogrammed spaces in events, the company of heretics and dissenters, or great events in which everyday rules are suspended.[15] As I'll show later, a more active social imagination also depends on being playful and indirect, opening up our minds in order to think in novel ways, and tuning down our linear, logical skills: escaping, in other words, from the captivity of daily life.

3

THE PAST

HOW IMAGINATION SHAPED OUR WORLD

If we go far enough back, imagination becomes woven into magic and mystery. The seers and shamans in prehistory looked in the entrails of chickens or patterns of smoke to see hints of the future. Agrarian societies produced prophets who claimed to speak for a single god, like Zoroaster speaking for Ahura Mazda, the Wise Lord, telling truths about the future. In the Old Testament, Isaiah spoke up for the poor and against the corrupt, talked of voices in the wilderness and of turning swords into ploughshares, and promised that Jerusalem would be punished and would then witness the destruction of its oppressor. Finally, a Messiah would come, bringing with him a new order.

Jesus, too, promised a renewal of society on earth and an imminent rupture in history. Then, when it didn't happen, his followers revised this into a purely spiritual rupture, but always with the sense that it might be literal rather than metaphorical. The Book of Revelations, for example, amidst its lurid talk of the horsemen of the apocalypse, promises a return at the end of time to an earthly paradise, with a long utopia: a thousand-year-long reign of peace when Satan will be taken and chained, before at last being set free and thrown into a pool of fire at the Last Judgement.

In these ideas we see themes that return again and again in social imagination: rising up against oppressive powers; the punishment of evil; an imminent world of peace and plenty. Perhaps it should come as no surprise that in the face of misery and broken dreams, people have always sought out prophecies that make sense of apparently senseless pain and chaos by offering a narrative arc in which the dark turns into light.

Imagination can also be found in fiction. In the English tradition, William Langland's *Piers Plowman* and Geoffrey Chaucer's *Canterbury Tales* both share revolutionary ideas about the possibility of a social order without oppression, and similar themes can be found in folk traditions and songs of all kinds, forerunners of John Lennon's song 'Imagine'.[1]

So the exercise of social imagination isn't new. Humans have always been able to conceive of different ways of doing things, to dream, create myths and reimagine a social order. But the idea that people could imagine a future society and could themselves then create it is quite modern. Although there are long traditions of ethical prescription, or the design of cults and communes, as well as ambitious political projects going back to Plato and Kautilya, these are different from the deliberate cultivation of social imagination, which is really a phenomenon of modernity, and connected to the ability to reimagine and transform the natural world.[2] This imagination has, at its best, liberated people from false truths—the claims of hierarchy, identity and more—and helped them grasp the deeper unity of humanity, and of nature.

Here I look at the many ways in which people have tried to imagine over the last few centuries, using the power of ideas to shift the course of their societies and prove that they are not slaves to fate or destiny.

Describe it—the role of utopias

The first way to change the world is to try to describe, literally, what it could become. The hope is that, somehow, the written word will then materialise through inspiration, rather as a Bible or Qur'an inspires people to become followers.

Edward Bellamy is a good example. He was an American author plagued by tuberculosis, who gave up journalism in the 1880s for the less physically demanding task of writing books. His most famous publication, *Looking Backward: 2000–1887*, published in 1888, became one of the three best-selling books of its time in the United States. It describes a future in which the US has been transformed by a peaceful revolution, which abolished private property and taxes, saw professions like lawyers and soldiers disappear, and enabled retirement at forty-five. In it, we can also find references to everyday innovations like home deliveries and credit cards, and machines which can play music at the push of a button.

Looking Backward tried to change the present by presenting a picture of a possible and desirable future. It's a tradition that goes back to Thomas More's *Utopia* (1516) and Plato's *Republic* (c. 375 BC), the first prescriptive utopia, governed by wise rulers imposing a plethora of strict rules. Many of the ideas found in these utopias look quirky and eccentric; Plato wanted to abolish the family, and in More's world, everyone had to be in bed by 8 pm. But they sowed many seeds that later germinated and flowered.

For example, later books would expand on island paradises stretching back to Plato's Atlantis and the Isles of the Blessed in Greek mythology, thought to lie on the edge of the earth out in the Atlantic Ocean. One of the most famous of these was Tommaso Campanella's description of a virtuous, theocratic utopia in his book *The City of the Sun*, written in the early seventeenth century. It portrayed a city with shared goods, a four-hour working day and special praise for those who had to work hardest, such as the builders. The walls of the city were painted with the best of the arts and knowledge—an encyclopaedia in physical form.

In England, later that century, Francis Bacon's *New Atlantis* offered a utopia shaped by science and experiment. Bacon was called the *buccinator novi temporis*, the 'trumpeter of new times', promising to extend the bounds of human empire by dominating nature using the method of constant testing. Bacon's contemporary James Harrington envisioned a very different kind of utopia which was equally prescient. *The Commonwealth of Oceana* presented a utopian republic sustained by a perfect constitution. Although it was initially censored by Oliver Cromwell, who then ruled England, a later version was dedicated to him. The book describes the limited rights of government and how officials should be treated and paid, and though largely ignored in England, it had a big influence more than a century later in France.

Feminism was foreshadowed in extraordinary early works, such as Christine de Pizan's *The Book of the City of Ladies*, published around 1405, and seventeenth-century English scientist Margaret Cavendish's *Blazing World*: a proto-science-fiction utopia full of talking animals. A century later, Sarah Scott, an English novelist and reformer, wrote *Millennium Hall* (1762), which offered a feminist 'bluestocking' utopia of education and improvement, with property held in common.

Other writers included Louis Sebastien Mercier in the eighteenth century, who promised a future where citizens would gladly overpay their taxes, and later on Henri de Saint-Simon, brilliant, depressive, suicidal, sometimes rich and sometimes poor, and the inventor of the new religion 'Nouveau Christianisme'. Étienne Cabet, another Frenchman, imagined a future of absolute cleanliness and absolute symmetry, helped by laws to specify everything from food to dress; his ideas prompted communes from Texas to California.

In the nineteenth century, utopias became very common, thanks to figures like the British textile designer and author William Morris, whose utopia had no laws or punishments, and the French philosopher Charles Fourier. Credited with coining the word 'feminism', Fourier commented that the 'level of development of any civilisation could be determined by the extent to which women are liberated'. The works of these thinkers reached large audiences.

Some utopias sparked counter-utopias. The success of Bellamy's *Looking Backward* prompted challengers, like Theodor Hertzka's *Freiland* (1889), which promised, instead of the end of private property, a free-market utopia. Inspired by the book, some 1,000 societies were set up to create a colony in Africa.

By the end of the nineteenth century, it seemed only logical for Oscar Wilde to quip that: 'A map of the world that does not include utopia is not worth even glancing at, for it leaves out the one country at which Humanity is always landing. And when Humanity lands there, it looks out, and, seeing a better country, sets sail.'[3]

The tradition of imagining utopias continued through the twentieth century. In her 1974 book *The Dispossessed*, speculative-fiction writer Ursula Le Guin described in detail the dynamics of Anarres, an anarchist-communitarian world. But over the last half-century, whether in literature or film, utopias have been far outnumbered by dystopias—perhaps appropriately, since the revolutionary utopias that existed in the twentieth century too often turned rapidly into dystopias.

Although it's easy to understand the appeal of utopias, like the religious promise of paradise or an afterlife, we now view them with a sceptical eye. Where the world progressed most in the last two centuries was through more piecemeal, incremental change, rather than the big bang of a utopian revelation followed by a political revolution. Indeed, the most admired countries today are no longer those with revolutionary histories—England, which decapitated its monarch in the seventeenth century, France, which did the same in the eighteenth, or the US and USSR, which were born in revolution—but rather smaller countries like Sweden, Denmark and Switzerland, which have been lucky enough to avoid such sudden shocks (and some of which even maintain a monarchy alongside their socialistic welfare states).

There have been a few recent attempts to revive the utopian tradition. One of the more interesting contemporary examples of writing that rethinks how a whole society and economy might work is Kim Stanley Robinson's *Mars* trilogy, published in the 1990s. A hundred people and plenty of equipment, from nuclear weapons to space greenhouses, land on Mars and have to do every-thing from scratch. Their work generating a habitable environ-ment, drilling tunnels, growing plants and producing oxygen is set out in detail; they build a closed economy but without money.

The early twenty-first century saw some novelists taking up the theme of how to rebuild out of the chaos of climate change, with the publication of Bruce Sterling's *The Caryatids*, Paul McAuley's *Quiet War* books and Ada Palmer's *Terra Ignota* series. This new strand of green utopias was described by one writer as offering 'visionary glimpses of how our real world could be changed', expressing the hope of sparking 'socio-political change by means of the aesthetic representation of a paradigm shift.'[4]

But I doubt that this is quite what they will do. None of the utopias published over the last 500 years accurately predicted how societies would change, and none were ever used as blueprints (the blueprints for Lenin or Pol Pot came from other sources). Their role was more modest and indirect. They helped clear people's heads, showing them the plasticity of the world, rather than serving as designs. As thought experiments, they brought to the surface surprising possible patterns, and some achieved what Frederik Pohl described as the essence of a good science-fiction story: the ability to predict not just the automobile but also the traffic jam.

I think of utopia as more like a verb than a noun, an activity rather than a finished product. We should emphasise utopia-making rather than utopias, and perhaps we need a word for this: 'utopifying'. The act of thinking about possible utopias is entirely healthy, indeed essential, particularly at a time like ours which is awash with dystopias. But the utopias that result are unlikely to provide detailed roadmaps for social change.

I'm sure that many writers of utopias (a surprising proportion of whom were involved in action and practical work) hoped that they would serve as manifestos. But part of the problem with utopias is that they are too complete: they make too much sense and so leave little space for the reader, or for society, to work out their own answers. A similar observation was made by Friedrich Engels in the late nineteenth century, when he commented of the social systems proposed by early socialists that 'the more completely they were worked out in detail, the more they could not avoid drifting off into pure fantasies.'[5] Yet Engels still saw a value in this kind of thought. It doesn't matter if we read these books in ways other than the ones envisaged by the original writers. They are useful all the same, acclimatising us to other possibilities. Spending time in another, imaginary world helps us to see how arbitrary our own world is. It breaks down our tendency to reify—to see relationships as things, social constructions as facts of nature.

But any utopias written now—and any utopia-making or utopifying—have to be nuanced, messy and contradictory. We are rightly suspicious of overly neat and perfect worlds, which are, in any case, boring. Instead, we want plausible pictures of the future, in which the unavoidable human patterns of frustration, envy and conflict are still present, but not dominant. This is why some recent authors play with alternative neologisms—'eutopias', 'neotopias' and 'protopias'—to hint at something more tentative and more evolutionary.

We might also want our future utopias to be global. It's no coincidence that so many utopias were conceived as islands. They work only because they are isolated, with no neighbouring towns or countries, no potential invaders, let alone shared ecosystems to worry about. This is a weakness too of many utopian communes: they imagine themselves as hermetically sealed off from the outside world, but in reality they are not. H.G. Wells was surely on the right track in arguing that global government had to be part of any plausible utopia; in the densely interconnected world of today, perhaps the only utopias that can make sense are ones that encompass the whole world.

Propose an idea—and let others apply it

So, utopias are both too complete and too insular. This is why their direct influence has been limited. A much bigger impact has come from generative ideas—ideas that spawn many other ideas. These don't need to be precise. Quite the opposite, in fact. The more imprecise the idea, the more chance it has of evolving and spreading.

The idea of human rights is a good example. It originated in the seventeenth century with the notion that we are all endowed with natural rights. John Locke argued that these were 'life, liberty, and estate [property]'. He believed that these rights were so fundamental that they couldn't be taken away by the state or anyone else.

This notion was embedded in bills of rights in the 1680s, taken further by the revolutions in the US and France, and then spread in many forms in the nineteenth century. Thanks to promoters such as the French jurist René Cassin, after three centuries the idea was enshrined in the UN Declaration of Human Rights, which Cassin drafted. From there, ideas about rights spread, pollinating in many directions to encompass civil rights, gay rights, children's rights, transgender rights, animal rights and now even the rights of robots.

Similar things happened with a number of other foundational ideas, including universal suffrage and representative democracy; parliamentary sovereignty; the joint-stock company; *habeas corpus*; and universal education. All are examples of ideas that spread in part because of their fuzziness and simplicity.

Some more rigid new frameworks have also spread, albeit usually more slowly. The permaculture movement was founded by David Holmgren and Bill Mollison in Tasmania in the 1970s and attempted to promote a systemic approach to agriculture, linking care for the land with care for people and a principle of returning surpluses to the soil. It was highly prescriptive, which probably limited its capacity to spread, but it resonated with a much broader shift in thinking about how farming should be done, with the rise of organic and biodynamic farming methods.

Less sweeping ideas have also proven generative, like the idea of making body organs available to others as a default, following the widespread acceptance of things like kidney donor cards; or of slowing down traffic to make cities more liveable; or of rewilding the countryside. Each is a simple idea that can be easily explained and extended in many different ways. For example, most traffic-calming or rewilding schemes are very different from their earliest iterations; the essential idea has been taken and adapted to new circumstances.

All around us are generative ideas that are already finding new applications. Some from the last couple of decades include nudge theory (the idea of subtly adjusting environments to encourage certain behaviour in everything from pensions to diets); effective altruism (the idea of systematically applying reason to determine how best you can help others); net zero (the idea of reshaping the economy and society to achieve carbon neutrality); co-creation (the idea of remaking public services so that they are genuinely jointly shaped by users and providers); privatisation (the idea of selling off public utilities and industries); and neo-nationalism (the idea of looking at everything from trade to migration through the lens of national advantage).

There are also genuinely novel ideas that could prove generative in the future. The idea that everyone on the planet should have a fixed and equal allocation of carbon certainly seems utopian now but may become tomorrow's common sense. The same may be true of the idea that everyone should control and even sell their own data.

In other words, if you want to change the world, you may have most influence by defining and promoting a simple idea, ideally one with enough ambiguity that it can grow and evolve, potentially far beyond what you might have imagined.

Invent a new a lifestyle or sensibility

An even better way to transform the world is to invent a new lifestyle or sensibility: to influence through habits as much as ideas by creating new ways of living. Veganism is a good example. It was invented in the 1940s by the Scottish teacher and farmer Donald Watson. He chose the name of the movement to be, literally, 'the beginning and end of vegetarian', and his mission was to emancipate animals from human exploitation. For many decades, veganism spread very slowly on the margins of vegetarianism. But it steadily gained ground in the 2000s as the damaging effects of meat both on the environment and people's health became more apparent (Watson was also a good advertisement for the health effects of veganism; he died in 2005 at the age of ninety-five). By 2020, between 1 and 3 per cent of the population were estimated to be vegan in the UK and the US, a figure that is rising fast—and in turn prompting rapid innovation in food production and provision.

Hacker culture, too, is as much an ethos as a programme. It emerged at the Massachusetts Institute of Technology in the 1950s and 1960s and promoted work done for curiosity rather than reward, as well as a belief in sharing, openness, decentralisation and bettering the world. It combined the discipline of engineering with the creative spirit of the arts. The movement, described by the writer Stephen Levy as a 'new way of life, with a philosophy, an ethic and a dream', has proved hugely influential. It provided an ideology for the open-source movement, whose technologies underpin much of the internet, and it continues to offer an alternative vision both to the surveillance capitalism of Facebook and Google and to the way digital technologies are used by governments like China's as a tool for control.

The hacker movement encourages us to make and shape the world around us rather than accepting the forms offered to us by governments or corporations. It emphasises how anything can be broken down and remade, and often how expensive things can be made freely available to all, an approach exemplified by figures like Aaron Swartz, a programmer and hacktivist who resisted the often absurd property rights of the digital economy. A more recent development is the biohacking movement, which augurs a future where people can remake and reshape their bodies with implants of all kinds (I have a small connection to this movement thanks to a tiny NFC chip in my hand, installed by a Swedish biohacker).

Social change can be fuelled by the combination of sensibility and practice, but sensibility on its own is not enough. Here is an example, written half a century ago by the evangelist of LSD Timothy Leary. He wrote of surfers as:

> the 'throw-aheads' of mankind ... the futurists ... leading the way to where man ultimately wants to be. The act of the ride is the epitome of 'be here now' and the tube ride is the most acute form of that. Which is: your future is right ahead of you, the past is exploding behind you, your wake is disappearing, your footprints are washed from the sand. It's a non-productive, non-depletive act that's done purely for the value of the dance itself. And that is the destiny of man.

Unfortunately, surfers didn't quite turn out to be the vanguard of any revolutions, though that spirit, of walking lightly on the earth, is very much part of twenty-first-century culture.

Create a new organisation that embodies an idea

A related approach turns imagination into reality through the vehicle of an organisation that then grows, inspires others to copy it or shifts minds. This is the method of social entrepreneurship: embedding an idea in a scalable structure. My mentor Michael Young was one of its greatest examples. Having experienced top-down change as author of the British Labour Party's 1945 manifesto (which promised amongst other things a National Health Service and welfare state), he became convinced of the virtues of bottom-up organic growth and went on to create nearly 100 organisations—the Consumers Association, Grandparents Plus, the School for Social Entrepreneurs, Education Extra—as well as persuading governments to give other ideas institutional form, most famously through the Open University.

Another leading social entrepreneur, Muhammad Yunus, won the Nobel Peace Prize for his creation of Grameen Bank in Bangladesh, a country that is also home to perhaps the world's largest NGO, BRAC. Other organisations that have sparked huge change include the cellular structures of Alcoholics Anonymous and its offshoots like Narcotics Anonymous, technology-based organisations like Wikipedia, and large service providers like the KIPP network of charter schools in the US.

In each case, the organisation embodies an idea and an ethos. Sometimes that can then mutate as the idea spreads. A good example is the University of the Third Age (U3A), dedicated to encouraging old age as a time for learning. Originally set up in Toulouse as an offshoot of a university, U3A reached the UK and took a radically different direction, becoming an independent organisation based on mutual aid (where both of my parents lectured).

I have been involved in setting up quite a few organisations, like Action for Happiness, which promotes the use of scientific knowledge of happiness (and has the Dalai Lama as a patron). It has reached millions of people through courses, tools and prompts. I also co-founded Uprising, an organisation that trains young people from marginalised backgrounds to become public leaders.

In the business world, organisations can become huge and change the world directly as their goods or services become mainstream. In civil society, this is much rarer, partly because capital is so much harder to raise, partly because of the challenges of ethos and culture, and partly because love and compassion are much harder to scale up than cars or software. Nonetheless, the organisational route is a good way to crystallise imagination fast and not have to wait for governments to catch up.[6]

Create an appealing neotopia

An even more concrete way for imagination to change the world is to build a real place that persuades others by force of example, influencing through its magnetic appeal. If the Greek origin of 'utopia' means 'no place', these are instead neotopias, places that aim to exemplify the new.

New Lanark, a village near Glasgow, is one of the best examples. Built by Robert Owen in the early nineteenth century, it aimed to show in three dimensions just how differently factories, schools and communities could be organised, applying new ideas of cooperation. Owen's other attempts—like the utopian settlement of New Harmony in the US—were dismal failures, as was his attempt to create an alternative religion (The Association of All Classes of All Fathers, with himself as the Rational Social Father). But New Lanark worked and was visited and admired, contributing to a legacy that was hugely influential—today, 3 million cooperatives employ nearly 300 million people globally.

More recently, radical ideas about place went on to have a huge influence. In the words of Peter Hall, the greatest historian of cities:

> Much if not most of what has happened—for good or for ill—to the world's cities in the years since WW2 can be traced back to the ideas of a few visionaries who lived and wrote long ago, often almost ignored and largely rejected by their contemporaries ... a secular version of the seventeenth century Puritan's Celestial City set on Mount Zion, now brought down to earth.[7]

Hall was thinking of figures like Ebenezer Howard, a contradictory combination who was both an anarchist *and* a planner. Horrified by the unhealthy and unhappy cities of Victorian England, he came up with the idea of the garden city—partly inspired by Edward Bellamy's novel *Looking Backward*. Garden cities would solve the problems of congestion and high land prices by moving the urban population out to new places where they would live and work surrounded by countryside and clean air. Howard's vision cleverly looked forward to the future *and* back to an imagined past where people led a more organic life. The goal was a society that would be 'neither capitalistic nor bureaucratic-socialistic: a society based on voluntary cooperation among men and women, working and living in small self-governing commonwealths'.[8] Nor were these only words. Ebenezer Howard was a rare visionary who was also practical (much of his original book set out calculations showing why garden cities offered such a good financial return to investors), and after his first success in Letchworth in England, hundreds of garden cities were set up around the world.

For the radical urban planners of the twentieth century, too, the city itself provided the ideal scale at which the imagination could come alive. Patrick Geddes, founder of environmental sociology and much else, described a more ideal city or 'eutopia' as lying 'in the city around us; and it must be planned and realized [with] us as its citizens—each a citizen of both the actual and ideal city seen increasingly as one.'[9] In his architectural designs for the city of Edinburgh, for example, he proposed that cities should contain civic observatories and laboratories, which would allow a fusion of the ideal and the real, theory and practice, to avoid the risks of these becoming methods only for professionals.

Freiburg in southern Germany is a good contemporary example, designed to show what a radically ecological community should be like, with strict rules on how people can behave, enforcing car-free lifestyles, intensive recycling and avoidance of waste. Sometimes, even the idea of such cities can be influential. Dongtan, the planned eco-city of half a million near Shanghai, is a particularly interesting case—much promoted by architects and visionaries in the 2000s and often presented at conferences and in articles as if it were a reality, when in fact none of it was ever built.

There are countless other examples of these kinds of imagined places and communities that hoped to prefigure a better future for the world.[10] Mahatma Gandhi, for example, set up a 'Tolstoy Farm' in South Africa in 1910, intended to embody Leo Tolstoy's vision of a society where people would love their enemies, return evil with good and avoid lust. Rabindranath Tagore, along with the British economist Leonard Elmhirst, set up a village organised around an Institute for Rural Reconstruction, Sriniketan, to serve as a model that would show the world how to 'vitalise knowledge' to overcome caste prejudice and poverty. The ideas of another Bengali, the Indian philosopher Sri Aurobindo, were put into practice in the new town of Auroville in southern India, where thousands were attracted from around the world.

Some have tried to prefigure a future of transformed personal relationships. The Oneida Community founded in upstate New York in 1848 opposed monogamy, with one member writing that 'the frost and ice of selfishness and exclusiveness melted' in their alternative of complex marriage. If any pair became too closely attached, a council intervened, and children were reared collectively. The commune soon dissolved, and today Oneida makes high-end homeware.

All of these experiments, to varying degrees, tried to prefigure the future society through their own rules and practices, to inspire others and then to be copied in the wider world. Few achieved their goals. Indeed, as a rule, the imagined places that were most sealed off from the world had the least influence (and the vast majority of utopian communes quickly collapsed). Those that were more interlinked with the world found it easier to evolve, adapt and influence by way of example.

A present-day equivalent of these new societies is the libertarian dream of creating new places without states or stifling rules and bureaucracy. Some are 'charter cities' that aim to create hubs of dynamic entrepreneurialism, a bit like Hong Kong. One example is the city of Próspera on an island off the coast of Honduras. The project is backed by the Honduran government and invested in by a group of American businesspeople. It's a particularly odd hybrid with governance arrangements that look more medieval than modern, giving landowners additional votes and the company a veto on any decisions.

Since all the land on our planet has already been claimed by states, some have taken to the sea, attracted by the promise of creating new utopias on boats or artificial islands. Over the last few decades, many proposals have offered the world's wealthy a chance to go literally offshore into such new communities, like 'The World', launched in 2002, which offered multi-million-dollar tax-free residences. Billionaire Peter Thiel is one of the supporters of this idea of seaborne utopias; he has funded the Seasteading Institute, which in turn supported the *Satoshi*, a cryptocurrency-oriented cruise-ship utopia. The *Satoshi* promised that its model of government would be suitably twenty-first century, unlike the eighteenth-century constitution of the US. But like so many such ventures, it soon ran into the practical problems of everyday cooperation (people can only live together on a boat with lots of detailed rules on everything from cooking and noise to pets). It foundered.[11]

An even more ambitious way to influence social imagination is to turn a whole country into a laboratory. Since my family comes from New Zealand, I like to see it as an exemplar. It was the first country to introduce universal suffrage (including women) in the 1890s and set up one of the world's first modern welfare states in the 1930s. Today it pioneers such things as 'well-being budgets', which reorient government spending from economic growth and towards happiness. It has also pioneered new ways of thinking about nature, giving legal personhood to a national park (Te Urewera in 2014) and a river (Whanganui in 2017). Finland is another small country that has taken up this mantle of being a pioneer, emboldened by coming top of many global league tables, whether for schools or happiness.

These countries combine highly educated populations; a size that allows for coherence; and successful positions in the global division of labour. They are sufficiently connected to the mainstream to benefit from its knowledge and sufficiently on the edge to think freely and experiment.

Many other countries have also exported their ideas, believing their own imagination to be of universal significance. France after 1789 was perhaps the first conscious exporter of revolutionary ideas, not least through the Napoleonic Code imposed on conquered countries. Maximilien Robespierre himself warned that 'no one likes armed missionaries'. Fyodor Dostoyevsky echoed his point: 'No nation on Earth, no society with a certain measure of stability, has been developed to order, on the lines of a programme imported from abroad.'

But imposed progress has not always been bad, though it may offend our pride to admit it. An interesting finding from recent political science is that those parts of Germany that had Napoleonic ideas forced on them were generally more prosperous and successful half a century later than those that didn't. Where I live in England appears to have been far more prosperous and peaceful during the few centuries of Roman rule than in the centuries either before or after. So even if, in principle, we may dislike the idea of imposition from abroad, history shows a more complex pattern than we might expect.

Put an idea into a political programme

Politics can appear to be the most direct route to turn imagination into reality, though in fact it's less direct than it seems.

Political movements have often put imaginative ideas into their programmes, sowing seeds that flowered much later. The English Chartists in the 1840s, for example, called for universal (male) suffrage and secret ballots. The Second International in the 1880s called for equal pay for women and men, an end to child labour and an eight-hour working day. All of these took a very long time to become reality, but eventually they did, and they justify the common argument of activists in social movements that it's only when you call for the impossible that the possible happens.

There are innumerable examples of quicker results—in the US, the G.I. Bill in the 1940s, which provided benefits to US war veterans, and Kennedy's promise to land a man on the moon; in the UK, the creation of the National Health Service (promised in the Labour Party manifesto in 1945), the right to buy council houses (promised in the Conservative Party manifesto in 1979), tax credits as a way to cut working families' poverty (promised by many parties in the 1990s and then implemented), and carbon taxes and allowances in the 2020s.

It is of course much easier to persuade a political party to adopt an idea if there's already a groundswell behind it, and none of the examples cited above came out of the blue; all built on decades of preparatory work. But connecting, through politics, to state power can dramatically accelerate the transition from idea to reality.

Organise exhibitions and showcases

Another way to promote an imaginative idea is to show it, literally, through an exhibition. Britain in the nineteenth century pioneered this way of inspiring the public and accelerating the enthusiasm of entrepreneurs, inventors and children. London's Great Exhibition of 1851, with its vast palaces of glass, showed the cornucopia of the Industrial Revolution and promised a better future through things, hoping to inspire not only its own population but the whole world. A similar approach was taken in Chicago during its world fair in 1893, with its phosphorescent neon lights and 27 million visitors (the spirit of indefatigable optimism only partially marred by the mayor's assassination just before the fair closed, and by the accelerated decay of nearby poor neighbourhoods as money poured into the immaculate exhibition grounds). The Paris Exposition in 1900, with 50 million visitors, was another example, again including ideas about where society might be headed in the future.

General Motors' 'Futurama' pavilion, built by the architectural firm Albert Kahn Associates, at the New York World's Fair in 1939 exemplified the strengths and weaknesses of such showcases. It attracted 30,000 visitors a day, who left with badges proclaiming, 'I have seen the future'. But it could only imagine the future in terms of plentiful new consumer technologies, with, of course, no mention of the flood of social reforms that would come only a few years later.

The more recent Expos have struggled with the dilemma of how to show intangible ideas. In principle, they are meant to portray a future society in the round, but the format limits them to showing objects. Shanghai's Expo in 2010 attracted 100 million visitors but had to drop its initial ambitious plans to portray a future circular economy, with low waste and reuse, in favour of a more conventional approach. The same was true of Milan in 2015 (partly devoted to ecology and food) and Dubai in 2021. All struggled with the constraints of state and corporate sponsorship and the limitations of presenting the future through the lens of objects and things rather than ideas and relationships. Even so, they were rare moments when possible futures were made tangible.

Tell a story

Fiction can influence imagination in ways that are much simpler than a fully formed utopia. A good example is a book by the French writer Jean Giono, *The Man Who Planted Trees*, which tells the story of a man who plants a hundred acorns each day in a barren landscape in Provence in southern France. In the story, this leads in time to the renaissance of the land and a return of insects, bees and birds. Many assumed that it was a true story; in fact it was fiction. Yet this fiction inspired many others. Wangari Maathai created the Green Belt Movement in Kenya in the late 1970s, which led to the planting of some 30 million trees (and won her the Nobel Peace Prize). There are now many examples of the use of tree-planting as a galvanising, restorative activity. They range from the very large-scale—Ethiopia claimed on a single day in 2019 to have planted over 350 million trees[12]—to the more local: one man, Jadav Payeng from Assam in North-East India, planted some 1,400 acres of forest to save an island on the Brahmaputra river from disappearing because of soil erosion. A glorious picture of the power of tree-planting can be seen in the final part of the film *The Salt of the Earth*, about the life and work of the photographer Sebastião Salgado, which documents how he helped to replant a barren area of Brazil. Each of these is an example of how a story sparks action, which in turn sparks new stories that are both literal stories of regeneration and renewal and also symbolic ones.

Analyse possible futures

The future is unknowable. Yet in the last few decades, a more self-conscious field of futures experts has emerged. Unlike that of the utopians, their work is presented as non-fiction rather than fiction. Some just focus on mapping out likely futures, but others try to encourage imagination, including figures like Bertrand de Jouvenel (and his Futuribles programme) and Gaston Berger (whose invocation was to use futures to 'disturb the present'). Their methods have an uneasy toe-hold in universities despite being frowned upon by the main disciplines.[13] However, there was a time when social scientists saw themselves as shapers and designers of possible futures rather than only as analysts. H.G. Wells, for example, wrote that 'sociology is the description of the Ideal Society and its relation to existing societies', a view shared by very few sociologists today.[14]

Another strand of futurism has been speculative design. Anthony Dunne and Fiona Raby of the Royal College of Art describe it in this way:

design today is concerned primarily with commercial and marketing activities but it could operate on a more intellectual level. It could place new technological developments within imaginary but believable everyday situations that would allow us to debate the implications of different technological futures before they happen.[15]

This may involve designing an object that doesn't or wouldn't exist in the real world and initiating a discussion around whether that object would be desirable, or playfully thinking ahead to how assistive technologies in the home or smart cities could evolve, showing how they might be experienced and what could go wrong. The approach is deliberately provocative rather than prescriptive.[16]

Fuel imagination with faith

Established religions have often been the source of a social imaginary, even if their primary purpose has been to offer an account of the cosmos and the afterlife. Some described a detailed hierarchical social order, like Hinduism or Confucianism. Others grew up as more rebellious, outsider movements, like Taoism, or early Christianity, which promised a break with history but later became an established religion, tied to land, buildings and treasure.

Much later, non-conformist Christianity was particularly fertile in social ideas, notably through the Quakers and Methodists, imagining a world of love and compassion through social reform. Evangelicals and Unitarians played central roles in the struggle against slavery, again in the name of a more just future. In the twentieth century, social Catholicism became a source of both radical ideas and action, and in the twenty-first century, Pope Francis has become a leading advocate for a different kind of economy that can act with decency and dignity towards the environment and humans.

The proposals of these religious movements have generally been fuzzy, as much about ethos and attitude as detailed designs.

This may be because the more detailed designs have generally failed. An extreme example of this, and of the fusion of religion and imagination, came after the French Revolution. The Festival of the Supreme Being was held in Paris in 1794, designed by the great painter Jacques-Louis David. It proposed a new secular religion to the newly liberated people and was matched by festivals across the country, which seem to have sparked some public enthusiasm for a novel fusion of God and revolution.[17] The enthusiasm didn't last long, however, and the festival's promoter, Robespierre, was guillotined a few months later. Not disheartened, France continued this tradition of religious innovation; Auguste Comte, founder of positivism, also attempted to invent a new creed, with roles, clothes and elaborate rituals.

Here were social thinkers trying to imagine new religions. None took hold. But older religions have not shied away from promising to describe, and run, a social order. Khomeini's Iran subordinated the state to the Ayatollahs and promised a return to an imagined past. More recently, the militant group Daesh adopted the name 'Islamic State' to claim authority over all Muslims across the world, with a promise that it would return to the halcyon days of early Islam, opposing all subsequent innovations. Daesh pledged to revive the Caliphate, which had lasted from the seventh century until 1924—again, a promise of return to an imagined utopia in the past. Not that they planned for their utopia to last long; instead, they promised the imminent arrival of 'end times', final battles of the apocalypse that would take place in the Middle East ahead of a day of judgement, an almost perfect mirror image of the optimistic social imaginaries described earlier.

Find new ways of seeing that prompt new ways of doing

New ways of seeing prompt new ways of understanding, and then of acting.[18] Indeed the best champions of social change are often the ones who are most attentive in every sense, spotting patterns around them that others don't see (and sometimes becoming obsessive about attending to other things, like the patterns of nature, the behaviour of birds or how plants grow).

The close links between seeing and doing are very evident in the history of science. Telescopes, microscopes, X-rays and electron microscopes each opened up new ways of understanding the world, first showing a new kind of reality and then prompting the formulation of theories and hypotheses. We see only a narrow spectrum of wavelengths but can now go beyond the infrared vision of snakes, the ultraviolet of bees, or the sonic sight of bats. Observing the red shifts in distant stars prompted new insights into the origins of the universe, while the achromatic-lens microscope developed in the 1820s by Joseph Lister led directly to germ theory, which many consider the most important breakthrough in medicine before 1900. In each case, a novel picture of reality sparked speculation about the meanings of what it revealed.

Climate change is a contemporary example. The world agreed to create an observatory—the Intergovernmental Panel on Climate Change (IPCC)—as a precursor to committing to action through the various treaties negotiated in Rio, Kyoto and Paris. The regular reports from the IPCC, fed by models, offered diagnoses rather than prescriptions. But they made it harder to avoid the need for action, helping the planet to see itself in a novel way and linking the 'is' of a clear picture of climate change, to the 'ought' of a moral imperative to do something about it, to the 'could' of plans for cutting carbon. In the near future, this might go much further as we come to witness more regularly in our daily lives the carbon impact of a short journey, the food we eat or how we heat our homes.

Something similar has happened repeatedly in the social world too. When John Snow mapped a cholera outbreak around Broad Street in London in the mid-nineteenth century and showed how the infections spread from a single water pump, he changed how we see the city. That new pattern of sight then prompted radically different approaches to the management of water and sewage.

A few decades later, statistical methods for measuring poverty paved the way for the welfare state. Charles Booth's great survey of east London in 1887, *Life and Labour of the People in London*, which employed, amongst many others, the young sociologist Beatrice Potter (later Webb), presented a portrait of a million Londoners in poverty and aimed to help society to see itself more clearly than ever before.

Using house-by-house surveys, Booth carefully divided the population into various categories. There were the 'young men who take naturally to loafing, girls who take almost as naturally to the streets'. These were considered the undeserving poor. Another, much larger group were described by Booth as 'shiftless, hand to mouth, pleasure loving and always poor'.

Such commentaries were very much of their time. But the detailed mapping and care with numbers were very much ahead of their time and showed how research could change the world. For example, the evidence showing that average life expectancy was only twenty-nine in poor districts compared to fifty-five in wealthier ones helped to justify large-scale provision of public housing and eventually paved the way for a universal health service.

This new way of seeing also helped to crystallise a new view of how the state might act in relation to society—with observation and research to guide it. Statistics played a central role in this shift, moving from being a way for the state to observe society into a way for society to observe itself. (On the meaning of statistics, Bertrand Russell is believed to have remarked that 'the mark of a civilised human is the ability to look at a column of numbers, and weep.')

More qualitative accounts could also shift hearts and minds—and, again, stir imaginative empathy. The Works Progress Administration (WPA) in the US in the 1930s brought the voices of the poor into the public realm and turned people who might otherwise be invisible, or merely statistics, into living flesh and blood. The Federal Writers' Project, which came under the WPA, aimed to produce a vast geographical-social-historical picture of the states, cities and localities of the whole of the United States, and as part of this work spread out to encourage a mapping of everyday life, folk memories, music and autobiographies, including memories of slavery, leading to the 'largest body of first-person narratives ever collected.'[19]

All progressive social change is preceded by a new way of seeing which then connects to a moral imperative. Recognising domestic violence, or the vulnerability of women on city streets; bringing gay love and sex out of the closet; acknowledging the trauma experienced by refugees; measuring and mapping carbon emissions; or taking notice of microplastics in the oceans—in each of these cases, something that was hidden in plain sight is spotted, recognised as a public fact and moral claim, talked about and then acted on. Our ideal might be a society where seeing quickly leads to action. Indeed, sometimes action is, as it were, automated. If a crime becomes visible, then the police and courts have to act. If a problem is formally identified, public bodies are required to respond. Such is one dimension of social progress (which is absent in regimes that are corrupt and authoritarian).

Often, these shifts in vision need new concepts as well as descriptive methods. The sociologist Judy Singer coined the term 'neurodiversity' in the 1990s, prompted by her experience of autism, and by what she thought was a misplaced 'social constructivist' view of her condition which denied its biological basis. Two decades later, the term is in wide use and believed to apply to as many as one in three people.

Today we might expect comparable breakthroughs to be sparked by the flood of new data, network analyses or semantic analyses that literally see the social world in new ways, or by the many movements to open up voice and decision-making to groups previously excluded from power. For example, the more detailed measurement of psychological well-being being conducted around the world is unfolding new ways of thinking about societies to complement the dominant accounts of GDP, income and wealth, showing the role that social security can play either in amplifying anxiety or dampening it, or shining a light on loneliness. Once you see that happiness and GDP are logarithmically linked, it becomes obvious that wealthy societies will do more for their well-being by focusing on the needs of the miserable and stressed, rather than helping the very rich become even richer, or even worrying too much about those on middle incomes.

Extreme Citizen Science, which involves indigenous peoples in creating and shaping new knowledge, for example about plants or fauna, is a particularly exciting example. Indeed, one way of trying to forecast where social imagination might go is to examine the frontiers of new ways of seeing: for example, the use of graphs to map relationships, cellular patterns of transmitting behaviours or new devices for mapping emotions through the face or patterns of brain activity.

My favourite example of how new ways of seeing can change how we think is the human body. We usually look at it as something fixed. But a little elementary science tells us that all of its cells regenerate, on average every few years, but some much more regularly. We better understand the body as a pattern that recreates itself, always with slight changes, rather than as something static. This is also a helpful way of thinking about societies and institutions—as patterns that much of the time recreate themselves but which, under the surface, are in constant motion.

Learning by doing?

I hope this chapter has given a sense of how much past imagination has shaped our present, from fictional utopias to simple, generative ideas, model towns to exhibitions, and new ways of living to new ways of seeing.

In each case, the imagination is only a spark. It is followed up by the hard work of design and then of implementation, which invariably changes the idea or reveals something about it that wasn't obvious to its originator: its gaps, flaws, contradictions or lateral potential.

Some of the methods described above attempted to impose an idea on others, whether through writing, imperial assertion or exhibitions. But the best ways to imagine may be the ones that position this work as a collaboration—done *with* people rather than to or for them—giving people and communities the freedom to learn by doing and to adapt the general into the particular.

4

PATTERNS

MAKING SENSE OF IMAGINATION

In the last chapter, I shared many examples of imagination from the past. How should we make sense of them? Are there any patterns? Can we reach any conclusions about which ones went on to have the greatest impact, and why? Here I suggest some of the ways we might approach and understand these many journeys from ideas to results.

Dreams and disappointments

The world of ideas and their implementation is one I've lived in for much of my life. I've had the good fortune to see how this works from the top down and the bottom up. I've seen again and again that although people usually overestimate how much will change quickly, we almost always underestimate how much can change over decades. One of the reasons is that big changes require many small things to shift in tandem, including how we think. That takes time. But once those changes have happened, the world really does look radically different.

67

Twenty years ago, I helped develop one of the first national climate change strategies—driving investments into renewable energy and encouraging changes in behaviour that are now becoming mainstream. I worked on ambitious programmes to cut poverty—like Surestart, which two decades later turned out to have transformed the lives of hundreds of thousands of children. The idea of everyone having a tradeable personal carbon allowance (which would decrease over time) was much discussed in the 2000s, and even floated in a UK government document later that decade. But even though it is much the fairest way to manage a transition to zero carbon, it still hasn't been introduced anywhere.[1]

I worked on radical ideas about how democracy could be reimagined and now can see dozens of examples in place around the world, from online deliberation and participatory budgeting to citizens' assemblies. In the late 1980s I worked on online music distribution and in the mid-1990s was part of a group developing online platforms for exchanging goods and services, an idea that then seemed utopian and now seems mundane.

A decade later I was working with data activists trying to invent new ways for us to take control of our own personal data. Hardly anyone was interested then, but now it's high on the political agenda. In between, I helped design a plan for sharply reducing the numbers of people living rough on the streets of English cities—and then saw the numbers fall by more than two-thirds as the plan was put into action.

I've also been closely involved in technological imagination ever since I was lucky enough to spend time with some of the pioneers of the internet in the 1980s. Digital technologies encourage you to break down familiar processes and see how they could be reconstructed in entirely different ways. One example is transforming the classroom with flipped learning—the idea that children can learn just as well through videos or online courses outside of lessons, so that time together in the classroom is used for discussion and absorbing the content, rather than consuming it. This was quite a marginal idea until the COVID-19 pandemic forced school systems all over the world to go online, accelerating a more thoughtful debate about both the potential and the limits of remote learning. Digital technology has also helped us see how healthcare could be changed, with a much bigger role for self-management and peer support, feedback on symptoms, and the potential to prevent illnesses rather than only attempt to cure.

I've also had my fair share of failures. I helped develop a new kind of school—the studio school—designed to better prepare young people for the worlds of work and life they were likely to face, built around project-based learning and teamwork. I was convinced these were the way to the future. For a time, they seemed to be succeeding. Dozens were set up and teenagers loved them. But then a sharp recession and hostility from government ministers meant that many closed down. Some are thriving, but it's still unclear whether the schools were just ahead of their time or whether the idea was flawed. The same was true of a project I helped to initiate to create a comprehensive data infrastructure for children—to link up many agencies so that they could spot problems earlier, and move to prevent future risks.[2] Again, this was shut down just as it was beginning to work. The world of imagination can be—and perhaps is always—a rollercoaster of dreams and disappointments.

We can't predict the future, but we can explore

Social change is far more complex than our capacity to under-stand it. The impossibility of knowing the future means that everyone sees the world and its future 'through a glass darkly'. Indeed, this is the paradox that faces anyone who studies history. On the one hand, there are steady long-term patterns of change: developments in consciousness, economy and technology that, while messy and uneven, are profound and inescapable and follow apparently consistent patterns (which I describe in more detail in Chapter 5). On the other hand, it is impossible to know what the future will actually bring. Few in 1900 expected a brutal world war and revolutions in the next generation. Few in 1925 anticipated a boom, a depression and then another war. Few in the 1950s expected the scale of cultural change of the 1960s. Few in the 1980s expected the imminent collapse of the USSR, resurgent Islamic fundamentalism, or the rise of personal computing and the internet. Few in the 2000s anticipated the scale of the financial crisis, or the boom in populist authoritarianism, or that the world would grind to a halt thanks to a pandemic. If anything, experts were worse at spotting these trends than non-experts, insiders worse than outsiders.

If nothing else, these patterns should warn us against any delusions of inevitability, whether the old communist ones (of inevitable revolution) or the more recent liberal capitalist ones (of inevitable globalisation), since these blind us to reversibility, fragility and sheer luck.

No one can see into the future and no one ever has, though many prophets believed they had the gift of foresight. Whether it's Nostradamus, Bellamy or modern futurists, it's noticeable that while they get some things right, they get many more things wrong.[3] Some are good at seeing things in the present that point to the future. But anyone who truly believes they have the gift of foresight is deluded. The patterns of change that shape the future are always vastly more complex than the human mind can grasp.

An important lesson follows from this. Precisely because the future is unknowable, the most useful imagineers may not be the ones who offer complete and coherent visions of the future, but rather the ones who provide ideas and tools that others can work with. The same is true in architecture: over-planned model cities rarely work as intended and are hard to love, whereas the best designs have built into them a capacity to adapt and evolve.

There is a wonderful comment by Bertolt Brecht on art: he asks which works of art endure, and answers 'those that are never completed'. Those that live, thrive and become meaningful to successive generations are the ones that leave them space to adapt, add and subtract (something always true of pieces of music and theatre, which have to be interpreted to live). This has important implications for utopias and detailed programmes. The fully formed utopia aims to offer a coherent, complete, usually closed picture. The alternative is fragmentary, suggestive and partial, whether in the form of single principles like the Levellers' call to abolish wage slavery or Thomas More's proposal to eliminate money, or ideas like Francis Bacon's on how to generalise the scientific academy to the whole of society. These incomplete ideas often go on to have much more influence than the complete blueprints.

That is why I tend to prefer explorers over prophets—explorers being people who set out to map the future through trial and error, who experiment, and who are humble in the face of complexities they can only dimly grasp. The prophets who believed they had unique insights that enabled them to paint comprehensive pictures of a desired future are, for me, more suspect. By contrast, the people who set ideas free into the world—from half-formed political concepts to urban designs—have turned out to be more useful to the future.

Another lesson flows from this. Dig beneath the surface of the utopias, philosophies and model communities and you quickly find that their creators have drawn on existing themes and ideas. Ideas never come from nowhere. They are always extensions, graftings or inversions of things that are already in the world. This is also true, of course, of music and literature: the greatest composers and writers play with existing elements, codes and grammars. Recognising this doesn't diminish our admiration. But it helps us to see their work less as magic and more as craft.

Social imagination can be thick or thin

Some ideas stand alone. Others form clusters or assemblies. And the most influential are thick, dense networks of ideas that feed off each other. When ideas first emerge, they lack this thickness. The proto-feminism of eighteenth-century writers was brave and pioneering but missing in complementary ideas. It was not yet an ethos as well as a programme, and it lacked exemplars it could point to, whereas by the end of the twentieth century it had many of these. So too with veganism, which only gained momentum when linked to a broader green movement and sensibility, an analysis of the wrongs of meat-eating, and then the practical offering of thousands of restaurants showing that vegan food could be pleasurable as well as ethical.

Any cluster of ideas or imaginaries can be pictured as a series of layers, stretching from a base that is practical, concrete and everyday to a summit that is aspirational but also misty. At the top, the first layer is ethos and vision, where imagination plays a role similar to religion. It provides an overall vision or direction for society that connects in a loose way to individual lives. That vision may be of the nation as a family; of society becoming ever more enlightened and free; it could be a promise of deep equality or future communism or ever greater individual freedom; of an individual nation achieving an historic destiny; of a society reunited with nature; or a technologically inspired vision of a future full of smart things and solutions. These ideas become part of people's identities; they provide a shape and meaning to how they interpret the world around them. Most cannot easily be refuted. They are often quite vague, even inchoate: more an ethos than a plan.

On the next level are the generative ideas. These are more specific concepts that can be applied in many fields and give substance to the broad visions. They include ideas such as universal human rights; national citizenship; needs-based welfare; social insurance; the circular economy; central planning; market-based solutions; conservation approaches to nature and animals; heritage approaches to cities and buildings; and organic or permaculture approaches to food. They often have roots in philosophical thought. These too are hard to verify or disprove. They exist at a level of abstraction and survive best if they have logical links to other related ideas.

Another level down are domain-specific ideas, or imaginative ideas for particular fields: ideas about how schools might be run, preventive healthcare, the practical organisation of democracy, or how a firm might be structured. This is the everyday currency of social imagination, and in a lively society there will be many thousands of these ideas bubbling up, sometimes spreading and sometimes waning. These are more easily refuted; if they are tried and don't work, they will generally be discarded.

Finally, there are specific applications of these: experiments, pilots, proposals and plans that connect the imaginative ideas to an everyday reality in a place and time, mobilising power, money and enthusiasm to make them happen. These are much more easily verified or refuted. They work or they don't—at least not enough to maintain the engagement of providers of money or authority.

The most powerful movements of social change are 'thick' and manage to function at all four levels. Robert Owen's cooperative programme is a good example. The vision was of a society based on cooperation rather than hierarchy or property; there were generative ideas of mutuality that could be applied to marriage, factories or schools. Then there were more specific ideas that showed how these would manifest in care for children or the organisation of production. And, finally, there were various implementations, some very successful (which inspired others

ANOTHER WORLD IS POSSIBLE

and spread across the world) and some very unsuccessful (which sank with barely a trace).

On the other side of the political spectrum, nineteenth-century Prussian militarism is a parallel example. Its social imaginary coalesced around a vision of victory on the battlefield and the conquest of territories. This was described in Bismarck's famous comment that 'not through speeches and majority decisions will the great questions of the day be decided ... but by iron and blood'. Its imaginary rested on the power of industry as well as armies, but also recognised the need for the cultivation of character, discipline and productive strength in the economy. That in turn required a welfare state, insurance for accidents and disability, and laws on health. This was partly to head off the threat from the liberals and the left, but it also contributed to productivity and national strength. A powerful state machinery was needed to implement these ideas—to train a workforce and harness technology—and to embed them in daily life. In all of these senses, Prussia combined some of the features of religion with some of the features of more experimental science. Defeat in the First World War partly invalidated its ideas, but many (including Adolf Hitler) were able to rationalise that defeat and blame it on betrayal.

I mention this imaginary—which was paralleled in different ways by Atatürk's Turkey and Meiji-era Japan (both of which imposed new dress codes and rules for language as well as new ways of running government and the economy)—because it may offer a template for some of the dominant imaginaries of the twenty-first century too, fusions of national mission and technology for the newer superpowers of China, India, Brazil and Indonesia (which I look at in more detail in Chapter 11).

All four dimensions of the imaginary need to evolve in harmony for imaginative ideas to last; they gather around them meanings and associations and become part of people's identity.

Visions that remain only visions do not survive, but equally, practical ideas that don't have any supporting superstructure of ideas tend not to thrive because they lack the emotional aura that a thick imagination brings. This becomes clearer if we look at some of the otherwise promising clusters of ideas that have not succeeded as they might.

Buddhism is a striking example. It has a very powerful diagnosis of the world and the causes of suffering, and its distinct ethos has had a big influence on me ever since I spent time in a Buddhist monastery at the age of seventeen. Its precepts influenced many rulers. But it has failed to generate a rich and detailed social imagination, a picture of how a Buddhist society might actually work. There are fragments of Buddhist economics (E.F. Schumacher's book *Small is Beautiful*, for example) and social thought. But there is no serious account of how a state might be run, or how justice, the family or businesses could be more Buddhist. This may be the result of Buddhism's stance that much of reality is an illusion. But it contrasts sharply with the traditions of both Christianity and Islam, which have produced detailed social and political designs, from the Catholic social thought that shaped the Christian Democratic parties of post-war Europe to the project of Shi'ite theocracy in Iran. As a result, although Buddhism has had great influence on personal lives globally and has even produced political parties in Japan and elsewhere, it has had very little influence on social organisation.

A very different example is the neo-conservatism that achieved great influence in the US at the beginning of this century; it had a strong high-level imaginary, of good fighting evil, but turned out to lack the practical ideas that could help with the rebuilding of states. The same has been true of anarchism: a powerful overall vision with some potent generative ideas, crystallised by great thinkers like Peter Kropotkin and Pierre-Joseph Proudhon, but that has consistently failed to turn these into effective practical ideas that could work at any scale.

Blockchain is a current, ambiguous example. The technology has prompted rich thinking about new ways of organising voting or governance without the need for a central state. The field of crypto has a strong ethos—usually libertarian and individualistic. And it is rich in experiments, from Bitcoin and Ethereum to applications in property and law. But it remains unclear whether the pieces fit together, or whether the promise of governance without a state can work reliably on a grand scale.

The same is perhaps true of data sovereignty, the idea that we should all control our own data. This has a clear vision and ethos, which can be translated into generative ideas; it can be applied in specific fields, from health to banking, and can benefit from hundreds of practical experiments.[4] But again, the practical limits of this imagination remain unclear: how far can anyone truly control data about themselves, from images picked up by CCTV cameras or satellites to traces of their movements or shopping?

Going with and against the grain

Some imagination points forwards and some points only backwards; some draws on the experiences and thoughts of the frontiers of its time—science, art, social organisation—and some rejects these. However, it's not enough simply to be 'for progress' or to seek to ride the tides of history. Instead, the most interesting patterns of social imagination draw on ideas at the frontiers of their time while also challenging them. They are, in other words, dialectical, rather than linear or deductive.

Dialectical thinking can mean many things. It is used to refer to the transformation of quantity into quality, the interpenetration of opposites, and even the 'negation of the negation'.[5] But at its core, it is a dynamic way of thinking that grasps tensions and contradictions rather than wishing them away.

This makes it different from more one-dimensional ways of thinking, like radical free-market capitalism, which offers markets as the answer to everything, or a naïve socialist communitarianism that argues that, if only we were nice to each other, everything would be fine. Instead, dialectics is a way of thinking that encourages us to think through how each action or new design creates its own dynamic and its own challenges.[6]

Much social and political imagination is not dialectical in this sense. Some just tries to go with the flow of change, widening or deepening already visible trends in technology, values or social organisation. These visions tend to align with the interests and values of the powerful, or with emergent powerful groups. Much traditional liberal thinking fits into this category, as does much 'futurology' which breathlessly celebrates rising power. When we look back, we can find equivalents—some written into utopias or fêted in great exhibitions. But these are soon forgotten; they date most quickly.

A very different approach deliberately goes against the grain and points in an opposite direction. Examples have been common since Romantic ideas emphasising the importance of nature were developed during the Industrial Revolution, or in more recent ecological thinking that encourages people to go off grid, return to small communities, create ascetic communes, or counter overcentralisation with radical decentralisation. Kropotkin and Tolstoy (and other aristocrats before and since) favoured an anti-industrial, anti-urban idyll of voluntary cooperation in the countryside, which would have been hard to square with the population levels of already industrialising countries. The advocacy of a new Islamic Caliphate is another important current example, deliberately and unambiguously reactionary in that it promises adherence to something from the past, not the future. The ascendancy of the Ayatollahs in Iran was equally reactionary in this sense, as are the strands of American Christian fundamentalism that seek to create a quasi-theocratic state, with laws derived from the edicts of the Bible.

A more dialectical approach goes both with and against the grain. This has been true of Marxism, which went with the grain of technology and industrial organisation in the nineteenth century but with a very different take on the options. Marxism saw in capitalism a great leap forward in human cooperation which could be taken in alternative directions; as a result, Marxists became at times infatuated with the frontiers of business, from Taylorism in the 1920s to post-Fordism in the late twentieth century, while also challenging the status quo.

Some strands of green thinking do the same today, making the most of science, data and new forms of economic organisation. All promise a step forward in human evolution but also a return to something that has been lost, an authentic, profoundly better way of life.

Dialectical thinking can take many forms. Fascist thinking was dialectical to some degree and attempted to draw on what were thought to be the frontiers at the time, whether of science (eugenics) or of art (the futurism of Marinetti, with its love of speed, violence and machines), while also promising a return to the glories of Imperial Rome. There are also odd hybrids that in their own ways attempted to go both with and against the grain: the Shah of Iran in the 1970s attempting to feed off the glories of ancient Persia and simultaneously to create a high-technology economy; the kings and sheikhs of the Gulf promising a fusion of medieval politics and twentieth-century business. But because these hybrids were and are so regressive on social and political issues, they have little to offer the rest of the world by way of inspiration.

Indeed, they help to clarify what makes an imaginary progressive. Ever since the days of the Enlightenment, the most progressive ideas of the future tried to show how the world could achieve its goals at a greater scale, and how complexity and differentiation could be combined with some kind of integration—the hallmark of all processes of evolution. They pointed, in other words, to ideas that were potentially universal and generalisable, rather than only relevant to one place and time. This seems to me to remain a pertinent distinction. It doesn't mean that universalisable ideas provide a precise blueprint; they can still leave lots of scope for societies to adapt ideas and bend the future rather than laying down a plan. After all, real societies are always impure hybrids of multiple cultures,[7] and overly static and homogeneous organisations or groups quickly fall apart. Wisdom is all about appreciating contexts. But the best progressive ideas are potentially relevant to anyone, and one lesson of the last two centuries is that many ideas—from the scientific method to parliamentary democracy, cooperatives to feminism—can thrive in the most unlikely places.

True conservatives, by contrast, believe that there are no such universalisable ideas; that any hope that rights, circular economies or politics based on well-being could become universal are at best fantasies and at worst dangerous.

Adaptation and assemblies

I've suggested that many of the most influential ideas are simple, even simplistic. They travel and spread because they can be summed up in a few pithy sentences, even if behind these sit vast tracts.

Yet it's a problem that our ideas will always be an order of magnitude simpler than the reality they seek to explain or shape. So will our models or algorithms. Our brains may be wonderful things, but they can grasp only a tiny fraction of what is happening around them, which is why we get by with simple heuristics that work much of the time but also repeatedly fall short. These are all reasons why we should be humble about cognitive capacity and always willing to learn, revise and adapt. It's never wise to attach your ego too firmly to any idea.

But this also has profound implications for imagination, and another kind of dialectic. Ideas, which are simple, meet the world in a dance, with an element of tension or give and take. In their manifestations, ideas always change. If they are forced too rigidly onto the world, then there are bound to be damaging results—the world bites back. This is why I advocate evolutionary, experimental implementation of ideas rather than diktat or elaborate five-year plans. It's through action on the world that we learn how the world works, not through detached reflection. As the great urbanist Patrick Geddes put it, 'By creating we think, by living we learn'.

It's tempting to design comprehensive proposals for the world. But a lesson of history is that it's usually better to combine broad generative ideas with more precise local implementations, fitted to context, and to combine the mindset of the searcher with that of the implementer. Parachuting the same model of school, hospital, parliament or elderly care into many different societies is likely to backfire. Many ideas work somewhere. Few work everywhere. As Francisco Varela puts it in his remarkable book *Ethical Know-How*, 'intelligence should guide our actions, but in harmony with the texture of the situation at hand, not in accordance with a set of rules or procedures.'[8]

This is why so many real social institutions are better understood as assemblies of many parts rather than as being logically deduced from a single idea. Think for example of the school that combines tuition, sports, activities of all kinds and engagement with its local community; or the parliament that combines roles of scrutiny and legislation, allowing a ruling party to rule and giving voice to society.

This character mirrors what we find with technologies. The car is much more than an internal combustion engine: it needs a chassis, wheels, electronic control systems, interior design and much more. A computer combines processing power, memory, visual displays, keyboards and, again, much more.

Real societies are also assemblies of very diverse, even contra-dictory elements. Although theorists like to claim they follow a single logic, reality is very different. Societies need different cultures and different moral syndromes in, for example, armies, intelligence agencies, auditors, doctors, entrepreneurs, carers and teachers, to mention just a few. The task of turning imaginative ideas into lived realities invariably involves assemblies that combine multiple things into a useful form rather than just extrapolation from a single idea.

Expanding possibility space

All of these examples confirm that the social function of imagination is in some respects quite simple: it widens the range of options open to us. Without it, we can still cope and adapt, but we will do so more cautiously and incrementally, tweaking here, adjusting there. Imagination creates a larger possibility space from which to choose, and if we can communicate our imagination in compelling ways, we open up a larger possibility space for others too, helping them to realise that they could overcome discrimination, adopt other diets, take pride in being transgender, or help to make digital commons.

Statistics and maths use a similar notion of 'possibility space'. In experiments or problem-solving, the possibility space includes all the possible results or outcomes (in maths, for example, all the possible results from rolling a dice). I use the term in a similar way to describe the options open to an organisation or a society at any point in history. The size of this space depends both on imagination and on the work done to translate imagination into practical options. In principle, we could map any society by the size of its possibility spaces, and we would expect those with larger spaces to respond better to shocks and surprises than those with smaller spaces. This, in essence, is the function of social imagination: it is a tool for generating options, many of which may be undesirable but some of which may be essential.

Evolutionary and network science provide useful insights here. Both have tried to make sense of how both biological and human evolution strike a balance between exploration and search on the one hand and exploitation of existing knowledge or resources on the other, for example between seeking out new homes and hunting grounds and making the most of existing ones.[9] When environments are changing fast, you're likely to need more exploration relative to exploitation—or discovery of more possibility space. But there will still be a need for the practical implementers to work out exactly how the group can move to a new home.[10] In this sense, imagination is an essential part of evolution, relevant to two of the four mechanisms of inheritance that Eva Jablonka and Marion Lamb describe in their classic *Evolution in Four Dimensions*: social learning (some forms of which can be found in many species), and distinctively human forms of symbolic thought.[11] Evolutionary theory also casts interesting light on cognitive styles. Some argue now that there may be good evolutionary reasons for the development of neurodiversity— dyslexia, for example, is often associated with a greater capacity to explore or see wholes, which must have been useful to groups during humanity's long prehistory.[12] The two halves of our brains also work in complementary ways, the one instrumental and linear, the other more holistic, creative and empathic; where the 'left hemisphere's relationship with the world is one of reaching out to grasp, and therefore to use it, the right hemisphere's appears to be that of reaching out, just that.'[13]

We each need both, and by analogy, within any group or team, too, you need people who can reach out, imagine and explore, as well as sceptics who can focus on the limits, risks and constraints. Getting the balance right is rarely easy, especially in bureaucracies that gravitate towards scepticism and caution. But this is an unavoidable challenge for any organisation or society.

We can look for inspiration from nature but probably won't want to emulate it. Nature manages this balance through a combination of profligacy and ruthlessness: thousands of frogspawn, only a handful of which will survive; countless seeds blown in the winds; and brutally high levels of child mortality in many species. Social imagination can be equally profligate, spawning millions of prophets without followers, movements that don't move, and bright ideas that briefly spark before disappearing. But it is only through multiplication and trying many things out that our world finds a way for a few to succeed, and the smartest organisations are the ones that learn how to balance imagination and realism without quite so much waste.

The anxiety of imagination

We have a desperate need for imagination to generate options, for everything has to be conceived before it can be tried. But imagination, like information, has both the strength and the weakness of being insubstantial, with no easy way to distinguish between truth, lies and half-truths.

This is the great challenge for anyone working on novel ideas. There is no easy way to discover if you are mad or sane, pursuing an illusion or a brilliant insight into the future.

Every idea will change when it encounters the constraints of the real world: material constraints, economic constraints and constraints imposed by human psychology. It is, then, the interplay between possibility and constraint that generates the real new as opposed to the imagined new. This is when interests and hypocrisy all kick in, as well as wise realism. Meek Christianity ('it is easier for a camel to go through the eye of a needle than for a rich man to get into heaven') ends up with the vast wealth, landowning and hedonism of organised churches. The frugal egalitarianism of communism ends with the extravagant waste of rulers like Nicolae Ceaușescu, whose 'People's House' cost €4 billion, or Kim Jong-Un. Well-intentioned moves to make firms accountable for their environmental or social impact end up in the 'greenwashing' of contemporary measurements—a conspiracy of pretence that bears scant relationship to reality.

But engagement with reality doesn't only bring ideas and idealism down. It also turns half-formed or unbalanced ideas into useful ones. The Chartist calls for universal suffrage quietly dropped the (not-so-wise) demand for annual parliaments. Appealing calls for flat incomes or flat taxes invariably have to adapt to a world of uneven needs and capacities, ending up anything but flat. Generous calls for borders to be open to all migration or refugees usually have to be tempered by the not unreasonable view that in a democracy, communities should have some say in who can join them.

Evidence is sometimes accumulated about what works—and not just that, but also what works when, where and how (since few ideas will work the same way everywhere). For example, the microcredit methods pioneered by Grameen Bank in Bangladesh, which won founder Muhammad Yunus a Nobel Peace Prize, worked very well there but much less well in neighbouring India. This evidence is then fed back so that ideas can be adjusted and refined.

These are just a few of the ways that the pure chemistry of ideas mutates into new compounds through exposure to the oxygen of real societies, patterns which mean that the originators of ideas can rarely know what will happen to them. Nor is there any easy way to situate imaginative ideas in time—to know whether they might bear fruit in a decade, a century or a millennium. You may look for corroboration from others, but we know from history that the most fashionable ideas are often the ones that disappear fastest. Being involved in this kind of work thus brings with it an unavoidable anxiety and requires a certain strength of character, a toughness and resistance to social pressures, to stick with ideas and help them grow.

5

THE FUTURE

HOW TO RE-ENERGISE OUR
COLLECTIVE IMAGINATION

How should we dream or imagine in ways that are useful? What methods encourage and quicken imagination, or help us in utopia-making? What are the options for a political leader, a funder of research, a social movement or a city that wants to expand its horizon of possibilities?

We know that creativity can be learned—it's not a unique attribute of a handful of people. And we know that innovation and creativity can be institutionalised, made part of people's jobs, as they are in TV and film, science and business. Creative people in other fields—like visual artists or filmmakers—depend on tools, palettes and paints, cameras and special-effects software. For society's imagineers, there are not so many obvious tools, the raw materials being life and society themselves; and there are few academies or colleges that teach the craft of change.[1]

But there are methods that can be used for the two steps essential to any process of imagination: first, distancing and questioning current reality; and second, designing an alternative.

These are designed to put into action Albert Einstein's comment that 'Imagination is more important than knowledge. Knowledge is limited. Imagination encircles the world.' Such methods offer a palette of tools which I think should be used much more widely to help us explore possible futures.

The universal grammars of creativity

Artists can draw on many frameworks for creativity that both describe and prescribe the steps that can lead to a novel, painting or film.[2] I like to use a simple one which mirrors those used in other fields of art. I think of this as a universal framework for creativity. It can be used to widen the possibility space for composing music, designing a home, doing graffiti or creating a recipe. It offers powerful tools for opening up new social possibilities. These help us to see both the constructed nature of the social world around us and how it could be changed.

The essential idea is to take an existing activity or function—like childcare, local bus services or the work of the United Nations—and then imagine a series of transformations being applied to it:

Extension
Grafting
Inversion
Addition
Subtraction
Mobilising metaphor and analogy
Using randomness.

Let's look at each of these in turn. *Extension* of an aspect of existing practice means taking it further. Examples from the arts include Bach's extension of fugues to six voices or expansion of the size of the orchestra. Something similar has happened repeatedly to ideas. A big strand of thinking on the radical libertarian right has played with extending the market into as many fields as possible. Others have expanded the range of fields where the concept of rights can be used (with rights themselves being an extension of theological ideas about human uniqueness). Extending school could mean adding on new hours to the day or weeks to the year. Extending suffrage might mean giving the vote to sixteen-year-olds, or six-year-olds. And much of our social imagination involves scaling up concepts from daily life—the camaraderie of friends, the competition of sports (the 'level playing field') or the care of the family—to the level of organisations and whole societies.

Grafting (or *combining*) involves taking an idea from one field and applying it to another. Again, this is very common in the arts—for example, grafting ideas from photography back into painting—and it's also common in the social field. Examples include the way that the idea of auctions was grafted onto the management of the electromagnetic spectrum (the radio waves used for mobile phones, satellites or television), or how the idea of the jury was grafted onto democracy in the form of citizens' juries. Thinking about grafting can also quickly generate new ideas. What if schools became places for health; what if democracy was introduced into the workplace; what if the provision of childcare or care for the elderly was managed on platforms like Amazon or Uber?

Writing on technological evolution, George Dyson commented that:

> sudden leaps in biological or technological evolution occur when an existing structure or behaviour is appropriated by a new function that spreads rapidly across the evolutionary landscape, taking advantage of a head start. Feathers must have had some other purpose before they were used to fly. U-boat commanders appropriated the Enigma machine first developed for use by banks. Charles Babbage

envisioned using the existing network of church steeples that rose above the chaos of London as the foundation for a packet-switched communications net.[3]

This insight is a good prompt for any exercise in social imagination. Are there interesting patterns in other fields that could be appropriated or adapted? What could be taken from airports and applied to hospitals to help the flow of people through the system; from the provision of food that could be applied to schools, such as calorie counts or diets; from healthcare that could be applied to relationships?

A more radical approach is to use *inversion*, as practised in the Middle Ages during Carnival, when for a day the poor pretended to be rich and vice versa. Inversion is a common theme in Christianity ('the meek shall inherit the earth') and has also prompted much radical innovation more recently. What if farmers became bankers (as happened with the microcredit provided by Grameen Bank); patients became doctors; or social care were provided by people who had themselves been recipients of care? What if the young taught the old? What if consumers became makers of things? What if data were used by citizens to oversee governments, not the other way around?

Addition and *subtraction* are also useful. Baroque and traditional Hindu architecture are good examples of extreme addition, and any social service can easily add on new elements—like a family doctor who also offers advice on welfare. Much modernist art and music favoured subtraction, leading to Kazimir Malevich's painting 'White on White' in 1918 or the silence of John Cage's 1952 composition 4'33''. This way of thinking can also be generative in social contexts: what if you took away half of the roles in a hierarchy or introduced a maximum income? Or what if you had to cut a budget by half, or could double it? What options would most preserve value? I've worked with public parks that faced a 50 per cent budget cut and were prompted to come up with dozens of creative ways of raising money, through events, music, festivals and food, leaving the parks more vibrant than they had been before. The cheap prices of today's supermarkets are only possible because Clarence Saunders in Memphis in the early twentieth century had the inspired idea of subtracting service staff and letting customers pack their own bags.

Sometimes, not doing things is better than doing them. A surprising example of this was found in the military's experience that taking immediate action to treat soldiers suffering from PTSD tended to make it worse. It proved better to let people mobilise their own resources and then to focus on the 4 or 5 per cent for whom that approach hadn't worked. Less can be more.

An interesting recent study showed that we find it much easier to add than to subtract when solving problems, even when this is less efficient.[4] But subtraction may be essential to the needs of our times. Veganism is an approach which subtracts—excluding meats and dairy products from diets—and much law and regulation is now focused on reducing energy use, carbon emissions and travel, rather than increasing them.

Creative thought is often helped by *mobilising metaphor and analogy*—seeing one thing and thinking of another (a variant of the grafting process described above). Much of social change comes from shifts in metaphors. Do we see society as a war, a body or an organism; a building, a machine or a family? Do we think in terms of journeys, or defence against threats? Is the economy analogous to a household, which means being very careful not to spend more than you earn, or is it more like an entrepot or trading post, in which case debt may be essential?

We automatically think in metaphors. We talk of ideas as illuminating and bright, fizzing and incisive, or flat and dull. We see our world in spatial terms—rising and falling, moving forward or back. We speak metaphorically, too—we 'ride' bicycles, though not cars; we 'harness' ideas to a new purpose; we let our imaginations 'take flight'. Biological metaphors are particularly powerful and universal—seeing social change through the metaphor of the butterfly and chrysalis, spring after winter, or planting seeds. These can be potent because we all know the everyday wonder of how nature can transform a barren place fast.

So, one approach to fuelling imagination is to deliberately use metaphors as tools. For example, take a live question or field and then reimagine it using a metaphor, perhaps seeing it as a journey, a landscape or a building. Or you can use combinatorial metaphors: reimagine your farm as if it were a factory or vice versa, or reimagine a house as an energy generator. This kind of exercise dislodges, throwing up surprising insights, combinations and angles, like a gym for the creative mind.[5]

Using randomness can be a way of throwing in surprise. In the arts, aleatory or randomising methods were widely used in music and painting in the first half of the twentieth century, from Arnold Schoenberg to Jackson Pollock. Similar methods can also help to generate new ideas. For example, pick a page on a website or a billboard, and find ways to use it to inspire novelty. The last billboard I saw before writing this was for an Evangelical Gospel church. Think of ten things your organisation or family might borrow from how they work.

Painting has an interesting history of encouraging such lateral, random methods. Leonardo da Vinci endorsed using random patterns such as the damp on a wall to spark inspiration ('by indistinct things the mind is stimulated to new inventions'), while Chinese painters recommended using the patterns of a falling-down building in the same way.

All of these tools generate ideas quickly, and the more you use them, the easier it is to expand the possibility space. They echo the transformations we see in the natural world: plants extend, add and graft. Hurricanes and forest fires subtract. The child becomes a man or woman, and then the elderly become child-like. Evolution throws in randomness.

These methods are only a starting point and a means to grow a bigger menu of imaginative options. Later on, I will turn to how to weave them together. But they can take you a long way, and they also serve as a kind of code for understanding past social change, which always involved applying some of these transformations to what already existed: inverting, extending or grafting the social materials already lying around.

Collections of tools like these can be found in many fields. Design has been particularly adept at gathering up methods and packaging them.[6] Some are conventional and mainstream, others exotic. For example, the 'mass dreams of the future' approach adapted 'past-life' therapeutic methods, which tried to help people explore their previous lives—a technique that only makes sense if you believe in reincarnation. Building on this, practitioners of this approach tried to prompt people to access their own lives a few hundred years into the future.[7] Susan Long and W. Gordon Lawrence have advocated what they call 'social dreaming' in a similar spirit. I'm quite sceptical of these approaches (and not wholly convinced of reincarnation of souls). But I like a related idea that comes from the Iroquois and other North American First Nations about the need to imagine those seven generations ahead in the future, as well as those seven generations behind in the past.[8] Reflecting on what they might think, say or suggest can serve as a useful corrective to the intense 'presentness' of generations immersed in digital media.

Psychodrama and embodiment

We can try to grasp future possibilities rationally. But we can also grasp them viscerally—feeling or even tasting them, as well as seeing. Methods from theatre can tap into the insights of the body, and participants are often surprised by the roles or ideas they find in themselves, stumbling on new insights that are out of reach when we only engage with issues cognitively. Some of these methods involve dance; groups interacting and making patterns; and occupying streets and bridges.[9] There are also methods that help people to see the world through others' eyes. In the twentieth century, psychodrama pioneers Jacob Levy Moreno and Zerka Toeman Moreno advocated spontaneous outdoor street theatre to enact arguments and explore political issues. They encouraged what they called 'doubling', in which a person's experience or thinking is clarified by someone else standing next to them. They also used role reversal techniques, as well as 'empty chair' methods, where an empty chair is placed in the room and participants take it in turns to try to speak for a missing person or interest. These methods can misfire, but at their best they help us to grasp possibilities below the neck as well as above it.

Patterns and pattern languages

The world is made up of patterns. The social world around us is the result of the various transformations of extension, grafting, addition and so on. Together these gave us the schools, hospitals, police forces, businesses and web services we use each day.

The architect Christopher Alexander took a similar approach when he analysed what he called the 'pattern language' of architecture and places, the elements of which can be assembled in different combinations. He advocated this idea in the 1960s, arguing that to design a new neighbourhood or city, we should avoid overcentralised planning because the city needs to be organic and multi-dimensional ('a city is not a tree', in his formulation). He encouraged looking at people's expressed preferences and behaviours—for example, drawing on where people actually chose to gather in a home, perhaps in a corner that caught the sun, or how they used public spaces—rather than an architect's assumptions about how the city should be built.

Alexander developed pattern language as a tool and believed that he was describing a universal lexicon. But his ideas make more sense as descriptions of particular cultures rather than as a generalisable language. Most places have developed their own pattern languages for designing buildings, towns and cities, finding particular ways of using available materials to shape doorways and rooms—the white stucco of southern Spain, or the elegant tiled roofs of rural China. Indeed, any new movement in architecture is in part the invention of a new language.

Alexander's ideas were influential in computing as well as in architecture, but this was partly because they were creatively misunderstood. Software evolved with modular methods and object-oriented programming that echoed the pattern language idea but didn't copy it.[10] The languages of software, as of architecture, turn out to be distinct rather than universal.[11]

But his essential insight—that every real building or city is an assembly of patterns and existing elements—was surely right and is useful for demystifying the creative process. Alexander also provided another insight that's relevant to social imagination. Throughout his work, he tried to explain which patterns had a more or less living structure and was often acute in showing why certain kinds of physical architecture feel more vivid and alive than others. As he put it, 'The more living patterns there are in a place—a room, a building, a town—the more it comes to life as an entirety, the more it glows.'[12]

Alexander's aim was to make it easier for us to feel at home in our homes and the places where we spend time. Again, there is an analogy in the social field: some societies are warmer, more convivial, full of feedback and life, while others are cool, detached and less engaged. The former will tend to have more centres and more living patterns; the latter may be neater and more logical, but they will be less alive.

Thought experiments

Thought experiments can help with the distancing and estrangement that are vital for more radical imagination, and they can unravel the logic of a new possibility. *Gedankenexperimente* have played an important role in science, like Einstein imagining trying to catch a ray of light, a thought which opened up lines of inquiry that ended up transforming physics. Good thought experiments take a small number of variables and play with how they might interact; in economics, they tend to imagine a world with one or two commodities, buyers or sellers, and then adjust variables. The imagined world is deliberately unrealistic but can throw up insights all the same. Such thought experiments can also go wider to address more fundamental questions: what if a society had to operate with no money but all the feedback tools of modern digital media? What if all pay levels were set collectively? What if there were zero growth for many decades?

The good experiments challenge dominant orthodoxies and take us through the discomfort this often brings. Another approach is to think four or five decades into the future and imagine relaxing key constraints or introducing new ones. Exercises of this kind show current orthodoxies more clearly and can spark more creative leaps into the mentality of other possible societies.

The work of synthesis

These methods all generate sparks, building blocks, elements for seeing and thinking in new ways. That may be enough to spark action and practical learning. But it can be useful to go further. A next stage involves merging or combining them, going beyond grafting or adding in order to create something new. This is what Samuel Taylor Coleridge called 'esemplastic power', the ability to shape disparate things into one, to take combinations and make a new whole.[13] The great educationalist and thinker John Dewey saw this as the purpose of imagination, which, he wrote, 'is a way of seeing and feeling things as they compose an integral whole. It is the large and generous blending of interests at the point where the mind comes in contact with the world.'[14]

There is a long philosophical tradition of thinking about synthesis and integration. Immanuel Kant wrote of 'the action of putting different representations together with each other and comprehending their manifoldness in one cognition.'[15] The synthesis captures the truth more accurately than a mere description of parts. Hegel was even more influential with his idea of a progression from thesis and antithesis to synthesis, where the synthesis contains the truth of both a thesis and an antithesis.

How to do this? Synthesis usually involves some analysis and then some recombination, breaking things down and putting them back together in a new way. So, a first step might require mapping all the relevant factors, inputs, ideas, models and relationships; then there is a stage of ranking them in terms of how useful they are; then of attempting mergers of combinations; and then of trying to leap up to a higher level of understanding or action.

This is often a circling process of trying things out, exploring and interrogating, seeing what works together. It can't be done as a one-off exercise and it usually requires a mix of methods, some analytic, others visualising how the pieces fit together. Our brains often find it easier to see new patterns and wholes than to work them out through logic.[16] The hope, then, is that a newly synthesised idea will be more useful, and more compelling, than the parts it is made up of.[17] What comes out may be a full synthesis, and something genuinely new, or it may be a new assembly of multiple elements. As Brian Arthur showed, this is how most technologies evolve—through shifting assemblies and subassemblies of elements that are put together to make a mobile phone, a truck or a ship. They don't all have to be similar or operate in the same mode. Indeed, the opposite is usually the case. Much the same is true of social and political innovations, which generally combine multiple elements into a rough synthesis rather than following a single logic.

This has big implications for attempts to create more ambitious, more structural propositions for transforming our societies. What if we moved to an entirely different way of organising property? What if accumulated privileges were dismantled? What if capitalism were replaced by an entirely different system?

Such synthetic visions help to free us from the unrealistic realism which presumes that our current arrangements will persist for ever—a perspective as misleading for capitalism now as it was for empire and monarchy two centuries ago. But it's quite wrong to believe that any society will be derived from a few simple principles. All real societies are assemblies of multiple elements. Capitalism as it actually exists includes large states, large religious organisations, publicly funded science systems, families organised on very non-capitalist principles and often a large social economy. A truly pure capitalism would quickly implode.

So, in thinking about the future, it's instructive to imagine radically different guiding principles and operating systems, but then to return to a more plausible picture of how multiple different elements may co-exist. Indeed, this is vital not just for plausibility, but also for ethical reasons. To impose a single logic on a society is a kind of violence. In 1925, Mahatma Gandhi famously included 'science without humanity' and 'knowledge without character' alongside 'politics without principle' and 'commerce without morality' in what he called 'Seven Social Sins'. He might have added 'singular solutions to complex problems' to these admonitions for anyone involved in social change or the design of social futures.

Forecasting, scenarios and futures

Another set of integrative tools tries to present synthetic descriptive pictures of the future. Many methods are used by companies or governments to help them cast their collective minds into the future. Older methods included astrology, the study of tea leaves or chicken's entrails, and even tyromancy, the study of cheese to find insights into the future. Newer ones include foresight, scenarios and simulations.[18] Scenarios are most commonly used by large companies, governments and NGOs. They help to acclimatise big organisations to possible patterns of change, though they are less good for imagining radical possibilities and tend to be bland rather than inspiring. Foresight methods try to map out what's likely to happen to technologies (such as quantum computing) or fields of application (such as mental health), primarily drawing on expert analysis and discussion.

A more creative alternative is the 'backcasting' method proposed by John Robinson and offered as an alternative to forecasting. This encourages starting with a vision of the future and then projecting backwards to the steps needed in the present to achieve it. This is useful as a prompt—policymaking is always better if it works backwards from desired outcomes rather than only working forwards from current conditions. But 'backcasting' methods quickly run into the sand for the reasons cited earlier—time moves in only one direction and all real-world processes involve learning, adaptation and evolution. The ideal of working backwards from a chosen end—the engineering model—usually needs to be combined with the mindset of a gardener, who focuses on beginnings rather than endings.

Finally, there are the various methods such as 'super-forecasting' and 'crowd predictions' which claim superior insight into what lies ahead. There is now some evidence that specialist forecasters outperform experts, and that the right kinds of crowd intelligence do so too. People too steeped in any one discipline or worldview, however expert, tend to perform poorly. However, the predictions of these new methods are still likely to be wrong more often than they're right.

The most useful methods try to bridge analysis and action, like the three horizons framework, which aims to connect the first horizon of the existing system, a second horizon of emergent innovations and a third horizon of radical possibility.[19] The idea is to help people think about a pathway from the present to the future, and to ask what we might want to conserve as well as what we might want to change.

Building worlds and narratives

Scenarios are essentially stories. Most of us find it easier to digest ideas in the form of narratives, and for an imaginative idea to be compelling, it can't just be a list or manifesto. The nineteenth-century utopians and twentieth-century science-fiction writers were often brilliant at reaching large audiences because of their skill with narrative. Nikolai Chernyshevsky's *What is to Be Done?*, published in Russia in 1863, and Edward Bellamy's *Looking Backward* were both huge best-sellers.

But how to make a story compelling? I have already suggested how metaphors can give shape to a story. We talk of nations rising (and falling) and of peoples 'breaking free' from constraints and bondage. There are stories of revenge and payback; restitution and purification. There are stories of underdogs standing up to power and sometimes overthrowing it. Some of these stories amplify the darker sides of human nature, with vicious punishment of enemies who are dehumanised. Others are more generous, seeing others as ends and not just means.

Often, we have to rid ourselves of older dominant narratives before we can be open to new ones—pushing to one side stories about the virtues of our nation, political system or economy that have become so embedded in our minds through constant repetition that we never question them (in the way that Germany had to 'unlearn' the idea of a superior master-race).[20] The most corrupting stories continue to be those that claim an eternal lineage for a nation, a continuity of blood and soil that not only defies all historical and genetic evidence but also justifies bigotry.

Many theorists have tried to define what makes a good story. Vladimir Propp argued that many folk stories had a similar structure, starting with a hero who seeks something, a villain who opposes them, a donor who provides an object with magical properties, and an array of helpers and hinderers along the way, with the hero being rewarded for their efforts in the end. This narrative structure has obvious echoes for anyone trying to advance a new idea, product or venture.

A few decades later, Joseph Campbell took a very similar approach, synthesising many myths and legends into *The Hero with a Thousand Faces*, a universal, archetypal story that was then used as a template for the Star Wars films and many others. It can be used to map possible journeys for new ideas, as they set out from a meagre start without resources or much hope, face down enemies and threats, and finally triumph. William Storr's much more recent book *The Science of Storytelling* takes a slightly different stance, showing how many of the most compelling stories involve a flawed person facing a unique challenge and then in some way growing as they overcome it.

If there is a common theme in all of these accounts, it is that the most absorbing narrative arcs involve struggle and barriers, enemies and demons.[21] The drama and the dynamic come from the tension these create, the sense that victory is unlikely. This is the case for at least some stories of social imagination that describe Davids against Goliaths, the little man and woman struggling against monstrous states, bureaucracies and systems that crush their humanity.[22] Political narratives, too, often draw on ideas of healing and rebirth; long-standing wrongs that need to be righted; barriers and blockages to be removed; or liberation to be achieved.

Just offering a pat picture of a lovely utopia means missing out on this narrative power. The communist movement succeeded where the utopians had failed in part because of the extraordinary power of their narrative, which fed off Christian stories of a Second Coming. It promised drama and struggle against powerful adversaries while also being sufficiently vague that millions of different hopes could be projected onto it.[23] Folk stories have also provided material for many revolutionary movements, with legends of revolts, bandits and outlaws standing up to oppression. All of these chime with the deep human tendency to resent oppressors, bullies and free-riders. In this way, even if people had to button their lips and restrain their impulses in the face of the superior force of the ruling classes, they could at least find salvation in stories.

Many different types of stories can be found in the literature of social imagination. The brilliant social thinker Albert Hirschman once described what he called the 'rhetorics of reaction' in conservative variants. These are all about resisting reforms which might jeopardise what is truly valuable (religion, nation, family, nature); or be futile; or risk perverse consequences. These are, as it were, the anti-imaginaries: arguments for sticking with the status quo. But there are mirroring 'rhetorics of progress', which claim that we need the next reform to consolidate the last ones, to right historic wrongs or to prevent slipping back. Recently, there have been many more narratives, around climate change, for example, that fuse the two, warning that unless we reform we face annihilation.[24] Yet these stories of the Anthropocene struggle with their own narrative arc, finding it easier to end in destruction than renewal, opening doors into the dark rather than doors into the light.[25]

Storytelling is instructive for anyone interested in social change, both because of the arcs that narratives form and because every storyteller has to summon up a convincing world, with forces and pressures working on their characters. Many manuals, classes and schools help people to create the fictional worlds into which they insert their characters, and some of these methods can be adapted to social thinking. They include the worldbuilding techniques that are used in film, TV and novels to create coherent environments for science fiction.[26] Typically, their focus is more physical than social, but some of the greatest films constructed holistic and convincing visions—like Fritz Lang's *Metropolis* or Hayao Miyazaki's *Laputa*. They're more often used for dystopias than utopias, but in a few cases, what results can be positive.[27] Ursula Le Guin described sci-fi as training for the imagination, and some immersion in these methods helps anyone interested in thinking far into the future.

So, stories are essential to social change. But we shouldn't rely on them too much. They are vehicles to be used and transcended, but not to be trapped in. Much of our world is influenced by powerful but deeply misleading fairy tales: for example, on the American right, the claim that capitalism has single-handedly given the world freedom, prosperity and good health, or the counterview that capitalism is uniquely wicked, the cause of all greed, inequality, poverty and environmental destruction. Many nations still take comfort in stories that emphasise the uniqueness of their values, their soul or their spirit. But we can only grow up and grasp the world as it is if we learn to transcend these stories and appreciate that stories deceive as often as they illuminate.

Institutions for imagination

Institutions sometimes seem like the opposite of imagination. They are formal and bureaucratic, stable and predictable. Yet they can help societies to imagine, and a few institutions have been given licence to think ahead freely, helping governing systems to keep an eye on the distant horizon. Finland in the 1960s, for example, set up a new public organisation, SITRA, as its 'Future Foundation' with a big endowment. The country's parliament has also had a Committee of the Future since 1992. Hungary had a Parliamentary Commissioner for Future Generations; between 2001 and 2006, Israel had an Ombudsman for Future Generations. Britain had a Sustainable Development Commission for a few years, abolishing it in 2011. Wales in 2015 passed a Future Generations Act and created a new post of Future Generations Commissioner.[28]

Laws can also give the claims of the future institutional form. Germany's Constitutional Court ruled some climate change policies unconstitutional because they shifted the burden to future generations.[29]

A few cities have also attempted to institutionalise imagination: Bologna has had a civic imagination office, while Adelaide in South Australia had a Thinker in Residence programme to feed imaginative ideas into the public sector. Singapore's Centre for Strategic Foresight has for the last ten years provided a space for imagination close to the core of government, while Dubai's Future Foundation and its Museum of the Future have been able to explore fascinating ideas around issues like AI, government and ethics. The UAE has even had a Ministry of Possibilities, designed to push government to think more creatively.

I ran the UK government's Strategy Unit for a few years, which included a similar role and connected futures teams in most of the big departments. Some of our work was very practical, designing and implementing policies that could be put straight into effect. Others set medium- to long-term strategies, expanding the UK's 'possibility space'. For example, we set in motion a strategy for renewables,[30] and another for seizing assets from organised crime. Sometimes we advocated inaction—like the recommendation for a five-year moratorium on reorganising the health service (my political bosses rejected that one, though I think we were right: fiddling with organisational structures all too often gets in the way of practical improvements).

Other topics we worked on were ahead of their time, like investigating the potential for fat and sugar taxes, which only became politically feasible over a decade later; designing systems for 'personal accounts' with government, which were implemented in Denmark and Singapore but not in the UK; or pioneering the ideas of behavioural economics, which became mainstream in the following decade.[31] In social policy, too, our aim was to design and set in motion long-term problem-solving, from reducing the gap between the poorest housing estates and the rest of the country; cutting teenage pregnancy in half; and cutting street homelessness by two-thirds within two years (all were achieved).

All of these institutions are granted licence to look ahead and to think heretical thoughts, and some have strong links to power. Any government which lacks the capacity to imagine and explore is likely to be condemned to responding to the world, rather than shaping it.

Meetings for imagination

How can a group work together to make their shared imagination more compelling and more plausible? Should they gather at workshops, conferences, retreats and walks, or just contemplate alone?

There are many ways to bring a group together that make it easier for them to explore and to avoid becoming too comfortable with old habits of thought. Pre-mortems, for example, were invented as a mirror to post-mortems: a method for thinking through everything that might go wrong in a project, but in advance. Red teams are a method developed in the military for challenging a group working on a project, again to show what they might have missed; and meeting devices like Edward de Bono's Six Thinking Hats and David Kantor's Four Player Model encourage people to play more creative roles.[32]

There are also methods for using walks, silence, switching between different numbers (pairs, groups of four, whole groups), reminiscence, game-playing or simulations. All try to challenge our tendency to conformism. Most people don't like disagreeing, or introducing discomforting facts and observations. This can be as true in apparently egalitarian settings as it is in hierarchical ones. Play and fun make it easier for us to suspend our tendency to edit out sideways thoughts, and all of these methods help to cultivate a more dialectical way of thinking rather than a linear one, and so feed creative imagination. Karl Marx and Friedrich Engels, for example, wrote *The Communist Manifesto* during a ten-day drinking binge, which is one way at least of avoiding the limits of overly logical thinking.

Some of the institutions mentioned earlier have overseen attempts to bring a much larger group of people into serious conversation about what's possible. Experiencing how to think about the future, plan and shape should be a normal part of democracy. But it's still quite rare.

When a big earthquake in 2010–11 destroyed Christchurch in New Zealand, for example, the city council created a massive multiplayer online role-playing game (MMORPG) called Magnetic South.[33] Nearly a thousand people took part over two days. Players generated cards, ideas and strategies for rebuilding the city, with nearly 9,000 micro-forecasts.

Future Design in Japan, a method established by Tatsuyoshi Saijo of the Research Institute for Humanity and Nature in Kyoto, runs citizens' assemblies in municipalities across the country.

One of its distinctive approaches is to recruit one group of participants to take on the perspective of current residents, while another group are asked to imagine themselves as 'future residents' from 2060, with special ceremonial robes to help them leap forward in time.

These 'participatory futures' approaches often use immersive physical or virtual environments, allowing people to place themselves in a future world and experiment with new values or behaviours. These might be interactive exhibitions, immersive theatre or digital simulations. The play *Early Days (of a Better Nation)*, a collaboration between Coney and the Cultural Institute at King's College London, transported people to a fictional post-collapse state and charged them with rebuilding it from scratch,[34] rather as, in the real world, Iceland after the financial crisis created a committee of a thousand members of the public to rethink their values and rewrite the constitution.

Another technique uses physical objects that represent the future. When I worked at Nesta, we commissioned 'objects of the future': imagined objects that could help people picture what might lie ahead, mirroring the way that objects from the past can be used to gain insights into the world where they were used.[35]

The methods of deliberative democracy can be combined with creative storytelling. In 2008, the government of the Dutch Caribbean nation of Aruba used these methods to chart a vision for the island looking forward to 2025 and addressing the existential challenges it faced, such as fragile ecosystems and vulnerability to volatile global energy markets. It aimed to generate positive visions for the future using scenarios and stories. More than half the island's 100,000 residents were involved, which meant that the national strategy that came from it could outlast the vagaries of the political cycle and a change of government.[36]

Australia 2020 was a much larger exercise (which I worked on), initiated in 2007 by then Prime Minister Kevin Rudd. It involved millions of people in thinking about the big issues facing the country, from ageing and climate change to water shortages. The media carried extensive sections on the issues; schools organised discussions; and a thousand people gathered in parliament with the prime minister to discuss the conclusions.[37]

In 2020, Britain's Lottery Fund supported fifty projects in what it called an Emerging Futures Fund to support local communities doing work of this kind: exploring and shaping plausible and desirable futures as an antidote to fatalism and learned helplessness, a good example of how philanthropy can, just occasionally, spread experience of designing new worlds.[38]

Children's imagination

Some of the most radical experiments have given children the chance to reimagine their own futures. One of the most famous was under the Polish writer and visionary Janusz Korczak, who created a republic for children with its own newspaper, court and parliament (he was later gassed by the Nazis in Treblinka, along with the orphans he looked after). His idea was that children should exercise sovereignty early on and might do a better job than the adults. Children find it easier to imagine and explore, and they will have to live with whatever futures are created. It's a cliché and, like many clichés, true that children can conjure up a world in an instant, play roles and easily immerse themselves in possible situations, just as they can more easily paint, sing, draw and sculpt than adults.

That imaginative skill is, all too often, lost as children grow up. They learn to focus but also lose some of their skill at daydreaming. Our minds are designed to wander and to see links and analogies, but this very fertility can also be a problem. It makes us easily distracted. It makes us restless mental nomads. This is why so much learning is needed to close imagination down or to achieve focus. It's only through the discipline of repetition that we learn to resist this rambling tendency and instead concentrate on our homework, playing a musical instrument or mastering a sport. Our world depends on millions of people who have learned to be disciplined, and we are all better off being served by surgeons, truck drivers, civil servants and bankers who can remain focused on their tasks.

But we pay a price for this as well, since if education is essentially about the transfer of knowledge, then by definition it must be knowledge of the past that is transmitted, knowledge that is held by teachers and elders or in textbooks. Success means being able to absorb and repeat that knowledge, with the maximum fidelity.

But imaginative learning can co-exist with more classical learning.[39] Where it takes us is to exercises or games that are more open, speculative and ambiguous. This is where we learn through questions as much as answers, and where the pleasure and satisfaction come from creating something new and uncertain, rather than alighting on the proven correct answer. We learn how to imagine 'what if?' sequences: what if the supply of water dramatically shrank, the climate worsened, or life expectancy doubled? What if we ran a hospital as if it were a school; a workplace like a playground; an economy like a garden or forest?[40]

In the last few decades, it has become obvious that children should shape their own choices and lives, with a voice in everything from family law to therapy. In the not-too-distant future, it may seem equally obvious that children should have votes. The argument that they lack the mental capacity to be full citizens would, logically, imply taking the vote away from the elderly with dementia, and of course, children have much more at stake than the old, since they will have to live with the results of political decisions. But even if you're not convinced by the need to change the rules of suffrage, I hope you agree that the shared ability, cultivated from an early age, to explore the possible future is a vital muscle for any democracy—and one that needs to be exercised early and often.

6

FROM IDEAS TO ACTION

POSSIBILITIES FOR THE DECADES AHEAD

What might we do with these methods? What might the imaginative landscape of the next few decades look like? There is a near-infinite range of possible paths for societies and the world to take. But the great majority of them will not be entirely novel—they will evolve from, or in response to, patterns that are already visible in the present. They will extend, graft, invert, add to or subtract from what's already around us.

A good example is the reimagining of welfare. Welfare states grew up to address a small number of widely shared risks, such as poverty in old age, unemployment and physical ill health. But today our risks are somewhat different; they include mental illness, precarious employment and the need for intensive care in old age as our faculties decline. Welfare systems are hard to change because the beneficiaries are loath to give up their rights. But they are also fields that badly need creativity and imagination.

In 2017 and 2018, 2,000 randomly selected unemployed Finnish people became part of one of the most important experiments in recent times. They were chosen to test out whether a universal basic income might be the answer to the problems of welfare states that no longer fit with the realities of a gig economy and precarious jobs. Each participant received a payment of €560 a month, with no strings attached and no questions asked. Over the next two years, researchers studied what happened to them—and how they compared with a much bigger control group of over 170,000 people left on unemployment benefits (at a similar level).

The results were modest but clear-cut. The people on basic income worked more than those on unemployment benefits—which was the opposite result to that predicted by many critics. They reported better financial well-being, mental health and cognitive functioning, as well as higher levels of confidence in the future.

This experiment, in addition to similar ones underway around the world from Brazil to Kenya, matters both for what it revealed and because of how it was done. It showed a willingness to think about the long term, picking up on ideas promoted by many who have advocated revolutionising welfare and doing away with conditions and checks. But instead of experimenting on a whole country at once—which is what most governments do—it started small. It has also sparked mutations—other experiments that try out variants, for example providing a basic income only for particular groups (such as children in care as they become adults), or for limited periods of time (perhaps everyone could be entitled to a decade of UBI). It presents a much better way to link imagination and practicality, and one that will be relevant to many of the biggest challenges that lie ahead.

The economist Milton Friedman once wrote:

> Only a crisis—actual or perceived—produces real change. When that crisis occurs, the actions that are taken depend on the ideas that are lying around. That, I believe, is our basic function: to develop alternatives to existing policies, to keep them alive and available until the politically impossible becomes the politically inevitable.[1]

This is surely right, and it was confirmed again by the COVID-19 crisis, which forced governments to consider policies that were previously unthinkable, whether guaranteed incomes and support for businesses or draconian restrictions on daily life.

We cannot know when the time will be ripe for any particular idea. The task of creators is to keep options alive and open and not to be too constrained by the limitations of a present that may be suddenly transformed—by a depression, war, a dramatic collapse of political trust, or a pandemic. In a much-quoted remark, Antonio Gramsci suggested that 'The crisis consists precisely in the fact that the old is dying and the new cannot be born; in this interregnum a great variety of morbid symptoms appear'.[2] But the new *can* be described before it's born. It can be sketched, interrogated, played with and observed, like a scan of an unborn child in a mother's womb.

Moreover, even if it is impossible to predict anything precisely, we know a fair amount about the *likely* direction of travel of many of the things that shape our society—the broad direction of technology, even if not the details; the likely scenarios for climate change; shifts in demography; and even values shifts and other long-term secular trends. We can always be surprised—some trends will stop, or bend, or turn around. But there is a reasonable likelihood that there will be forty-plus megacities with populations over 10 million in the next few decades and that we'll see rising carbon emissions; the population growing before it shrinks; continued ageing; and a further shift in the world's geopolitical centre of gravity away from North America and Europe. So our imagination should at least be compatible with the more probable environments of the future even as we try to be ready for shocks, surprises and jumps.

Modern societies have succeeded to a remarkable degree in solving many of the problems of the past: extremes of poverty; vulnerability to infectious disease and early death; everyday

113

violence; and many of the risks of oppression and exploitation. For many people, this is an era in which we can celebrate the absence of war, the absence of poverty and if not the absence of disease, then at least the absence of the crushing fear that most children will not make it to adulthood.

But alongside these successes, societies have stumbled into new problems and created their own. We now need to imagine solutions to the rather different issues that surround us, from new forms of psychological poverty and economic insecurity to ecological vulnerability and digital misinformation.

In what follows, I look at different domains of life to suggest sketches of what could lie ahead: options that can prompt thinking, design and action.[3] The physicist Wolfgang Pauli once said of an unimpressive theory, 'It's not only not right; it isn't even wrong,' meaning that it wasn't sufficiently sharply defined to be proven either true or false.

Good theories aren't always right, but they can be useful. Utopias tend to be wrong, but they can be useful even in their wrongness if they are sharply formulated. That's why it's useful to map out possibilities with some precision; then, they can at least be interrogated or disagreed with. Too much recent futurology has been frustratingly opaque and therefore not much help to the job of designing a better future. My hope is that if we can map out richer shared landscapes of the possible, these can then be used to shape political programmes and social projects of all kinds—and to help us know better what we may need to resist.

What changes the world in the end is the generative ideas, not the detailed blueprints. But the blueprints are useful tools for thinking with—they help to clarify ideas and can show unexpected consequences. Developing them is part of being positively engaged with the world. It's easy to be against things and easy to be a critic; much harder to offer answers. We live in a world of cheap opinions, mostly negative. Imagine if our physical world were the same—rich in critics and demolishers, poor in architects and builders, where anyone could tell you why a building was horrible, but no one could say how to build a better one. That is roughly the state we have reached in social design. So here are a few sketches, of both the questions and the answers. They're exercises in asking, 'What if...?'

Surplus time

Let's start with the question of surplus time. Two centuries ago, people on average worked around 60 hours a week in the UK, then the world's first industrial nation. This number has fallen steadily to not much more than 30 hours now (and below that in a few countries, such as the Netherlands).

Meanwhile, life expectancy continues to rise, going up faster than retirement ages, so that millions, soon perhaps billions, can realistically expect to reach the age of 100 or more. The result could be a huge and growing quantity of surplus hours that could in principle be used for anything: playing golf, watching films, gardening, hobbies, volunteering, mentoring, romance or fun.

For more than a century, utopians have promised a future where we would be liberated from drudgery and toil. In an essay in 1891, Oscar Wilde wrote, 'Just as the grass grows while the country gentleman sleeps so all the dirty and unrewarding work will be done by machines.'[4] But past promises of a leisure society turned out to be misleading. People certainly want to be freed from dull or meaningless work, but a life of pure leisure is unsatisfying. This is one reason why working hours at the top of society have tended to move upwards, not downwards.[5] Amongst over-65s, one of the activities most associated with life satisfaction is paid work, not its absence—one reason why so many start their own businesses in retirement (and generally have a better success rate than entrepreneurs in their twenties).

In his famous reflections on the 'Economic Possibilities for our Grandchildren', Keynes wrote that in the future:

> for the first time since his creation man will be faced with his real, his permanent problem—how to use his freedom from pressing economic cares, how to occupy the leisure, which science and compound interest will have won for him, to live wisely and agreeably and well.[6]

Keynes underestimated the many roles that work plays in our lives beyond our economic needs, but the question he raised was the right one: how will we organise liberated time in ways that are meaningful and satisfying? Will we see ever more refined subcultures of hedonism, around food, fitness or drugs? Or, just as the job market is full of agencies, coaches, mentors and platforms, will we see the growth of comparable institutions to mobilise spare time in meaningful ways? Will localisation change again, as more people choose to devote time to where they live, perhaps through allotments and community gardens? Will schools as a matter of course make use of older volunteers? Will new currencies be used to reward these older workers, in the way that timebanks already do on a small scale?

No one knows the answers to these questions, and they may be very different in a big city or a remote region, a rich country or a poor one. But they are likely to require new social arrangements. For example, one option is to create parallel currencies and a parallel economy distinct from the formal money economy. In this economy people can exchange time or locally produced goods, as already happens with some local currencies, like the Bristol Pound in England or the Sardo in Sardinia. In some places people can pay a share of local taxes in the local currency and take a share of their income in it, too.

In the future we might imagine people in their sixties and seventies reducing their traditional paid work and becoming more active in this parallel economy, doing odd jobs, providing child-care, growing food in their allotment, and reconnecting with their local community. The idea of retirement would lose its meaning and working lives would more closely resemble those in the pre-industrial era, where the elderly continue working and contributing as they can. We might expect a great expansion of education for this age group, building on initiatives like the University of the Third Age, in which the elderly teach each other in classes and courses not unlike a traditional university; after all, we know that curiosity is vital for staying fit and healthy.

If some of the promises of a radical extension of life expectancy materialise, such a reimagining of the shape of life will become even more vital: we might have multiple careers rather than just one; multiple life partners; multiple passions in every sense. The key point, though, is that if such a dream is to be accessible to more than just the very wealthy, our social arrangements will have to change, from pensions, care and tax to the physical design of towns and cities.

Feedback and social credit

A very different example is feedback. We're becoming used to more feedback on social media, or from wearing digital devices on our body. Restaurants and university professors get rated all the time. China's social credit systems, first proposed around 2007 and implemented after 2014, went a step further. They score people's behaviour, from traffic violations and late payment of bills to donating to charities or volunteering, and then offer benefits and penalties in terms of access to credit or public services. It's a complex and opaque system—partly run by private companies and partly involving local and national government.

Most media coverage in the West has been critical of these systems, presenting them as a new form of Big Brother-like oppression (indeed, the European Union plans to ban any use of artificial intelligence for social credit systems). But any society needs some ways of rewarding and penalising behaviours, and there are many ways of imagining feedback systems that sit somewhere between the full force of law and existing commercial credit systems. They could reflect different value systems, for example prioritising ecological behaviour, or disciplining offensive comments and abuse. Imagine the idea of systematic feedback becoming ever more the norm. In every job, everyone would get 360-degree feedback, including the boss (and perhaps in some variants that feedback would be made public). Every doctor would get feedback not just on whether treatment has worked but also on how the patient felt. Every teacher would get feedback on how their students are coping and feeling. Or imagine if every dating website included feedback on past dates and relationships.

We're familiar with some of this already. Extending feedback may seem like utopia or hell, but it would certainly lead to a more aware society, even if it were vulnerable to game-playing and score-settling. The benefits might depend on encouraging many more people to give constructive, thoughtful feedback (at present only a small minority bother). But if that happened it would become harder to get away with unpleasant or abusive behaviour. It would be a less favourable environment for bullies of all kinds. But it would also mean an end to the privacy and anonymity that many people value.

New rights

We're used to the idea of rights and equity extending into new fields, and there is now a vast literature bringing human rights into many different areas. One subject to which these notions haven't yet been applied is to matters of beauty or attractiveness, which are treated as entirely personal and subjective, unsuitable for public policy, laws or rights. Yet they matter greatly to billions of people, who are shaped profoundly by how they feel about their own attractiveness to others. They feel shame when they see endless pictures of beautiful models and film stars, or footage of charismatic figures who make them seem boring. Their partners may be less satisfied with them because of their greater awareness of the alternatives. And so, a new hierarchy or class system opens up, one that is very visible in fields like online dating.

What if we concluded that this was a crucial inequality, an inequality that separated out the beautiful and attractive from the ugly or just plain, the charismatic from the dull? What if that led to a deliberate attempt to redistribute beauty and attraction? So, for example, subsidised access to plastic surgery might be offered to the least attractive individuals to level them up. They might get free makeovers, advice and support, which could extend to voice coaching or posture.

You may think that this sounds ridiculous. But why is it inherently obvious that unequal access to education or income inequality matter so much more than these, or that the right to fix a broken leg is so much more self-evident than the right to fix an ugly face?

Truth backed by law

We know that one of the unforeseen effects of the internet is that lies and half-truths travel much faster and further than facts. We also know that disinformation can have a profound and damaging effect on social norms, fuelling polarisation and distrust. Traditional liberal tolerance and the belief that free speech is more important than truth look ill equipped to cope with this environment.

There are many things that could be done to reduce the harmful impact of social media, including building up new public interest media, funded by taxes, donations or recycling of advertising from the big online platforms. But these may not be enough, particularly when a new generation of artificial intelligence is even more effective at feeding addictive behaviours. So, what if the law were brought into truth, so that it became illegal to knowingly propagate untruths through public media? If publishers and platforms failed to correct false information, they would face fines. Courts would adjudicate—after all, they are set up to sift through evidence and make judgements, and they may find it easier to judge on truth than to judge on harms as they are often already required to do (for example, through UK laws on online harm). This would be challenging on a large scale but not impossible—China already employs hundreds of thousands of people to monitor social media, though for dissent rather than lies. A democratic equivalent might combine automated fact-checking and teams of professionals and volunteers.

A milder version of this requires signposting towards truths. An example is the Belmont method of redirecting people to relevant information—for example, if their online actions signal that they may be at risk of suicide, they are gently directed towards suicide advice; or if they click on unreliable information, at the same time they are given options to find more validated information on the same subject.

All of these ideas—and laws that criminalise 'knowingly false' communication—are at odds with traditional liberal notions of free speech, which include the freedom to propagate lies (though not ones with very obvious harms, such as shouting 'fire' in a cinema). But they may be essential for more knowledge-based societies that are challenged by strong institutions seeking to disrupt truth. In the near future our lives will be profoundly influenced by new generations of AI-GAN (generative adversarial networks) and GPT (Generative Pre-Trained Transformer) 3—which can create convincing prose that is, at best, indistinguishable from a human author. These will be powerful weapons for disinformation by states and campaigners, and they could take us even further towards a world where no one knows whom or what to believe, an ideal climate for rogues and charlatans to thrive. Sweden was, as far as I can establish, the first nation to create a national Psychological Defense Agency to protect against the many attacks it was experiencing (many originating in Russia), while its neighbour Finland was the first to build into its school curriculums rigorous training to help children spot fake news and disinformation.

Net zero

All over the world, countries, cities and companies are trying to work out how to reduce net carbon emissions to zero. A myriad of different innovations are evolving in tandem. Some are about transforming the big systems of energy, buildings and transport, moving towards renewables, or promoting electric cars, cycling and walking. Some are about everyday life—such as weaning people off meat. And some are more legal, like the idea of giving everyone a carbon allowance and charging them if they use more, with potentially penal costs for the most frequent fliers.

I've had some involvement in net zero strategies for a quarter of a century, since helping to frame the UK's first plan for sharply reducing carbon emissions in the early 2000s. Later that decade, I was also involved in China's ambitious plans to expand solar and wind power, ramping up building standards.

I remember being fascinated in the 1990s hearing figures like Amory Lovins talk about how energy grids could be restructured to promote cuts in energy use rather than increases (the idea of 'negawatts'), and how to think of a whole economy in terms of all its material flows, the coal, oil and gas, the steel and plastic used to make a car, including the vast majority which is thrown away.[7]

Because big systems are so slow to change, there is no option but to look far into the future, to 2050 and beyond. Some of the creative work on circular economies with greatly reduced waste provides good examples in this respect, asking what jobs might look like (will there be many more in maintenance?), how tax systems should work (should they penalise goods that are hard to maintain or reuse?), and how standards should be set (will we need much more standardisation of things like plugs to reduce the mountains of e-waste?).

I've argued that serious strategies for net zero will, for example, require radically different ways of organising data and knowledge. Few of these ideas are uncontroversial. President Emmanuel Macron of France sparked the 'gilets jaunes' revolt when he tried to raise taxes on petrol as part of a programme to fight climate change. But it's unlikely that the easy steps will be enough on their own.

Holistic health

Net zero is an example of a shift in how things are framed which then opens up new possibilities. Health is overdue a comparable shift. The evidence on premature death is quite clear. A large proportion is caused by behaviours, environmental factors, social factors and genetics. The quality of health services probably explains at most 20 per cent of premature deaths. Yet our health systems and our health research systems are almost entirely focused on parts of that 20 per cent, in particular through pharmaceuticals. Advances in drugs have had a huge—and hugely positive—effect on our lives. But there has been a steady decline in the productivity of research, so that each billion invested in new research delivers much less benefit today than the same investment fifty years ago. So, what would a health system look like that was genuinely evidence-based in the deeper sense of directing brain power to the most important causes of early death? What if we addressed exercise, loneliness and dietary needs as well as conditions that can be dealt with through surgery and prescription drugs, and with the same rigour and seriousness? Would this change how we built cities and homes, or how we thought of the regulation of markets? Imagine, for example, if health considerations became as prominent as economic ones are now.

Population mental health

When modern welfare states were designed, the overwhelming priorities were to meet people's material needs; housing, healthcare and income support for unemployment and old age were what mattered most. Policymakers could assume that many people who were materially poor lived in reasonably close-knit families and communities that could provide emotional support in hard times. The state's job was to meet physical needs and to insure people against material risks; society's job was to meet most of the psychological and psycho-social ones. The solidarity that underpinned the welfare state was based on a shared understanding that for a majority of the population, the serious risks were those of unemployment, poverty, sickness and destitution in old age.

Seventy-five years later, the picture is very different. Some people are still homeless, and classic poverty has not disappeared. We depend as much as ever on the state to protect us if we lose our jobs or fall ill. But relatively few people in rich countries go seriously hungry or have nowhere to sleep. In countries like the UK, decades of economic growth have created a society which by past standards is materially abundant, indeed one that is as concerned with excess consumption, whether in the form of obesity, smoking, alcohol or gambling, as it is with underconsumption. Over the last decade, the proportion of people unable to afford essentials has come down sharply. And although nearly half of the adult population has little or no savings, a substantial proportion of the population now owns significant assets.

Yet during this same period, society's ability to meet people's psychological and psycho-social needs appears to have declined. There has been a rise of individualism. A more overtly meritocratic society has encouraged people to be more ambitious for themselves, but it has also made them more vulnerable to failures—and more likely to blame themselves (rather than fate or the class system) if things go wrong. Some of the shock absorbers—from faith to family—that helped us cope with setbacks in the past have atrophied. It's possible that a new basis of solidarity is slowly coming into view in which we are bound together by a new set of shared risks: the risk of loneliness and isolation; the risk of mental illness; the risk of being left behind. But these risks are not yet reflected in political settlements, and they are inherently harder to reach through the standard tools of public policy and provision.

What if governments took psychological prosperity as seriously as material prosperity? This is beginning to be talked about as more governments are starting to measure well-being. Some are looking in more detail at how policies affect well-being—for example how social security can affect anxiety as well as material poverty. We could imagine much more serious programmes focused on population mental health, addressing the anxiety or depression affecting 10, 20 or 30 per cent of the population and not just the intense needs currently served by health services (which rarely reach more than 1 per cent of the population in any one year). Such programmes would be likely to combine face-to-face therapy, online support and peer support. They might involve a big role for employers, some of which already support mental health first aid, and for schools, given how much these issues affect teenagers.

At present we lack the evidence to know exactly how such programmes would be put together. But it is plausible that within a generation, it will seem obvious that governments should take psychological health and well-being as seriously as they now take physical health.[8] According to one recent global survey in low-income countries, 58 per cent believe that mental health is more important than physical health (in high-income countries the figure is 28 per cent, but another 69 per cent believe mental health is as important as physical health). Inertia, however, means it could take decades for that preference to be fully acted on.[9]

Reimagined public spaces

What of public spaces? Imagine what public beaches might look like in fifty years' time. They will probably be hotter thanks to climate change; people may be more aware of the risks of too much exposure to the sun. But their organisation could take many different forms. They could be more segmented by age, with areas for the elderly, for families with children or for teenagers wanting to have fun. They could concentrate on pleasure or sport or silence with nature. They could be devoted to expressing an idea; as Rebecca Solnit put it, 'if war has an opposite, gardens might sometimes be it, and people have found a particular kind of peace in forests, meadows, parks, and gardens'.[10] They could be open and free or paid for. They could, like most current beaches, deliberately include everyone together, or they could offer highly customised experiences.

Alternatively, imagine that all public libraries closed down and you were given their former budget and a blank sheet of paper— what would you put in their place? It's highly unlikely that you would rebuild them just as they were. You might, for example, reimagine them much more as places of education, with stimulating learning materials, quiet places for study, and rooms for small groups to discuss lectures they have watched online. Or you might reimagine them through the lens of physical and mental health, relocating public and primary healthcare and building new ways to offer advice and self-diagnostics. Or you might emphasise their role as community centres—hubs for neighbourhood activity with books much less prominent.

Or think about the corner shop and what it might become. Already, it has been partly bypassed by the internet in much of the world. To generate ideas, you could observe how people use existing corner shops and talk to them about their everyday needs—and which ones can't easily be met online or through the high street. That might take you to a very different view of what functions need to exist at the ultra-local scale of walking distances. So, for example, farmers are now subsidised (by the European Union and national governments) to be guardians of land as well as makers of food. Might something similar happen to corner shops, which would be reinvented as neighbourhood concierges, taking in deliveries (as many already do) and keeping an eye out for people with dementia who are lost and confused (as already happens in parts of Italy)? The recent fashion for the 15-minute city—the idea promoted by Paris Mayor Anne Hidalgo and others of putting as many functions as possible within 15 minutes' walk—could point in this direction.

In Appendix 1, I share a longer list of ideas and prompts, from property rights to bodies, care to ecology, democracy to law. In each field we can deliberately try to push the boundaries, developing sketches of alternative routes to see if they make sense, if they would work and if anyone would feel at home in a world where they were implemented. By multiplying these ideas across different fields, we create larger 'possibility spaces', a bigger menu of options for our societies to adapt and evolve in the decades ahead.

7

SOURCES

WHERE DO IDEAS COME FROM?

Modules in the mind

Ideas don't come from nowhere. Instead, all social imagination feeds off not only what's already there but also our own memories and the everyday heuristics and modules that are built into our minds, products of our long evolution as a species. Some come from our intuitive physics—how we think about force, or how objects influence each other, achieve balance or resist gravity. We talk of people being 'pushed' by others to do things, the 'pull' of attraction, 'pressures' to act, some 'standing over', others under.[1] We think of power as a force or a thing—something that can be held, taken and used. We think in terms of lifting weights and burdens and rising up, and often we see the world in terms of cosmic balance—with wrongs needing to be balanced by rights.

Then there are our everyday social heuristics. We are strongly predisposed to cooperation and almost effortlessly pick up on apparent social rules. We have a powerful sense of justice (even if that includes some contradictory elements, like our intuitive sense of ownership and our equally intuitive sense of fairness). We are good at fitting into hierarchies with complex divisions of labour, recognising that others may be better than us at some tasks. Human societies long ago learned the tricks that make it harder for people to defect, exploit or free-ride (and we are innately very inclined to punish free-riders). We automatically see groups as things with a mind of their own and with moods, wishes and fears. Hence the everyday talk of 'business believes x', 'the working class want y', 'farmers are unhappy about z'.

These are the 'minds that make societies', to use anthropologist Pascal Boyer's useful phrase. They have allowed humans to engage in complex collective projects for imagined future rewards. It's perhaps not surprising that our social imaginaries draw on this stock of material—whether it's to amplify a particular idea of justice or to replicate everyday love and care at the scale of the whole society.

Indeed, one classic social analysis argued that dominant ideologies often mirrored dominant family forms; what we see as natural or imagine as desirable is shaped by our early experiences of equality, authority and property in the family home. People brought up in families where authority passed from the father to the eldest son viewed the world quite differently to those brought up in families where the children were treated equally, or where they were expected to compete with each other. Communism tended to thrive in nations (from Russia to Vietnam to Cuba) where exogamous family forms in which sons bring their brides back into the parental home had mutated into more egalitarian family forms, combining habits of deference to external authority with equal sharing.[2]

All of these underlying ideas can be thought of as a kind of folk sociology or political science. They are everyday explanations of how the world works that sit alongside the folk economics that makes people think, for example, that there is a fixed stock of jobs at any one point or that a nation's finances should be run in the same way as those of a household. These can be powerful forces; as George Akerlof and Robert Shiller observed, 'we will never really understand important economic events unless we confront the fact that their causes are largely mental in nature'.[3]

A more developed social science challenges these folk beliefs. Some of the greatest social science breakthroughs showed counterintuitive patterns—like Keynesian arguments for spending more during a recession, or sociologist Émile Durkheim's demonstration of how very personal decisions about suicide were highly influenced by large social patterns.

Yet when it comes to social imagination, folk ideas—themselves based on more basic mental modules—are still the main ingredient. A restoration of balance; renewal and regeneration; lifting of weights: these are common frames. So too are more conservative ones, like an emphasis on purity—removing what's alien or toxic—or rewarding loyalty and punishing disloyalty. These are sources of our shared hopes and fears. Societies are societies of minds as well as materiality, and that makes them susceptible to the push of powerful ideas as well as to psychological shocks.

Collective unconscious

For this reason, what can be *collectively* imagined is severely constrained. Individual imagination can run riot, but shared imagination cannot. It is constrained by the direction of the underlying forces of society, the slow grind of the tectonic plates which determine the boundaries of the possible, the habitual patterns of thought and shared concepts.

An interesting current in social science has tried to map and understand how these shared imaginaries work, where they come from and how they shape collective thought and action. This tradition is associated with figures including Benedict Anderson, author of *Imagined Communities*, which described nations in these terms, and the philosopher Charles Taylor. Their interest is in how imagination supports the present order. Shared imagination (or 'necessary fictions') allows people to endow constructs such as the nation, the rule of law or democracy with an air of solidity. Indeed, all social institutions are essentially shared fictions which we agree to believe in.

This work is impressive and convincing. But these writers showed less interest in imagination of the future.[4] For them, imagination is a conservative and conserving force. But in any modern society, this collective unconscious, or imagination, is more fluid and open, with a stock of codes and symbols that can challenge orthodoxies. Beneath the surface of news, commentaries and political discussions lie these deeper shared ideas, ideals and pictures—some essentially about conserving what exists or what's past, and some groping towards the future.

These can be seen in arguments of the ecological movement and feminism which resonate with ideas that have been in circulation for a long time (as I showed earlier, for example, feminist utopias date back many centuries). In other words, ideas work best when they echo parts of this social or political unconscious—shared but hidden views of hope and fear. Fredric Jameson wrote of this from a literary perspective, suggesting that:

> behind such written traces of the political unconscious as the narrative texts of high or mass culture, but also behind those other symptoms or traces which are opinion, ideology and even philosophical systems ... [are] the outlines of some deeper and vaster narrative movement in which the groups of a given collectivity at a certain historical conjuncture anxiously interrogate their fate, and explore it with hope or dread.[5]

For Jameson, the unconscious is just there—something to seek out, beneath the surface. But for others, it is something to be influenced through new dreams and nightmares. These take time to evolve but they become a fertile soil into which new seeds of social imagination can be planted. A good example is how we think of data. We now have quite developed nightmares of Orwellian control and corporate abuse, surveillance and predation—and the beginnings of a contrary vision of data as either under personal control or as a commons. Twenty years ago, ideas for such things as 'personal data stores', data commons and data trusts failed to take hold because they lacked a supportive mental framing or unconscious to resonate with. But as the deeper-level ideas become more common and more internalised, they then create new, unconscious homes in which radical ideas of this kind can take hold.

The material base of imagination: time and money

So imagination happens in the mind, often involves a new way of seeing, both literally and metaphorically, and feeds off a deeper shared unconscious. What else does it depend on? Everyone can imagine to some extent. We are all endowed with an ability to picture things which don't exist. But social imagination—the ability to picture a future society or way of life—is a highly specialised activity. It surges in particular places and at particular times, like the booming industrial cities of the eighteenth and nineteenth centuries or the hotbeds of digital creativity in the twenty-first.

There are some obvious reasons for this. You need at least a modicum of security to be able to free your mind to imagine. We now know much more about how stress can diminish IQ; people who are focused only on their next meal, or on avoiding crushing debt, are less likely to care about the distant future.[6]

Then there is the need for free time, which is harder to come by if you're working a 14-hour day or looking after ten children.

It takes time to think hard about the future and it takes time to conceive, design and describe imaginative possible options and get beyond daydreaming or the odd flash of inspiration.

There are other practical constraints—like literacy, or access to libraries and books—which have excluded most of the world's population until very recently. Indeed, the lesson of the arts is that it is difficult to create compelling works of imagination without hard work as well as resources. It's not surprising that the same is true of social imagination, which also requires time and resources—and space for criticism and trial and error. The great social visionaries of the eighteenth and nineteenth centuries often depended on private wealth or patrons. Saint-Simon and Kropotkin were aristocrats; Marx depended on funding from Engels, an industrialist and heir. Mary Wollstonecraft was a relative exception in having to fend for herself through much of her turbulent life. Meanwhile it was the relative prosperity of the most highly skilled manual workers of the nineteenth century who flocked into utopian clubs of all kinds that gave them the space to imagine and explore. Most of their peers were just too busy and exhausted to join in.

Milieux—the social character of social imagination

If these are some of the material conditions, there are equally important social ones, in particular the presence of a surrounding network or milieu. It's rare for people to develop compelling and coherent ideas on their own. Individuals and teams flourish best in a vibrant milieu that brings together comment and criticism, competition with peers, and the feedback of an informed audience. The occasional genius may be able to imagine when detached from such a milieu. But they are the exception, and usually when we look closely we find that they are, in fact, connected to other thinkers.

As Nietzsche put it, 'Companions the creator seeks, not corpses, not herds and believers. Fellow creators, the creator seeks—those who write new values on new tablets.'[7] So, although plenty of innovation does happen in rural areas, it is not surprising that most of the people cited in the previous chapters were based in the great cities of their eras—Paris, London or New York; Mumbai, Nairobi or Beijing—and were also tied into multiple networks. Sir Thomas More, for example, was in correspondence with many of the leading thinkers of his time across Europe. Ursula Le Guin drew on ideas from anthropology through her father, from Taoism, from the sci-fi writing community and from the emerging feminist movement. Mahatma Gandhi straddled an equally diverse range of networks in theology, politics and law, from South Africa to England to India.

Lewis Mumford wrote, 'The chief function of the city is to convert power into form, energy into culture, dead matter into the living symbols of art, biological reproduction into social creativity'.[8] Cities' metabolisms take energy and turn it into knowledge, and bigger cities proportionately generate more patents, more ideas and more GDP, helped by density and combinations.

In the 1950s, sociologist Robert Merton coined the ugly but informative term 'serendipitous socio-cognitive microenvironments' to capture a similar idea: that some settings seem to encourage discovery and creativity, random encounters that lead to new ideas. Peter Hall's list of the great creative cities in civilisation—from ancient Athens to Manchester to Chicago—roughly but not precisely aligns with this notion that new ways of thinking can flourish in urban societies with the right mix of freedom, free money (from philanthropists or universities), argument and disputation.

These places tend to attract the energetic and young. Here may be one partial explanation for the slowdown of creativity discussed earlier. The philosopher of science Thomas Kuhn argued that paradigm shifts—the fundamental advances in science—don't happen because people are persuaded by reason. Rather, they depend on the guardians of the old orthodoxies becoming tired, and dying. Kuhn quoted physicist Max Planck's comment that science proceeds 'one funeral at a time'. It follows that if there are fewer funerals as people live longer, then the youthful vibrancy of those less steeped in orthodoxy will be rarer, and cities less dynamic.

In the work of Geoffrey West, these links are direct; scale almost automatically leads to prosperity and innovation, regardless of age. But the actual patterns aren't quite as simple. One of the oddities of big cities is that although greater scale tends to correlate with greater productivity and creativity, it has the opposite effects on capacities for problem-solving. As well as opening opportunity, larger scale generates larger frictions—too many boundaries, organisations, egos and interests, which is why cities like New York and London are often worse governed than their smaller counterparts and are more prone to lasting problems of poverty, infrastructure or education.

Moreover, some big cities are rich in connective institutions that multiply the space for serendipitous encounters; others lack them. In other words, the link between scale and results depends on qualities as well as quantities.

These, however, are only partial caveats. The broader picture in which the most prosperous cities also tend to be crucibles of imagination, able to generate resources and intellectual fizz, still holds. They do so in part because of their relative privilege: more surpluses, more free time, more chances to experiment.

All of this has important implications for the diversity and inclusiveness of social imagination, or rather for its lack of inclusiveness. Unequal capacities to dream, imagine and shape arguably constitute a deeper inequality than present material inequalities, a deeper constraint on freedom because of their dynamic effects.

Compare the torrent of work on the future that flows from Silicon Valley, often financed by successful investors and entrepreneurs, with the much scanter materials produced by more populated places like Pakistan or Nigeria. Or consider the vast outpouring of ecological imagination over the last fifty years, much of it encouraged by the wealthy—aristocrats as well as activists—compared to the much lower level of attention paid to imagination around poverty. Observe too how these skews lead to slightly hypocritical patterns, like the common demand for shorter working hours taken up today, as in the sixteenth century, by privileged workaholics, or the way that rebellious writers in the nineteenth century so often became very bossy in prescribing how their idealised worlds should work.

Today, too, futurology is dominated by highly educated white males and reflects their worldviews (though recent science fiction has also been a powerful outlet for feminists). A healthier, happier world depends on opening the space for social imagination to multiple voices and experiences. Here there are interesting analogies with the opening up of other kinds of creative production. Mass literacy and the printing press achieved this for writing, while cheap paints, pianos and accordions and more recently digital photography and technology have all empowered millions to create.

But in each of these fields, mass creativity has depended on mass access to methods, tools and guidance. It has depended on social contexts too: milieux of other, equally interested people, who can share ideas, comment, praise or criticise, in a realm of dynamic creativity that has complemented rather than replaced the specialist and professional production of films, music and books.

On the cusp of the inside and the outside

Some people are much more comfortable exploring and searching for new things than others. There are good reasons for believing that evolution has encouraged a minority to think in these ways, with more curiosity, peripheral vision and hunger for novelty.[9]

But the most influential are not necessarily the most creative. Instead, we see an interesting pattern by which imagination is plentiful among people who are simultaneously insiders and outsiders. Some of the writers mentioned earlier held powerful jobs. Sir Thomas More was Lord High Chancellor to the King of England. Three centuries later, William Morris, author of the utopian novel *News from Nowhere*, was commissioned to make wallpaper for the Queen. But in different ways, they also saw themselves as outsiders, at odds with the dominant currents of their times. Thomas More ended up having his head cut off. Morris hated the industrialisation he saw around him. Gandhi was a very successful lawyer, Tagore a wealthy Brahmin who also studied in England and travelled widely—again, both insiders and outsiders at the same time.

I've seen the same pattern with social entrepreneurs and innovators. Some come from the grassroots, but the majority straddle insider and outsider status, combining some links to the elites with links to the communities in need of social action.

On the cusp of the normal and the strange

The kinds of people who are able to leap out of the assumptions of their time and imagine a distant future also sometimes sit on the boundary between sanity and madness. In the words of Shakespeare's Theseus in *A Midsummer Night's Dream*: 'The lunatic, the lover, and the poet / Are of imagination all compact.'[10] Pioneers in the worlds of medicine, business, politics or education often pay a personal price for their divergence; there is a popular saying among scientists that warns, 'When you work at the cutting edge, you are likely to bleed.'

This is perhaps even more true if you are trying to shift history in a different direction.[11] In these instances, you don't only face enemies and obstacles, which is true in every field. You are also threatening power in all its forms, including the power that has a monopoly of violence. To assert that the world can be remade and reconfigured rather than only analysed from a detached distance, and to show that current arrangements are not natural, makes you a threat.

We tend to reify the social world—to think of groups as persons and institutions as things. But an oddity of social imagination is that it has to see these constructions as artificial and unnatural. Here we come to a deep paradox in how we, as social creatures, learn to reject and remake social meanings. In our everyday lives, we exist in what Heidegger described as 'worlds'—each with its own equipment, purposes and identities. As he pointed out, these worlds are made by the activities we take part in—caring for a child, cooking food or running a school—and this is how meaning arises. Things which have no place in these worlds are alien to us, baffling or exotic, in the way that an object from a civilisation we don't understand is inert and may literally make no sense. In the same way, our own identities as worker, friend, parent or neighbour are shaped by activities most of the time, rather than by an inner personality.

Everyday life in any society is the life of these identities, roles and worlds, and to be a social creature requires us to understand and internalise them. Yet social imagination necessitates that we suspend this normality and learn to question society's elementary building blocks instead.

A similar process happens in literature. To Russian literary theorist Roman Jakobson, literature represents 'organised violence committed on ordinary speech'—it has to unsettle and disturb. The Yugoslav critic Darko Suvin described this in science fiction as 'cognitive estrangement' and saw it as an essential part of the creative process. The balance needed is subtle: enough estrangement to generate novelty, but not so much as to lose connection to others. Like humour, it requires knowing how to walk the line between what's acceptable and what's transgressive, and being willing to challenge our social relationships, though not to the point where they are broken irreparably.

The most radical ideas have their roots in some level of distance or estrangement. This motivation to see the world as strange may be encouraged by blockages, humiliations, disappointments or suffering (as it was for Mary Wollstonecraft, whose father regularly beat her mother), or shock (Darko Suvin was almost killed by a Nazi bomb as a child). Such experiences fuel courage.

Our natural conformism is a major constraint on social imagination. Yet the message of the fable of the emperor's new clothes, and one that has been reinforced by modern psychology, is that it may only take one person to question an apparent orthodoxy to encourage others to do so, and a small group can dislodge the certainty of another small group, which in turn dislodges others. Thus do apparently solid dogmas unravel.[12]

On the cusp of rationality and intuition

The usefulness of taking a stance between the familiar and the strange suggests a very different view of creativity and invention from conventional accounts of how change happens. To a rationalist, change should come from diagnosis followed by prescription: understanding social ills and then proposing suitable remedies. This was the promise of Auguste Comte, that there could be a true science of society and a rational practice of social improvement—a belief later upheld by Sidney and Beatrice Webb in England. The business theorist Peter Drucker described entrepreneurship in a similar way, as a rational activity a bit like medicine that involves a disciplined search for symptoms and principles for diagnosis and cure. In the world of business, whoever gets the first sense of a change in the facts, and then responds fast, gets an advantage. As new needs arise they are market-researched, and entrepreneurs respond.

Sometimes, this is indeed how imagination works. In business, it may become apparent that there is an emergent latent demand for high-quality home-delivered food, and entrepreneurs flood in trying to meet it. Or, in society, there may be growing evidence of loneliness or depression, and policymakers and social entrepreneurs design competing remedies.

But this is at best a very partial description of how change really happens. Needs are not facts until they are recognised as needs. No market research showed a need for the Beatles or Greenpeace. Most radical social ideas were inconceivable through the frameworks that preceded them—they were, literally, hard to think of. Yet it is not rational deduction but rather the step of asking a new question or seeing in a new way that usually leads to imagining new answers. Creativity depends on integrating rationality and imagination, logic and intuition, the visible and the invisible, or grasping that apparent opposites may share a deeper unity.

Many problems appear to lack any solution, and there is an extensive literature on so-called 'wicked problems'.[13] It used to be thought that these were inherently insoluble; and they were indeed very hard to solve in direct, linear and logical ways. Yet many apparently very wicked problems have in fact been solved, or rather more often have been outgrown or displaced. Mass unemployment, homelessness, domestic violence and poverty have all turned out to be amenable to action, even if in ways that were not always expected and that sometimes have led to new problems. Sometimes, such issues were addressed by reframing the question rather than attacking it head on. For example, homelessness is not always the result of a shortage of homes; it can just as much be an effect of family breakup, prison discharge, mental illness or substance abuse. Unemployment turned out to be strongly shaped by macroeconomic forces rather than by the incentive, or laziness, of individuals. Again, the problem had to be looked at in a new way before it could be solved.

The most striking example is overpopulation. Many utopian writers, as well as generations of analysts and commentators, thought this the world's most pressing and wicked problem— one that would require strict limits on reproduction such as through China's one-child policy. Yet in much of the world, birth rates have fallen below replacement levels, the effect of women's empowerment and changing social values. The problem appears to be being outgrown, confirming how wrong it is to believe that there is a category of inherently wicked and insoluble problems.

Anyone wanting to change the world needs to cultivate a mix of rationality and intuition, as well as a mix of arrogance and humility: the arrogance to believe that they may be able to alter the course of human history, but also the humility to observe and change their views. American investor George Gilder wrote about entrepreneurship that 'the first law is to listen', emphasising the importance of a willingness to learn alongside the need to 'act boldly in the shadows of doubt'.

On the cusp of connectedness and isolation

Creativity of all kinds is a social activity—but only up to a point. Although imagination is encouraged by being connected to other people or living in lively milieux, it's also helped by separation. Too much connectedness drowns out originality; it encourages conformism and even groupthink, denying new ideas the space they need to develop.[14]

Silence also has its place in the imaginative process. New thoughts might only take shape once the noise is shut off; they may not emerge so easily from rapid-fire seminars or discussions, or from the speed of social media. Action researcher Otto Scharmer once commented: 'What happens at the beginning of any creative process? Nothing! Creativity requires that we create space and wait for something to emerge.'

Here we find a paradox very like that for art. Lively social imagination depends both on being embedded in a supportive society that provides food, shelter, argument and company, and on a willingness to reject, transcend or simply ignore that base. In other words, we need to be safe enough to play with being unsafe, secure enough to leap into insecurity.

8

PATHWAYS

WHERE DO IDEAS GO?

Ideas go into the world. But most evaporate, like rain hitting a hot pavement. So why do some spread while others disappear?

The philosopher A.N. Whitehead suggested that learning happens in three stages: first there is romance, then there is precision and then comes generalisation. Something similar happens with ideas. Utopia is part of the romance, the spark or dream. Then comes precision with experiments, showcases and prototypes that refine the idea. Finally, for a few, comes generalisation into political programmes that spread and scale the ideas.

Most ideas face resistance; few don't threaten someone's power and status, and any radical idea will be baffling to people steeped in the conventions of their time. But others become common sense, part of the furniture of daily life: kindergartens and hospices, recycling bins and bicycle lanes.

Many ideas look quaint and eccentric in retrospect, like Étienne Cabet's promise of absolute cleanliness and absolute symmetry, helped by laws to specify everything from food to dress (though his promise that all citizens would be engaged in government as well as voting, supported by a Department of Statistics to provide them with the facts they needed, looks less quaint).

Other ideas had a slow-burn influence. For example, James Harrington's *The Commonwealth of Oceana* was influential in France a century after it was written, thanks to the work of Abbé Sieyès, author of one of the greatest political tracts of all time. This pamphlet, *What is the Third Estate?*, the manifesto for the French revolution, answered its titular question with the declaration: 'Everything. What has it been hitherto in the political order? Nothing. What does it desire to be? Something.' Sieyès used the utopia of Oceana as a model for his 'Constitution de l'an VIII' (though the constitution which actually resulted turned out very different, recast by Napoleon, whom Sieyès had helped into power). Harrington's ideas were also eagerly absorbed by John Adams and Thomas Jefferson and their echoes can be found in the US Declaration of Independence and in various American political institutions.

Some were prescient in their faith that powerful ideas could progress and be extended—for example, spreading democracy or extending notions of rights or voice to nature. But others were not so prescient. Michel Foucault advocated paedophilia, thinking that sex with children had been acceptable in the past and would be again, putting it in the same broad category as gay sex and on the way to becoming socially acceptable.

Push and pull

To understand why some ideas survive and prosper, we need to look at both how they are pushed and how they are pulled—pushed by advocates and evangelists, pulled by the needs of society. In other words, in order to spread, ideas need both what I call 'effective supply'—a practical working model that can convince people to invest in the idea—and 'effective demand', which usually means the willingness of an audience to pay for the service or product being supplied, or to give their time and commitment to it. The great majority of ideas, however good in some respects, fail to achieve one or both of these.

William Blake was the most single-minded believer in the virtues of pushing. He saw imagination as a force in its own right: 'Then I asked: does a firm persuasion that a thing is so, make it so? He replied, All poets believe that it does, and in ages of imagination this firm persuasion removed mountains'.[1] Some political leaders have acted in this spirit, confident that, with enough charisma and energy, innovations could be spread and become a common sense. National ideals; 'the New Soviet man'; the marriage of Mr Science and Mr Democracy promoted by the Chinese intellectuals of the May Fourth Movement: all are examples of this faith in imagination from above. So too was the aesthetic programme of Nazism, which hoped that its portrayal of a coherent worldview, embodied in crowds, films, uniforms and slogans, would shape a world in its image.

Other versions of the push model can be found in economics and sociology. One recent writer commented that 'power in the economy is exercised to the extent an actor can make his own imaginary of the future become influential and mobilize others to turn it into the future present'.[2] This is the 'push power' of a firm promising a future of driverless cars, hyperloop or smart cities—if it can activate enough capital, then reality may well take shape around it, just as happened with the pioneers of railways or mass ownership of cars in previous eras. This is the sense in which Blake and others were right. Imagination does shape the world, and we are creatures of mind as well as matter, suggestible and wanting to conform.

Evidence also plays its part here. If there is strong evidence that a drug or a treatment works, it's far more likely to be taken up. But it's not quite true that if you build a better mousetrap, the world will beat a path to your door. Very efficient goods and services can languish, unappreciated; inferior standards can prevail over better ones. The push of hard evidence is rarely enough, though we should want a world where it is taken more seriously.

Meanwhile, what's pushed may be beautiful or ugly. We long ago lost any hope that beauty and truth are connected. But the beauty of ideas—their character and resonance—does influence their appeal. Social ideas that feed off deeper notions of communion, unity, love, harmony, equilibrium and self-organisation seem to engage people, as do those that offer simplicity, symmetry, karma and universality. Stories involving threat and protection; about overcoming struggle to reach liberation; or invoking modes of sociality like the nation and the family are also popular. The ideas that are most animating may be the ones that have the greatest strength, a strength that derives from a philosophical ontology—a view of what is, or what matters. Indeed, many of the future visions that had most impact in the past were consciously built on such foundations—liberal, socialist or anarchist—or on a belief in unrealised human potential and, at the extreme, the potential for people to become god-like.

Pull theories, by contrast, focus less on the inherent appeal of ideas and more on the needs and demands they satisfy. The pull of profit motivates firms to adopt new ideas. Electoral politics makes governments hungry for new ideas to convince electors to keep them in power. Wars and crises force adoption of new measures—like rationing in the UK during the Second World War, which led to substantial improvements in children's diets, or the COVID-19 pandemic, which dramatically accelerated vaccine development. Fear of imminent disaster can be a good spur for imagination. The threat of invasion forced many countries to rethink how they worked, for example pressuring them to improve public health. The Great Stink in London in the 1850s forced a radical rethink of public sewage and health. Today the threat of species extinction, the loss of bees and other insects, soils turning into dustbowls, and cascading disasters as food becomes scarce, combined with furious competition between nations for remaining resources, are all prompts to experiment and explore, creating a pull for new ideas.

How do ideas keep flying?

Muhammad Ali said that 'the man who has no imagination has no wings'. But once it has taken off, what makes an idea fly—and keep flying? Social science offers many answers to these questions. It's much easier to see in retrospect why particular ideas were appealing than it is to see this in advance. Nevertheless, there are some reliable ways of thinking about this question of how ideas are pulled and spread, and understanding these can be useful for anyone wanting to promote a novel idea. The spread of ideas like income tax and welfare states, recycling laws and bans on plastics, feed-in tariffs and bitcoin combined both push and pull factors with problems that the new ideas helped to solve.

To the extent that there is a serious theory of the spread of ideas (set out in books such as Peter Richerson and Robert Boyd's *Culture and the Evolutionary Process*), it emphasises such things as frequency bias (the more common an idea is, the more likely it is to survive); prestige bias (ideas associated with highly prestigious people are more likely to spread); and content biases (some kinds of material are just easier to grasp—like catchy tunes).

Some of these explanations are not new. Tocqueville, in trying to explain the conformism he found in nineteenth-century America, gave a good account of this. He thought that people:

equal in condition ... see things from the same angle, their minds are naturally inclined towards analogous ideas, and while each of them may diverge from his contemporaries and form beliefs of his own, all end up unwittingly and unintentionally sharing a certain number of opinions in common.[3]

So, if a new idea gets widely adopted, many others will adopt it if only to avoid being ostracised. Here, we see a combination of external peer pressure and a fairly rational association of truth with the majority (if others are flocking to stand in a queue or to escape a cinema, we are probably wise to go with them).

Another explanation focuses on how well proponents of ideas show others that they are valuable. Michael Spence's signalling theory looked at situations of asymmetric information where signalling is needed to show the value of what is being offered. Originally, the interest was in things like the quality of a job applicant. But the idea also applies to advocates of any novel idea. Somehow, they need to signal to audiences that the idea is worth taking seriously. Imagination may be free, but taking up ideas can be costly. This signalling can take place through validation by others (perhaps the endorsement of eminent professors and Nobel Prize winners) or through costly behaviours that are hard to fake. At the extreme, it can be achieved through a willingness to be a martyr. Less drastic signalling devices include giving up one's possessions, deciding to live on a commune, or committing to do a course (for example, in permaculture or cognitive behavioural therapy). These are all ways of telling a sceptical new audience that a novel idea has something going for it.

Another bundle of answers focuses on networks. The sociologist Mark Granovetter put the thesis clearly: 'Whatever is to be diffused can reach a larger number of people, and traverse a greater social distance, when passed through weak ties rather than strong.'[4] In other words, ideas will spread through loose networks of acquaintances, and through them can travel far and fast. This theory worked well in explaining, for example, how information about job opportunities is transmitted, and it led in turn to the 'small world' theory of Duncan Watts, which looked at the crucial role played by some people in acting as bridges between otherwise separate worlds. I have already highlighted how some of the most influential imaginers were well positioned in just this sense, sitting astride multiple fields. Together, these and other theories of modern network science have become good at showing, at least in retrospect, how ideas, facts or memes can spread across the world.

But these accounts only go some of the way. These theories have turned out to be less successful at predicting how more profound behaviours change, particularly ones where the change involves some cost, or risk, or requires other things to change in tandem. Studies of, for example, the spread of the Paris Commune, Swedish trade union recruitment or US civil rights activism showed that they diffused through neighbouring densely knit communities—that is, through the influence of strong rather than weak ties.[5] The same appears to be true for many other behaviours that matter now, like adopting radically less carbon-intensive lifestyles or profoundly changing one's diet and relationships. The reasons are obvious. When the costs of change are higher, we are more likely to adapt if we receive messages, again and again, from people we trust. Gentle nudges or reading a single post on social media are unlikely to have much effect. Instead, changes spread in much more cellular ways.

These different patterns are likely to be mixed up in practice. Veganism spread for several decades in a cellular way but later spread along weaker networks, amplified by its visibility in the mass media.

But it remains impossible to predict which ideas will catch fire, and anyone who claims to have reliable insights into this is either deceiving you or deceiving themselves. Radical ideas may start off very rare, may be complex or hard to grasp, and are, almost by definition, not backed by those with the most prestige. Yet sometimes, they too spread.

Ideas travel in groups

Both push and pull are easier when ideas travel in groups—when they are 'thickened out' with complementary ideas, concepts and techniques. Few travel well on their own. Ideas spread more easily when they have a surrounding architecture that makes them easier to absorb. The prophets of monotheistic religion depended on precursors, who had warmed up their audiences with similar ideas. Feminism took two centuries to acclimatise women to new ways of seeing their roles, their oppression and their options. There may be a parallel with the famous saying about travel: if I want to travel fast, I travel alone; if I want to travel far, I travel with others. The ideas that travel furthest are the ones that find companions, partner ideas with which they resonate.

The most successful new ideas also usually complement rather than replace older ideas. Executing innovation is much easier if it can be grafted onto existing systems. That is another reason why smashing the system is risky. Even if the alternative system may end up far superior, there is bound to be a transitional period when things work less well.

A new idea about education can mobilise an existing network of teachers, schools, exams and pupils, making it easier to execute than an idea that needs an entirely new infrastructure. The Khan Academy, an educational organisation that offers short video lessons and a very different approach to teaching, was helped by big philanthropic funding and was also able to piggyback on the internet during a period when millions were becoming more familiar with the idea of learning online.

Another good example is the idea of equal pay, promoted from the mid-nineteenth century by socialist parties and eventually implemented through an array of legal, regulatory, inspection and other capacities that didn't exist in the 1840s. Universal basic income is a modern example which struggled to find the right fit within other systems but may now leap ahead, since COVID-19 has forced many countries to provide large-scale stimulus payments to their populations (though my guess is that what results from this encounter with real governments and real needs will be very different from the standard proposals for UBI). The circular economy concept, which first crystallised in the 1980s, is likewise now being enacted and grafted onto existing capabilities in production engineering, supply chain design, project management methods and so on. In each case, we can see imagination co-evolving with material systems.

The cool and the hot support each other. The most compelling imagination combines the heat of emotion with cooler analysis, integrating these in ways that are cognitively and emotionally coherent.[6] The importance of complementary systems also helps to explain why timing matters so much. For an imaginative idea to spread, there may need to be complementary technologies in place, complementary institutions or attitudes, or a shared sense of need. Many social ideas are imagined too far in advance of conditions becoming ripe for their implementation.

Alternatively, ideas may just lack the money and power needed to take them to necessary scale. I remember commissioning and publishing a proposal for 'guaranteed electronic markets' in the mid-1990s, which aimed to create online platforms on which people could rent out goods (such as cars and equipment) or time, with clever devices to handle quality and reputation. A few years later, thanks to billions of dollars of investment, Uber, Airbnb, TaskRabbit and others entered exactly this space with very similar ideas, but by then helped by the funds, technologies and attitudes needed to make them succeed.

Embedding ideas

Embedding a new idea is hard work. Early on, it requires agitation, campaigns and disruption. The most successful movements have radical flanks as well as moderates, the radical flanks creating space for the moderates to compromise. But later on, agitation has to be followed by cooler work, turning ideas into routines, institutions and jobs. Who will deliver it? What will the buildings look like, or the flows of money?

So, to achieve impact in the world, ideas require the hard work of implementation (indeed, we could say that social change is 1 per cent inspiration and 99 per cent perspiration). Both God and the devil are in the details. This is why all histories of ideas should highlight the role of the organisers who transform ideas into laws, rules, protocols and institutions, the builders who start with the architects' sketches. It takes hard work to promote, adapt and evangelise ideas. As the Bible puts it in James 2:17: 'Faith by itself, if it does not have works, is dead.' Michael Dell, founder of the computer company that built the machine I'm writing these words on, observed the same point: 'Ideas are a commodity. Execution of them is not.'

Revolutions have all faced a similar challenge when the adrenaline begins to wear off and difficult decisions have to be made: how to distribute food, how to organise transport, what to do about money. This is when the practical people come into their own, though they are not always immediately appreciated. When, inspired by the Paris Commune, young revolutionaries in 1960s China chose to smash the old system rather than just reshape it, the same problem immediately arose: what, exactly, to do. But it took them some years to recognise the nature of the challenge. There is an intriguing quote by Chairman Mao from this very moment, at the peak of the Cultural Revolution, which is not, I think, intentionally ironic: 'At first I did not quite understand ... How was it possible to have a thorough grasp of principles and yet be incompetent in handling concrete problems? Now I see that there is something in that statement ...'.[7]

In the end, imagination has been most powerful when its ideas have become second nature, no longer thought about so consciously. The first forms that imagination takes are one-off events, fragments of ideas, books and programmes. But these come to influence the world when they become repetitions and habits, cycles that are so embedded in the rhythms of daily life that we don't even think about them. To do so, they have to become shared frames—ways of seeing and thinking that are then organised as ways of doing. It's often assumed that we conform to norms because we have internalised them or fear external sanctions. In fact, we tend to follow them quite automatically, regardless of incentives or personal commitments. This is the sense in which social norms really are social.[8]

So, imagination on its own is like thin air and clouds; it may shape how people see, but not how they act. What we think is not the same as what we do. Yet imagination can change the world when its ideas become ingrained and unconscious, like the way we ride a bicycle or play a musical instrument.

9

THE LIMITS OF IMAGINATION

The boundaries of the possible

How far can imagination go? How diverse can societies be? There are few limits to what we can dream. As the neurologist Robert Sapolsky put it, 'on a certain level, the nature of our nature is not to be particularly constrained by our nature.'[1] Recent prehistory confirms the astonishing variety of human social organisation.[2] We now know that democracy was far more common globally than suggested by the traditional account of its invention in Athens; rather, it had antecedents from Persia to northern India. Elected monarchies and republics were also common long before the modern era. Cities and monuments preceded agriculture, contrary to conventional understanding.

But there are limits to what can be done and also limits to what can be thought; it is in the nature of any culture that it constrains. Pharaonic Egypt couldn't suddenly switch to become a Scandinavian social democracy (and couldn't even make the switch to monotheism that Akhenaton attempted). Karl Marx asked, 'Are men free to choose this or that form of society for themselves?' and replied emphatically, 'By no means'.[3] Indeed, one of the striking patterns of history is the strong trend of iso-morphism, or convergent evolution, that pulls apparently diverse societies in similar directions, and suggests limits to social imagi-nation. When Christopher Columbus reached the Americas, for example, civilisations that had been wholly separated for at least 15,000 years, on opposite sides of the Atlantic, turned out to have some very similar forms: governments, urban planning, schools, taxes, organised religion, roads, writing and slavery.

Many of these were practical solutions to problems of scale—how to organise large settlements with food, housing, water, energy, mobility—for which there are only limited options at any particular stage of technological development. Today, too, even apparently very different societies share a lot; much of North Korea doesn't look so different from dozens of other countries. The same might be true in 2100; there may turn out to be rela-tively few stable ways of organising societies flooded with data, full of advanced AI, managing behaviour to sharply cut emissions and waste, or caring for large populations of the frail elderly.

Imagination is also constrained by past choices. Every society gets locked into systems; an oil-based economy, inherited sys-tems of taxation or welfare, or dominant methods of transport all preclude some alternative choices. It's not just that some of these require very long-term investment, and so can't change quickly. It's also that so many other institutions and habits adjust around them. So a car-based society gets locked into supply chains of petrol and metals; the skills of drivers and mechanics; habits of shopping and commuting; cultures that make the car a source of meaning and status; and much more. All of these can, and do, change (today, many fewer young adults are choosing to buy a car than a generation ago). But they can't change fast. All of us are prisoners of the locked-in choices of the past.

If we look at individual domains, it can also be surprising how little variety there is, not how much. Schools look similar the world over, and not so different from how they looked fifty or 100 years ago. So do activities and institutions as varied as tax collection, cinemas, public beaches, prisons, offices and factories. The reasons for this convergence are many: they include both functional and practical constraints, on the one hand, and suggestibility and conformism of the kind described above, on the other, including the influence of more prestigious nations.

This last point opens up many questions for imagination. The extraordinary technological, economic and military dominance of the West in the eighteenth, nineteenth and twentieth centuries forced the rest of the world to respond. The Turkish writer Ahmet Hamdi Tanpınar, author of the extraordinary book *The Time Regulation Institute*, described this as 'the awful thing we call belatedness', the experience of coming late to modernity and then having to learn its lessons fast as the only protection against domination. The reformers of Emperor Meiji's Japan, Atatürk's Turkey and even Lenin's USSR were evangelists of isomorphism, of catching up, better late than never. In each country, their evangelism sparked a reaction—a nostalgic assertion of the unique soul and spirit of the nation in literature and politics and a denunciation of the cold, heartless logic of modernisation. Later on, each country found ways to fuse the past, present and future in ways that were less about slavishly copying, and more about adapting. But their experiences open up the counterfactual question of whether there were alternative imaginaries open to them, less about fixing belatedness and more about a distinctive route to development.

Both poles of this argument now look anachronistic: on the one hand, the idea that there are fixed stages through which societies evolve, as of necessity; on the other, the idea that every society can choose for itself from an infinite menu of options. Instead, the real options open to any society are constrained by the resources available, the choices made before, inherited mentalities and the actions of neighbours and competitors.

There are plenty of other obvious limits, too, to the options available to any society at any point in time. There are ecological and material limits to how any society operates. None can defy the laws of physics, and we can only denude the earth of its natural resources for a limited time. The great acceleration that has been underway for two centuries in growth, knowledge, energy and material use inevitably hits limits; exponential curves relating to material facts have to either flatten or crash down at some point.

Human nature, along with the social organisation that it both shapes and is shaped by, may be flexible and fluid (for example, population densities are now about a million times higher in some cities than they were for hunter-gatherers). But it is not infinitely flexible, and societies which depend on implausible views of humanity don't last long. Other limits include basic biological needs, needs for meaning and recognition, and needs to organise reproduction (many communes could work while maintaining strict celibacy rules, but, for obvious reasons, this doesn't work for whole societies).

Some schools of social science strongly emphasise path dependence, which when applied to ideas means that the routes that societies have already taken make them in turn more or less receptive to particular ways of thinking. The options open to any society are greatly limited by where that society has been; one that has trained thousands of doctors in the methods of Western medicine cannot suddenly jump to Chinese medicine.

But, again, timing is everything. Too much emphasis on path dependence makes it easy to underestimate how much societies can reinvent themselves over a generation. It was assumed, for example, in the 1960s that East Asian societies were condemned to economic stagnation because of their Confucian roots. By the 1980s, the same Confucian values were being cited as reasons for their explosive economic growth. In the eighteenth and early nineteenth centuries, it was assumed that Germany was far too romantic, fragmented and backward-looking ever to become an industrial power. Again, history mocked this prejudice. The old saying 'culture eats strategy for breakfast' is appealing, but if it were true, cultures would never change. Instead, recent history is full of successful attempts to transform cultures (not always for the better).

Isomorphism has its own limits too. Extreme theocracy should have been unsuitable for late-twentieth-century Iran, a highly industrialised country. But it nevertheless became its ruling ideology. For a time, the Islamic State group recreated the Caliphate in parts of Iraq and Syria that had had plenty of engineers, scientists and office workers.

Escaping from path dependence may rely on strong social consensus for change and mobilisation across sectors, but it does happen. Indeed, one of the things governments can, occasionally, do is to utterly shift the direction of travel of a society, as Meiji, Atatürk and Stalin did.

Yet it's worth paying respect to the past, and to the paths already taken, so that in any project of social imagination a balance is struck between freshness on the one hand and conservation on the other. 'Year zero' thinking tends to be brutal and inefficient. Nowhere starts with a clean sheet. Everywhere people have histories, attachments and belongings, and these can be a strength and not a weakness. So, we should think of healthy social imagination as not discarding the best of the past, but rather finding ways to conserve the most resonant traditions, the fertile rather than sterile heritages, and combining them with the new. Indeed, even Marx suggested that revolutions adopt the languages and symbols of past ones (the 'poetry of the past', he called them), rather as people learning a new language have to start by translating word for word from their own language, and only later can invent their own sentences.

This has been quite common in architecture, which has often recycled old styles: Neoclassical, Tudor, Gothic. For example, the City Beautiful Movement of the early twentieth century used ideas from Renaissance civic architecture combined with naturalistic park and road design. Some of the social thinkers of the late nineteenth century tried to revive medieval ideas, like the guild. Democracy was often presented as a revival of ancient rights rather than something entirely new. Now, too, it is often wise to present new ideas as returns to older ideas rather than emphasising their absolute novelty.

Intentions and results are distant cousins

Hegel once joked, 'We learn from history that we do not learn from history.' If we did, we would find that prophets are liable to be surprised or disappointed by what happens to their prophecies. History tells us repeatedly that the possibilities that materialise have only a tenuous connection to the aims of the imaginer. Hegel called this the 'ruse of reason' in history. Contemporary examples would include how America's actions to wipe out terrorism in the Middle East had the opposite effect, or how Hitler's aim of destroying communism instead strengthened it.

Some revolutions have echoed the shape of a Möbius strip rather than a straight road, so that moving in one direction ends up taking you to a destination almost opposite to the one you expect. Fighting for freedom ends with dictatorship; fighting for equality ends with new inequality. More often, the results are just a more bureaucratic version of the intentions. The desire for greater respect and recognition ends up with a panoply of laws, inspectorates and procedures.

In Leo Tolstoy's *War and Peace*, the great Field Marshal Kutuzov, the much-derided old leader of the Russian forces who eventually wins the war, describes the world as made up of complex messy and chaotic events that are far beyond human comprehension. They look like a fog. But on rare occasions, Kutuzov suggests, the mists clear and it becomes possible to see the underlying reality, and then to act decisively in ways that transform the shape of history. These moments of sudden change (the weeks when decades happen, in Lenin's adage) transform what's possible and realistic.

Yet such moments are impossible to predict, the world being so much more complex than our minds or our models. The many conditions described in Chapter 8 make it more likely that an idea will flourish. But they are not the whole story. Sometimes, the world moves on its axis and suddenly becomes ready for what a few months prior was almost unimaginable.

10

DANGEROUS IMAGINATION

The devil has the best tunes

Hannah Arendt was perhaps the twentieth century's most articulate critic of faceless power. For her, imagination was at best ambiguous, at worst an ally of evil. Describing Nazism and other totalitarian movements, Arendt argued that 'sheer imagination' was deployed so that 'uprooted masses can feel at home and are spared the never-ending shocks which real life and real experiences deal to human beings and their expectations'.[1] The Nazis' imagination created a 'lying world', she wrote, distant from the real world, both factually and morally.

In any field, imagination can be good or bad, healthy or pathological, though it may be hard to reach a consensus on the boundary lines. That something is novel doesn't make it desirable; imagination can easily conjure up nightmares, dystopias and horrors of all kinds. Utopia for one person may look like hell to another. In a poem about Hollywood, Bertolt Brecht wrote about how utopias can be heaven and hell simultaneously, suggesting that God's heaven could also serve as hell by being visible but out of reach for the unprosperous and unsuccessful.[2]

ANOTHER WORLD IS POSSIBLE

Unfortunately, human imagination has been able to create much more appalling hells than this, often amplifying the worst and not the best of human nature. Human selfishness or will to power are sometimes imagined as fundamental truths and all of a society's institutions are then built around these ideas, or, as with Pol Pot's Khmer Rouge, whole groups of people come to be seen as enemies who must be wiped out in the name of a utopian vision.

Hitler's biography is the definitive riposte to anyone who believes that engagement with high art promotes humanity and enlightenment. He consistently claimed that he really wanted to become an artist again, poured money into arts projects of all kinds, personally intervened in hiring decisions and exhibitions and viewed much of his work as a kind of performance, from the aesthetics of uniforms, symbols and architecture to grand rallies which embodied the dissolution of the individual into a collective people. His ideas for creating the institutions and buildings for a thousand-year Reich were nothing if not imaginative.

In his famous painting of the same name, Goya depicts on the desk of a scholar the words 'the sleep of reason produces monsters'. Many horrors arose from the combination of reason with imagination, such as mass bombings by the US and the UK in the name of democracy, Nazi death camps justified by a warped version of eugenic science, and the forced subjugation of indigenous peoples in Australia and North America.

There is no doubting the imaginative reach of some of the death cults that have been so influential over the last two centuries. The fascists and Nazis believed that death and war were purifying: 'Long live death!' was a Spanish fascist chant. The Islamic State group, promoters of a revived Caliphate, are also lovers of death, reflected in their imagery, rhetoric and actions. Such movements attract the psychopaths.

Other ideas attract the clever while being equally morally suspect. Eugenics pulled in many of the most impressive thinkers of the time, from leading scientist and statistician Francis Galton to H.G. Wells, who favoured sterilisation of the 'undesirable'. Their social imaginary included much more deliberate management of who could breed with whom, and they influenced not just the Nazis but also some US states, as well as Sweden, which for a time implemented eugenicist policies.

Bad imagination can be morally bad, but also bad in another sense.[3] Fertile imagination is sometimes taken as a substitute for knowledge or real insight, and bad ideas have a habit of spreading. There is a maxim only half-jokingly known as Brandolini's law which states that it takes an order of magnitude more energy to refute bullshit than it does to produce it.

Then there is the imagination of pushing things to extremes—like imagining no property, no government, no police, no rules, no secrecy—which can be useful as a thought experiment but less so as a practical programme. Ursula Le Guin, again, put her finger on this ambiguity: 'My imagination makes me human and makes me a fool; it gives me all the world and exiles me from it.'[4]

Sometimes it's good to explore the folly. Our imagination usually seeks to tame unruly, random nature. The capriciously merciless patterns of the natural world—full of plagues, droughts, floods and famine—makes us want to imagine turning wilderness into orchards, deserts into oases, recasting hostile landscapes as friendly, warm and giving. Much of what we call civilisation is the story of how such work has made the world ever more comfortable as a home. Yet one of the reasons that utopias are often unappealing is that they are too neat and too tamed, leaving little room to breathe. So, we need an opposite imaginary—one that has been present at least since the Industrial Revolution—which celebrates our animal nature and the spaces in which we can be allowed to go crazy or break free from restraints. Festivals, parties, raves and orgies give us a hint of a primordial communal wildness, as do landscapes that bring back the wolves, bears and birds of prey, reintroducing teeming life to city centres and providing an alternative to the serried ranks of business organisations, suburbs and towns built on rigid grids.

In short, imagination is necessary, indeed vital, and sometimes we have to explore its boundaries. Sometimes we have to clear away familiar ideas and institutions to make way for the new. In the words of Dee Hock, the founder of Visa (a truly radical idea when it first launched that imagined banking as a network of protocols rather than as institutions with buildings), 'forgetting, not learning, is the real—and fiendishly difficult—trick.' All that imagination can do is widen our menu of choices. It then remains for us to have the wisdom to choose well, avoiding the bad, the bullshit and the ugly.

Do we have to destroy to create?

Every new idea faces enemies: blockers, barriers and diverters. Some resist because their minds are narrow, others because their life depends on it. As Upton Sinclair wrote, 'It is difficult to get a man to understand something when his salary depends on his not understanding it.'[5]

Because resistance is natural, it's easy to conclude that blockages and barriers have to be destroyed to make way for the new; as Lenin put it, you can't make an omelette without breaking eggs. Sometimes shocks can be constructive. A study of 850 enduring inter-state conflicts that occurred between 1816 and 1992 found that more than 75 per cent of them ended within ten years of a major destabilizing shock.[6] Societal shocks can break in different ways, making things better or worse.

The benign, pacific hope that sweet reason is enough to bring change finds little support in the historical record. Instead, anger, like fear, can be a great motivator of imagination, and violence can help to make the imagined real, as people imagine a world where rights are wronged and vengeance is wreaked on the powerful and privileged. Guillotines, firing squads and citizen courts translate that anger into justice and humiliation. The Chinese Cultural Revolution is a recent example, urged on by an imaginary of purifying and purging, removing the old, the corrupt and the domineering.

In the nineteenth century, the anarchists, of whom there were many, were similarly attracted to the purifying potential of the murderous violence that was essential for the promise of their political and social imagination to be realised. For several decades, anarchist cells ran a successful programme of assassination, aimed mainly at kings and emperors. They thought that violence could free the mind from its shackles and assumptions—indeed, that nothing else could. Hans Magnus Enzensberger, writing of two such anarchists, Vera Sassulitch and Jegor Sasonov, commented that they:

> were not interested in party lines or political recipes, nor in a social doctrine. What was at stake for them was their and everyone else's weal and salvation: a salvation that was of this world and which could be achieved only at the price of their life. In that second of truth, when they tossed the bomb, they realised their salvation and anticipated that of others.[7]

Karl Marx, writing earlier, described people like them as 'dreamers of the absolute'. One such dreamer, an anonymous one in the crowd, 'suffices to instil dread into all those who hold power on this earth.'[8]

Many others took a similar view. Frantz Fanon believed that states with a monopoly of force had to be confronted with an equal and opposite will to violence. More recently, the believers in a revived Caliphate have proclaimed violence as purifying, redemptive and clarifying. For Fanon, the old had to be demolished before the new could be built; for the Islamic State group and their like, the new must be demolished so that we can return to the old.

The problem with violence is that it tends either to be pointless or to become habitual. The strongest political leaders are able to keep their military wings under control. But often, the means becomes an end. And since the foundation of most social imagination is a world where we learn better to live together, cooperate, share and love, violence is far more likely to be the problem than the solution.

The deeper weakness of these political movements is also the weakness of all anger, whether in daily life or for whole societies. It promises a reckoning, a payback after wrongs. But it doesn't offer what philosopher Martha Nussbaum calls 'the transition' of moving beyond anger to thinking about what lies after. In this sense, the very fierceness of imagining the moment of violence crowds out imagination of the world beyond.

Revolutionaries in the tradition of Gandhi, Martin Luther King Jr and Nelson Mandela, by contrast, advocate generosity towards the formerly powerful, in part because that is the only route to future harmony and a world where, in King's famous words, we 'rise to the majestic heights of meeting physical force with soul force'. Such generosity may be emotionally unsatisfying when we seek justice and a restoration of cosmic balance. But without it, we risk passing on hatred and mistrust through the generations.

11

COMPETING POLITICAL IMAGINARIES

In this chapter, I explore the contending political imaginaries of the years ahead—attempts to fuse ideas together into coherent and compelling pictures. In George Orwell's *Nineteen Eighty-Four*, the Party's slogan was 'Who controls the past controls the future: who controls the present controls the past.'[1] But whoever controls the future can also dominate the present. This is why the future has been a battleground, a place for competing visions, ideas and ideals, and why Lenin at one point worried that there was too little dreaming in his movement.[2]

As I suggested earlier, imaginaries can be thick or thin. The thick kind is rich in myth, generative ideas, domain-specific concepts, and models of implementation. We prefer to forget, but fascism in the 1920s and 1930s was in this sense quite thick. It combined artistic sensibilities in architecture and futurism; philosophical ideas loosely drawn from Nietzsche; an historical analysis of why liberal democracy was bound to be weak and to fail; a programme for government; and practical examples, like efficient railways and later autobahns. The whole package was appealing to many—from British aristocrats to the leaders of anti-colonial movements.

By the mid-twentieth century, fascism had almost disappeared thanks to defeat in war. Instead, communism and capitalism faced off as dense bodies of ideas that worked at each of the above levels. Some other contenders failed. Gandhian ideas had some influence through the concepts of non-violence, civil rights, intermediate technology and the green movement, but in India they were more significant as symbols than as guides. Maoism briefly offered itself as a global imaginary, but China opted too for the symbolism of its founder's philosophy rather than the substance, and today it exports state capitalism with hardly a trace of Marxism in programmes like the Belt and Road Initiative.

For the next few decades, we may be left with a very different landscape of contending imaginaries. Some will be 'anti-imaginaries'. Politicians can choose to concentrate on dreams and hope on the one hand or fears and nightmares on the other, or they can opt for a pragmatic middle ground (perhaps one where the public are asked to slumber quietly). Many contemporary politicians have opted for an essentially negative stance: a permanent campaign against the present and a switch from the positive politics that emphasises the openness and possibility of the future towards a negative politics that emphasises risk and harms, is defensive, sceptical and nostalgic, and remains convinced that the best years lie in the past. Here I am more interested in the positive contenders in a century when the world's centre of gravity is likely to move steadily eastwards.

At the frontiers

Karl Marx thought that the leading edge of the new economy was where the future of politics would be determined. As the economy evolved with new models of production and technologies, it would create new political actors but also new tensions. In his time, it was the tension between wage labour and capital that was most apparent at the leading edge of production, which meant the factories making iron, steel and textiles, not where the majority still worked in agriculture. This new tension—exploitation by owners in the factory—would generate not only political movements but also ideas about how a better society could be designed, precisely so as to solve the problems that had newly arisen.

While many of his predictions were wrong, Marx was largely right about this. Negotiations between working-class masses and a capitalist class came to dominate the century after Marx and led to working rights, universal suffrage and a welfare state. This movement was led by the relatively skilled workers—the aristocracy of labour, as they were called—who became the bedrock of socialist societies and trade unions, urged on by the pamphleteers, believers in a future where labour would become autonomous. Their experiences became pointers for a much more general reality a generation or two later.

Many of these workers were required to invent, adjust and improve in their professional roles, for example as artisans and engineers. Indeed, this is the defining characteristic of the frontier at any point in history, so it is not surprising that such experiences at work spill over into active imagination about the whole of society, a dissatisfaction with current arrangements and an intuitive feel for the malleability of the world.

Looking to the emerging economic forms on the frontiers now may also provide pointers to future imagination. Conflicts here may, in time, become the dominant conflicts, the ones that get attention. And at the frontline, there will be many who will have the power to achieve change, unlike the very marginalised.

One comparable group today to the nineteenth-century skilled professionals are people working in high-end manufacturing, where, under advanced systems like that of Japanese firm Toyota or the Third Italy's 'flexible specialisation', workers are allowed to stop the production line or otherwise have a high degree of autonomy. These models in which responsibility is shared among highly skilled workers have achieved big jumps in productivity.

Another group with even stronger parallels are the millions working in software, logistics, retail, surveillance, marketing and data. The open-source movement represents one ideal for this group, just as their nineteenth-century equivalents in the aristocracy of labour were attracted to anarchist and socialist ideas. Again, the ideal model for work is self-organising teams, founded on deep knowledge and experience, and without too much of a role for formal property rights.

For those working in data and software, the commitment to autonomy leads to a belief that whoever is controlled by algorithms should control the algorithm, and that those whose data is being used should have some control over that data. In the life sciences and genetics, we can see a similar spirit, which also leads to similar tensions—over reward (who counts as the inventor?), over safety and over purpose (why should the supply of essential drugs be restricted?).

Perhaps even more than their late-nineteenth-century equivalents, these workers today—whose daily tasks involve knowledge, design and creativity—experience a world that can be reprogrammed and remade, and so they naturally extend these ways of thinking to the society around them. While their relative privilege cuts them off from others, the nature of their roles makes them natural pioneers of new, generalisable principles that could empower everyone.

The story of the confrontation between communities in Toronto and the attempts by Google's Sidewalk Labs to create a new kind of smart city in the late 2010s was authentically Marxist in this sense. Google had promised to build a new model city in a central part of Toronto, a project that was launched with great fanfare and championed by Prime Minister Justin Trudeau. But it steadily became clear that the community would have little control over the data that would be collected and that Google had given little thought to questions of governance and accountability. In early 2020, the project was dropped. This was a battle at the frontiers over radically different imaginaries: on the one side, a corporate, more authoritarian vision of the smart city; on the other, one with connections to anarchist sensibilities and demanding community control.

The battle confirmed that this frontier is still struggling to find its political expression. It has sometimes shown up in small parties across Europe, like the Pirate Parties in Iceland and elsewhere, or in aspects of the programme of the Five Star Movement in Italy, which committed to using digital democracy for all decision-making. In Germany, the Greens dominate this conversation. In the US, the movement tends to be Democrat, with estimates suggesting that well over 90 per cent of employees in the big digital firms are Democrat voters. In Taiwan, a group of hackers were incorporated into the government and, led by the minister Audrey Tang, introduced a new politics focused on collective intelligence, social innovation and radical transparency.

But those working at our contemporary frontiers have yet to find a fully coherent political expression that generalises their own experiences into the promise of greater freedom for everyone, and so far these visions offer little to manual workers or care workers, whose bargaining power is so much less.

Classic conservatism

In direct opposition to a politics of the frontiers is classic conservatism, which, by definition, is sceptical of change over time. One form is dogmatic, asserting a return to a lost ideal, like the Caliphate or a romanticised vision of the 1950s. An example is seen in radical Islam, which remains a powerful force across the world, supported by strong networks of websites, madrasas and mosques funded in large part by the Saudis. These ultra-conservatives, from Salafists to Deobandis, seek a return to an imagined past and claim the authority of God to define themselves against a range of enemies, such as secularism, consumerism, communism and feminism. A decade after the Arab Spring, there are surprisingly few competing imaginaries in the Islamic world. In the Middle East there is the consumerism of Dubai and the stagnant monarchies of Morocco or Jordan, but nothing comparable to the pan-Arab socialism that moved millions in the 1950s and 1960s and for a time offered the promise of a reunited Arab nation.

Classic conservatism is often deferential to tradition—as is Confucian philosophy—and it can be overtly hostile to modernity. Indeed, it's not hard to imagine future fusions of conservatism and populism that would take on the many excesses of modernity with aggressive confidence. Bans on pornography, prostitution, drugs and gambling are one obvious route. Another is challenging the power of Big Tech companies with stringent taxes and regulations. Yet another would demand more accountability of the experts of the modern world—imagine if architects were held liable for the damaging effects of their buildings, scientists for the side effects of drugs, or CEOs for corporate harms. In each of these cases, a populist conservatism would find allies across the political spectrum as well as significant public support.

But conservatism can also take much more pragmatic forms. Edmund Burke's conservative ideals included respect for tradition and learning, as well as a belief that there must be good reasons behind any existing arrangement. This kind of conservatism can easily reinvent itself—promising to protect traditional values, such as family values, against individualism. It can be sceptical of migration and globalisation, but also ready to embrace some of the gifts of modernity. Its golden ages tend to be imagined in the past, but it can still compromise with the future.

174

COMPETING POLITICAL IMAGINARIES

A new neoliberalism

In competition on the right, and still battered and bruised, there is the very unconservative imaginary of global neoliberalism. This became influential in the 1980s and 1990s, promising frictionless trade and movement, a world dominated by open markets and an optimistic account of technology. This was the perfect ideology for global corporations and investors, and it found a natural home at gatherings like the World Economic Forum.

But neoliberalism has been in retreat for nearly two decades. As a political offer, it proved too narrow in its appeal and was partly dropped even by the British Conservative Party, once its most ardent champions, who tempered its ideology with promises of a revived civil society, protecting welfare and embracing environmentalism. At a global level, the Washington Consensus, which came to be seen as a manifesto for neoliberalism, had largely been rejected by the 2010s, as waves of privatisation in Latin America backfired.

Neoliberalism advocated the free market, monetarism and free movement of goods, capital and people as the model for a future world. Its theorists failed to deepen or humanise its often rather cold appeal, and its advocates offered little to those who lost out from the changes it brought. Yet neoliberalism is the closest thing to an operating ideology for large sections of the world's elites, the Davos men and women, the multinational corporations and the big philanthropists. It is possible that it will be revived, perhaps integrated with new visions of digital technology. Some of its building blocks are available to draw from.

One is the idea of free cities, promoted in recent decades by the Nobel Prize winner Paul Romer. Inspired by the Hanseatic League and the examples of Singapore, Dubai and Hong Kong, Romer advocated charter cities—self-governing port cities—as a way to accelerate economic development. A more extreme variant, like the Próspera experiment mentioned in Chapter 3, consists of the perennial attempts to create new floating cities for the wealthy that would be free from any government or taxes.

Often these ideas appeal to people who see digital technology as a tool to escape the dead hand of state bureaucracy. Blockchain technologies have sparked a wave of often imaginative thinking about new forms of companies, money, law and organisations, a stateless order that fits neatly into libertarian ideology.

These imaginaries may have only minority appeal, attracting men more than women, the single rather than families, the highly educated and well-off rather than the poor. But precisely because that minority is likely to include many wealthy individuals who would be happy to fund associated think tanks and research, their ideas are likely to remain prominent in the decades ahead.

Authoritarian nationalist technocracy

Today's frontiers include strong challengers to Western liberal orthodoxy. These include many expressions of technological nationalism, usually with an authoritarian undercurrent, which echo the nineteenth-century nationalism of Bismarck. Each tries to fuse a sense of the nation's unique history and mission with military prowess and industrial strength.

Perhaps the most important exemplar of such nationalism today is Xi Jinping, who has also helpfully published many examples of the 'Xi Jinping Thought' that is now an official part of the Chinese constitution. This thought is vague in the extreme as to what the future might bring. But rather like his antecedents, Xi has attempted to weave various threads together. He pledges, plausibly, to eliminate poverty, just like Bismarck. He highlights continuities, speaking of how 'the Chinese nation has created a splendid civilisation' that can be traced back over

5,000 years. He promises 'a moderately prosperous society' (which means a more equal society than that of recent decades) and 'seeking truth from facts', while washing away a century of humiliation. Like a good nineteenth-century Prussian, he stands against corruption and for the rule of law and virtue, and promises that his nation will be a world leader in science and technology, never again to be pushed around by other nations.[3]

There are some differences. No contemporary imaginary can say nothing about the environment, and so Xi Jinping quotes Engels' warning against celebrating humanity's triumphs over nature, since 'for each victory, nature takes its revenge on us'. Xi also advocates renewables, recycling, a circular economy and global leadership on climate change. He promises a distinct approach to cyberspace, a vision of the internet as a tool of governance, offering to 'let a healthy internet guide and reflect public opinion' so that people should not be 'permitted to conflate right and wrong, circulate rumours, cause trouble, violate the law or commit crime'—a promise of control that appeals to many rulers. On the global stage, China offers a vision of interconnected infrastructures through the Belt and Road Initiative— roads, rail, ports and digital infrastructure, all financed by Chinese money and linked to Chinese interests, again with remarkable echoes of the rail networks promoted by nineteenth-century Germany.

China puts itself at the heart of these visions, using the ancient Chinese idea of '*tianxia*' or 'All Under Heaven'. This is now being extended into a vision of a future global order in which China will lead the world from an age of chaos through an age of order and into an age of great peace.[4] In the past, these ideas were associated with sharp distinctions between 'Hua' (civilised Chinese) and 'Yi' (uncivilised barbarians), between 'inner' (central) and 'outer' (marginal) Chinese, and between 'superiors' and 'inferiors'. It's not hard to see a new and expansionary imperial logic flowing from the revival of such ideas, a very different vision to that of national self-determination or universal human rights.

Xi's chief ideological adviser, Wang Huning, has summarised China's current ideological imaginary, partly in opposition to the US, where, he wrote:

> the family, has disintegrated ... everything has a dual nature, and the glamour of high commodification abounds. Human flesh, sex, knowledge, politics, power, and law can all become the target of commodification [which] corrupts society ... We can say that the American economic system has created human loneliness.[5]

Such thoughts justify the Chinese Communist Party's crackdowns on big business, entertainment stars and the internet.

Yet these techno-nationalist imaginaries are fuzzy. There is scarcely a hint of how the state might be run in fifty years' time, or education, or health, or justice. But with a state propaganda machine in harness, the constant repetition of memes like the 'Chinese dream' makes these imaginaries powerful. Many people want to believe in them, and the costs of visibly doubting them can be high. Indeed, the costs of non-compliance with the official view mean that even if you don't believe the official story yourself, it's hard to gauge whether others don't believe either or whether you are exceptional. This, of course, is why communist regimes made so much use of ritual and formulaic propaganda. They may not convince people rationally, but they reinforce the sense that most other people must be believers (even in societies where there are few spies, most people tend to overestimate others' commitments to social norms).[6]

Moreover, there is a substantial demand for such rule and leadership. Perhaps a third of the population in many countries is predisposed to authoritarianism, which comes with a dislike of differences of all kinds. In the words of political scientist Karen Stenner, they are best understood as 'simple-minded avoiders of complexity rather than closed-minded avoiders of change', and their beliefs are activated by perceived external threats.

Ecological imagination

A very different imaginary comes from ecological thinking, which offers answers to the question of how humans relate to the ecology that we are part of. The starting point is nightmare—the nightmare of a silent spring, of pollution, climate change and accelerating species extinction.[7]

The alternatives promise to put industrialisation into reverse—organic farming in place of agribusiness; vegetarianism instead of meat-eating; cycling and walking instead of car-based cities; an economy without waste—new systems helped by science and technology. The imaginary promises a return to community, equity and the warmth of mutual care, and usually a rediscovery of the spiritual, including sensitivity to nature.

The political challenge of the ecological imaginary has always been what to do with the people. In the language of the Extinction Rebellion movement, humans are sometimes portrayed as a virus or cancer (which implies they must be eliminated), echoing many other imaginaries of purity that are usually associated with the conservative right. I remember a general election in which the British Green Party promoted the idea of bringing the population down by two-thirds, but, unsurprisingly, struggled to say who should be kept and who should be let go. Moreover, in the worldview of green movements and parties, hierarchy was always bad (which was why such groups avoided having leaders) and structures should always be flat, but this often made it hard to make decisions or to build up personalities in the media.

Some of these dilemmas echo those faced by the Gandhians in India in the middle of the twentieth century: how to reconcile a philosophical worldview suitable for a small rural population with the reality of a large, predominantly urban population. They have been partly resolved by parties like Die Grünen in Germany, with a much more mainstream, pragmatic synthesis of ecological concern with centrist approaches to welfare, economic policy and tax.

These emerging political imaginaries take on the intellectual work of breaking out of the polarisation between a wholly human-centric worldview (of the kind found in orthodox economics and most twentieth-century politics) and the extreme ecological view in which humans are to be despised and rejected. Such a reconnection was the promise of complexity systems and theory, cybernetics, and what biologist E.O. Wilson called 'consilience'.[8]

Here we see another dichotomy in social imagination, perhaps replacing the old one between freedom and the machine, which centres on whether we see humans as part of nature or even as subordinate to nature. One route leads us to despise fellow humans, who cannot help but destroy, vandalise and disrupt. A good future puts humans back in their place, restores the planet to wildlife, and shrinks the cities, which return to forest or swamp. This is the potent vision of much radical ecological thinking.

In another view, humans are part of nature but also superior to much of the rest of nature, at least in intelligence. Nature produces advanced forms of consciousness and indeed will produce kinds that far supersede humans. We should respect and care for the natural world on which we depend and for the many creatures we can love and learn from. But we shouldn't pretend that we are the same as them, and we shouldn't confer on them purely human constructs like rights. This is the logic that has been pushed by some of the more rigorous thinkers on animal rights such as Peter Singer, who takes the clear view that there is a hierarchy of consciousness, even if there is no hard boundary between people and animals. The German green philosopher

Reinhard Olschanski makes a parallel point that 'the human is that part of nature in which it becomes aware of itself'.

In this worldview, the ecological and social imagination of the twenty-first century should be concerned with how we can advance our consciousness further, integrating it with machines rather than standing against them, and aspiring to greater wisdom rather than a return to a pre-industrial halcyon age. This is a view compatible with decisive action to contain climate change, but as much because it threatens humans and our long-term survival as because it threatens animals and the rest of nature.

Social democracy: timidity, purity and pragmatism

Where do the more traditional political parties of the left stand on these questions? One of the oddities of the first decades of the twenty-first century is the timidity of the progressives in contrast to the confidence of the techno-nationalists and greens. Once, progressives were full of bold and sometimes dangerous ideas. Now, the horizons have closed in, with a remarkable degree of conformism around a few, fairly old ideas. The standard progressive manifesto now cites some kind of variant of universal basic income—an idea that has been in widespread circulation for half a century, promoted by figures on the right and the left. It includes the goal of achieving a circular economy and reusing waste, an idea first adopted by the Chinese Communist Party in 2002 when the 16th National Congress put it into law as a national priority. Usually, there will be some reference to a shorter working week—which has been an important part of progressive politics since the nineteenth century—and some sense of a need to recognise different kinds of labour, at home, in care or in the neighbourhood. Add to these support for decentralisation; a bit more generosity in welfare; a preference for a bigger role for government and the public sector; a

stance that is generally pro-immigration but vague on practicali-
ties; and a conventional social democratic view of arts and libraries, and of university education as a right.

There is nothing wrong with these ideas—indeed there is
much that is good about them. But it says something about lack
of imagination that these remain the left's primary ideas. Few
parties can combine practical steps that could be introduced in
the near term with a clear picture of what they aspire to a generation from now. They fear being thought of by the people and
mocked by the media as impractical or unrealistic. But voters
understand very well that some goals may be desirable but not
achievable quickly.

The de-energising of progressive politics has many causes. As
I have shown, the progressive left and green movements have in
many ways thrived best when they have found a dialectical position, simultaneously going with and against the grain of deep
currents of change in technology and values, while expressing
the progressive interests of some of the workers on the frontiers
of the economy.

But like all movements, they tend to gravitate towards less
dynamic positions. Tepid oppositionism blames everything possible on capitalism or neoliberalism, a comfortable space which
requires no serious self-criticism. Timid incrementalism advocates
keeping everything as it is but with a few modest tweaks; this is
a comfortable space in another sense, in that it requires so little
change. Historic defensiveness protects the interests of particular
groups—those with influence in the parties—against any changes
that could weaken them, for example a group of workers resisting
any use of new technology that could reduce their numbers.

Progressive movements—and perhaps all political movements—have a tendency to purity. They take pride in the eternal
sunshine of their spotless virtue, and sometimes come to believe
that if only their virtue can be made pure enough then change

will come. So, they sniff out heresies of all kinds, demand self-abasement and flagellation, which often ratchets upwards in a competition to be the most pure. This happened quite fast in the early years of the French Revolution as the guillotine consumed the revolution's makers. It is a common pattern in cults and religions of all kinds and turns the imagination into a courtroom, with most seen as guilty until proven innocent. It squeezes out any space for exploration, discovery and surprise.

My hope would be that more parties try to work out where they want to go—how they might reimagine welfare, or the governance of technology, or the everyday workings of democracy—and my guess is that all of them would find this energising. The more they can involve the wider public, and particularly young people, in these exercises the better, not so as to dream up a singular utopia, but rather to become familiar with the many diverse options which will need to be assembled together if our societies are to prosper.

To fuel these exercises, parties need not just analysis and argument but also empathy—part of imagination is imagining how the world looks to someone quite unlike you. This is ever harder in the era of social media and filter bubbles, as well as in cultures that pursue the politics of purity, seeking out heretics and traitors. But it's a vital step towards a more generous, and inclusive, social imagination.

It's particularly vital for understanding some of the new divides, like that between the fast and well connected on the one hand and the slow and less connected on the other. This first struck me hard in the mid-2000s when I conducted many ethnographic interviews with people of all backgrounds in London and found just how many felt that they had been bypassed by the city's extraordinary dynamism.

Part of that divide simply mirrors economic privilege, but it's also become a cultural divide—between elites with university degrees and geographical and professional mobility and more manual workers living in towns and rural areas. These groups tend to develop different social and political values from each other. The cognitive elites tend to be younger, more urban and more educated. They are highly interested in the dynamics of identity, sensitive to microaggressions, tolerant of migration, and relatively unsympathetic to manual labour or to traditional bonds and attachments, whether to religions or nations. For them, the world is one of speed—the internet and easy travel.

For older, less urban and less educated people, by contrast, the fast world has partly passed them by. Many have struggled during the years of deindustrialisation and the rise of a knowledge-based economy. They often feel disrespected, have seen their incomes stagnate or decline, and tend to care about crime and migration. They tend to feel quite rooted where they live and objectively lead much slower lives than the first group. The result is a new fissure that was warned of by Christopher Lasch back in the 1980s and has undermined the electoral coalitions of the progressives, contributing to the dramatic losses and eclipse of French and Greek socialists, Italian communists and the UK Labour Party, and the rise of competing movements like Podemos, the Five Star Movement and Die Grünen.

It is also a divide that threatens action on climate change, as large groups now take pride in climate change denial and make it as much part of their identity as climate action is for the Extinction Rebellion marchers. What has been an argument about science, evidence and the future risks instead becoming one about identity and culture—and therefore much less amenable to evidence, facts or logic.

This is a challenge for political creativity—to construct an imaginary that recasts the shift to a zero-carbon and circular economy in a more inclusive vision. This should not be impossible. Many of the new jobs needed in a low-carbon world will be traditional manual ones: construction workers retrofitting homes and buildings; electricians installing renewable and community energy schemes; repair and maintenance of consumer goods and cars. We already know that new jobs can be created if it becomes a priority to extend product lives, such as the highly skilled jobs that have been newly made to deal with the mountains of e-waste that come from disposed laptops and iPhones.

Indeed, these movements towards remanufacturing and refurbishment, such as movements for 'right to repair' in the US and Iron & Earth in Canada, should provide a way to bridge the gulf of understanding between the climate activists and the climate resisters. The alternative of berating the climate resisters for being stupid or immoral probably won't work very well. Here, in other words, is an example where the social imagination of progressives faces an acute challenge and demands creative responses that don't just preach to the converted.

Everything connects—but not as much as we like to think

At this point, I want to posit what may seem a surprising conclusion. We might think that imaginaries need to be coherent, and certainly intellectuals like me tend to want to weave together disparate elements into a pleasing pattern. A good contemporary example is the idea of the 'just transition' that simultaneously solves climate change and issues concerning social justice, and many books by intellectuals try to show the connections between apparently disparate problems and solutions, in meta-statements that show why, for example, the various ingredients mentioned earlier—UBI, co-creation, circular economies, new metrics—fit together.[9]

There are indeed many connections between ecology, social justice and political reform, and showing these is deeply appealing to our search for meaning in the world. But there are major problems with this tendency. It always overstates—for example by seeing capitalism as much more coherent than it actually is (all major existing capitalist economies include a state that is responsible for between 20 and 50 per cent of GDP and that heavily regulates and taxes the remainder), or by presenting capitalism as uniquely harmful to nature, ignoring thousands of years of environmental destruction in human history. Claims that everything connects skate over trade-offs and tensions, like those between the speed of progress towards net zero and effects on social justice. Such views can also encourage a hermetically sealed network of ideas, incapable of engaging with enemies or learning from them, since if these ideas really are so pure and harmonious, they will be damaged by adding in ingredients from competing traditions.

The tendency to believe that everything connects in congruous ways is appealing to writers, whose metier is the word. But it is at odds with what practitioners learn all the time. Engineers, politicians and civil servants soon learn that not all good things come together. Programmes that try to solve everything risk solving nothing.

It should also already be apparent that many of the most influential social imaginaries are capacious assemblies of multiple elements that contain within themselves the contradictory nature of the world. Bismarck fused traditional nationalism with a welfare state and modern administration. Communism offered equality but with rigid hierarchy. Margaret Thatcher offered liberalism and open borders for the economy along with the traditional values of family and nation. The new techno-nationalism of President Xi promises the rule of law and facts, and deference to Mao and Marx as well as to the market, while guarding plenty of presidential discretion to decide how any of those may be deployed. In other words, the most successful imaginaries are impure, mongrel hybrids, whose tensions and contradictions reflect those of the societies they seek to shape.[10]

IMAGINING GOVERNMENT IN NEW WAYS

Governments often look like the sworn enemies of imagination. They can be distrustful of new ideas, dissent or heresy. They are prone to bureaucratisation and well designed to crush spontaneity through planning. It's fashionable now to emphasise their mistakes, with a deluge of books and reports on government disasters, failures, blunders and blind spots.[1] The tone of much commentary emphasises crisis, sickness and decay rather than renewal or creativity.[2]

This is not the place to discuss whether these views are accurate or better understood as a cultural bias of our times. They are certainly at odds with objective facts—a world with unprecedented levels of health, prosperity and security, much of which correlates with good governance—and at odds with what we know of the effectiveness of many governments' responses to the financial crisis of 2007–8 and the COVID-19 pandemic. But it is fair to worry that governments have lost confidence to dream or imagine.

In much of the rich world, where most of the time government works fairly well, the causes of cynicism include the wave of anti-government sentiment that peaked in the Reagan and

Thatcher era. Recent years have brought shrunken horizons with far less space for strategic and long-term thinking of all kinds. Elsewhere, a more authoritarian political climate has made it harder for civil servants and politicians to think heretical, creative thoughts. Instead, they self-censor or take refuge in the safe space of orthodox technological determinism, talking about how AI will solve the world's problems.

Meanwhile, in much of the world, it's not imagination that is in short supply. Having worked directly with many dozens of governments around the world, I'm often struck by how simple the elements of good government are: placing a priority on basic education and health, and not just on the army or police; raising enough tax, particularly from the rich, to pay for basic infra-structures of road, rail, water and electricity; penalising corruption; ensuring that justice is fair and fast. Sadly, there are far too many countries where none of this can be taken for granted.

The result of all these trends is an odd distortion in our perception of what governments can and should do, and a stunted imagination in relation to what it could be. I like the idea that our relationship to the state is a bit like that of a house cat to its home. The cat believes itself to be fiercely independent. Yet in truth, it is utterly dependent on its owner to provide food, protection and warmth. And so, even as we depend for almost everything on systems and bureaucracies, we like to think ourselves free and independent, with government as an annoyance or oppressor.

The great sociologist Max Weber wrote of modernity as an 'iron cage' in which societies come to live as 'specialists without spirit, sensualists without heart'.[3] The state played a central part in his story, multiplying bureaucracy everywhere and believing itself to be the answer to every problem. Indeed, in Weber's account, 'this nullity imagines that it has attained a level of civili-sation never before achieved', oblivious to what it has destroyed.

But to the extent that civilisation has advanced in its ability to preserve life, promote prosperity or educate, the state has indeed played a central role. So, part of any social imagination has to be a view of how the state can operate.

Contrary to conventional wisdom, the state in many ways preceded both society and the market. The first recorded states in Sumer managed grain supplies in elaborate detail, as well as irrigation, and ordered many aspects of daily life. A long strand of social imagination has denied this. For the anarchist and libertarian traditions, and recent movements like the attempt to create free ships or charter cities, the state is a problem to be eliminated, a brutal and unnecessary imposition. They are right to observe that states have often been the preserve of small groups—families, cliques, invaders, autocrats and kleptomaniacs—and that they have often made life miserable for everyone else.[4]

But no large-scale societies have functioned without institutions that look like states—able to organise justice, welfare and protection. States are ubiquitous because we know no ways of running societies without laws, without protection against free-riders, and without some protection against risk and much more.

What could and should states look like? We have glimpses of some possible futures in the technology-enhanced authoritarianism of modern China, a state with greatly enhanced powers to observe, coerce and oppress. Some believe that this may be a superior model in the face of the challenges that lie ahead. Britain's Astronomer Royal, Martin Rees, warned that 'Only an enlightened despot could push through the measures needed to navigate the 21st century safely',[5] imposing the sacrifices, constraints and honesty about choices that may be needed. But we don't have to be so pessimistic.

Democracy is founded on the idea that it is not the state as such that is the problem, but rather how it is run. The promise of democracy is that the state can become a possession of the people—indeed, that was an animating ideal for social imagination in the eighteenth and nineteenth centuries, and a further evolution of that ideal gives us at least one possible future for this century.

How governments mutate

There have been many times when the forms that states took mutated, sometimes strengthening their muscles the better to bully the people and sometimes being reshaped to serve them better. The great expansion in the European (and later other) states in the late nineteenth and early twentieth centuries was mainly a response to pressure from below—the need to avert revolution by expanding welfare, education and health, with large bureaucracies, social observation and analysis.

In the 1930s, the Great Depression brought other leaps in the state's form, both its coercive powers in the USSR and its interventionist capacity to address social problems, notably in pioneers like New Zealand and Sweden. The state grew under Roosevelt in the US, in both armaments and welfare, while in the UK, war and its aftermath led to a massive remaking of the state, including a jump in the directive power of government, requiring employers to ensure health and safety, pensions and rights at work. In each case, thinking about what government was for, how it could operate, and how it could work with society was transformed. The acceleration of life expectancy, education and prosperity that most of the world has seen over the last 150 years cannot be understood without acknowledging this, the role of more capable states.

A decisive question for the twenty-first century is whether states will continue this evolution, becoming ever less defined by their roles as coercive, military forces, and ever more integrated into society as partners and servants. This could point to future states that are transparent, not opaque; responsive, not distant; and humble, not arrogant. There are plenty of states which are the opposite of this ideal, shored up by new generations of technology and concentrating power in the hands of a very few people. But the idea of a more enabling, relational state has enough real-world elements to make the imaginary plausible.

Some of these ideas invert the old assumptions about how government should work. Intelligence, instead of being something gathered and then hoarded within the state, would be shared with society. Communications, instead of being a one-way process from teams within government, would be two-way, as users of services become co-creators.

Just as important are the directions of travel that invert the tendency of some states to enrich their leaders. Vladimir Putin is sometimes estimated to be one of the richest individuals in the world, inheritor of a long tradition of predatory government (the author of the first multi-volume history of Russia summed up its message in two words: 'they steal'). But states can also direct their energies towards reducing poverty, and the COVID-19 crisis forced many governments to create huge-scale income support schemes, some inventing welfare systems almost from scratch, others having to transform what had been support systems for a small minority into support for the majority.

The unique power of governments to create money opens many opportunities for them. It means that they can offer job guarantees during recessions, and that they can achieve perpetual full employment, with guaranteed salaries that are modest but better than unemployment, deploying labour either to private firms or for public activities. They can also be more creative in how they lend money to people, helped by new platforms which allow them to give each citizen a personal account, perhaps to finance university, training or a first mortgage. Governments can also learn new ways to influence behaviour—whether through the full panoply of social credit systems described earlier or through simpler nudges offered by text message or email.

China has shown just how far state action can go in alleviating poverty, implementing programmes in both cities and rural areas that provide direct support from the municipality to named individuals and families—a fascinating example of how, helped by data, government can become much more fine-grained in its action for good, as well as more coercive.

Government as brain

These imaginaries of the future state have at their heart a transformed view of government intelligence, seeing the state as a kind of brain that shares intelligence with society rather than only wielding it as a tool against society or against enemies. Parts of this idea of government as brain are very old. The early Sumerian symbol of the ruler was the rod and line, signifying a surveyor and not a warrior: analytical, cognitive and controlling. For millennia, government was imagined as a head, with the ruler's head put on coins, and an assumption that states had to organise intelligence to know their enemies or whom to collect taxes from. The inversion of this idea gives us a future imaginary of a state whose intelligence is merged with that of the society. What might that mean?

A starting point would be observation, which is the foundation of government intelligence. From the Domesday Book used by medieval kings of England to map every taxable building, field and animal, to the eighteenth-century pioneers of statistics, to intelligence agencies today, this has been at the core of how governments work. The COVID crisis reinforced how vital it is to observe the right things, with some governments incredibly energetic in testing and tracking, and others wholly lax. Taiwan's 'digital fences' and Singapore's use of mobile phone data to trace contacts show just how powerful the right kinds of observation can be. They point to a future where states could use multiple forms of observation—feedback from citizens' lived experience; data from sensors or satellites; citizen-generated data; and 'sous-veillance', or surveillance from the bottom up rather than the top down—and then organise the data received as a commons, open to anyone.

That vision would require a revolution in how data is governed. It would mean new laws and institutions to guarantee that data is not misused or shared in inappropriate ways. It would imply changing both *what* government observes—a good example being loneliness and isolation, which in the recent past were not measured at all but are now seen as hugely important to physical and mental health—and *how* it observes, for example, by scraping the web or using images from microsatellites. The net effect could be to enhance society's shared intelligence.

The next elements of a shared intelligence are models, or tools to think with. A big lesson of recent neuroscience is that models precede observations; they determine what we see as well as what sense we make of it. The mark of smart government, then, is that it has many models and constantly refines and improves them. A government that shares its intelligence with society also shares its models and encourages people to make improvements. Again, COVID re-emphasised this, highlighting the risks of overdependence on single models. As Scott Page put it in his brilliant book *The Model Thinker*, for any complex phenomenon we need many models that can challenge each other, in this case including not just epidemiological models but also economic and social models. So, we could imagine the future state setting out its many models and views of causation, encouraging an open dialogue about their accuracy.

Then the shared brain needs to be able to create. Governments need to be able to tap into new ideas, to experiment and invent.

Many have innovation labs, teams and accelerators of various kinds, designed to speed up the generation of ideas. COVID forced an extraordinary acceleration of innovation, from India turning 10,000 train carriages into ambulances; to Bogota quintupling bike lanes; to Rwanda introducing hand sanitisers in urban centres; to astonishing efforts to speed up the production of ventilators or the development of vaccines.

In much of business, innovation and R&D (research and development) are taken seriously, with big investments of money and time. Governments are far less systematic—even in the best cases, innovation is piecemeal, ignored in public finance and rarely linked to strategic priorities like solving the care crisis. The UAE remains the only government with a significant (1 per cent) budget allocation for its own R&D. And while some public agencies have embraced collective intelligence—like NASA, which has opened innovative tasks like designing space suits or writing code to anyone anywhere—most lack anything comparable. Yet the future government we imagine surely needs to be one that can itself imagine and create, in partnership with its people.

One aspect of this is experimentation, of which some very old traditions exist. Ancient China's highly centralised bureaucracy also used experiments, an approach revived by Mao and then Deng Xiaoping as *youdian daomian*, or moving from 'point' (the experiment) to 'surface' (a policy for the whole country).[6] In the seventeenth century, Francis Bacon developed an entire scientific method based on experiments; John Stuart Mill promoted 'experiments in living' in the early nineteenth century; and, in the mid-twentieth century, philosopher Karl Popper proposed the importance of experimentation for falsifying scientific hypotheses, but argued that such theories could never, by contrast, be proven true. These ideas pointed towards a state engaged in continuous experiment and learning, rather than convinced that it already has all the answers or a monopoly over truth.

One positive recent development is the greater use of experiments in governments and beyond, notably in Finland, Canada, the UAE and the UK.[7] This change has been aided by the award of the 2019 Nobel Prize in Economics to Esther Duflo, Abhijit Banerjee and Michael Kremer for their 'experimental approach to alleviating global poverty'. Interesting recent work from the Japanese government points in this direction too. Using the label of 'Society 5.0', it suggests a framework for rules to constantly be updated, rather than laws being fixed, with some governance run through algorithms (where physical space and cyberspace come together, such as in transport systems), and more use of 'soft law' to complement hard law. Penalties for companies would reflect the quality of their governance and how they respond to an accident or failure, rather than just looking at the rights and wrongs of any particular instance of corporate wrongdoing.

The shared brain also needs a shared memory—of what was tried in the past, or how to respond to unlikely but threatening risks. A well-organised memory is one justification for a permanent civil service. But few governments organise their memories very well, and many large organisations struggle to know what they know. One recent answer has been to externalise that memory through creating repositories of evidence, or 'What Works Centres' in the UK, that bring together what's known about topics such as care for young children or policing and make this freely available. This is a healthy example of a more open, porous state.

Next, we might want any future state and its employees to be well versed in empathy. Robert McNamara, who served as the boss of Ford, the Pentagon and the World Bank, commented that lack of empathy—the ability to feel and see from the perspective of another, whether a villager in Vietnam or an unemployed fifty-five-year-old—often lay behind the biggest failings of governments. Empathy can be cultivated, for example by encouraging civil servants to spend time watching, listening and talking on the frontlines of the services for which they make policies. I've long advocated this approach, arguing that civil servants, politicians and advisers should never believe anything the system claims unless it has been checked first-hand, whether in a local school, business or GP surgery. Sitting in an office and relying on papers and emails guarantees a distorted view. Reality and representation are rarely identical.

Finally come good judgement and wisdom, which, as in other fields, draw on experience, ethical sensitivity and the ability to take a long view. These qualities are often best cultivated by being quite explicit about what you expect to happen and then having open ways to assess why things turn out differently. This helps protect against the delusions and illusions to which we are all prone.

Add these together and it is possible to imagine a future government as an expression of collective intelligence that can sense, feel, remember, create and share its consciousness with its citizens, sensing problems or pain, drawing on the wisdom of its people and grasping threats. Fragments of this are already present and take us away from the linear, administrative state whose only concern is control towards a state that governs with rather than over its people, sharing in their wisdom and creativity.

An inherent capacity to change

Many societies have changed fundamentally after a breakdown. Wars, depressions, revolutions or civil wars so undermine the confidence and legitimacy of the old regime that people are willing to contemplate radical alternatives.

These moments are so rare partly because the people who have state power tend to grip it tightly. They only give up when they have run out of alternatives. Some are willing to drive their nations into the ground if only to preserve their power—and their ability to cling on to power, even in the face of disastrous failure, has increased in recent years in examples as varied as Belarus, Syria and Myanmar.

But we might hope for a way of organising societies that doesn't require collapse to trigger necessary transformations. One of the virtues of well-functioning markets is that they can cope with far-reaching changes without foundering. New firms come, old firms go bankrupt or are taken over, jobs change, but everyone can still rely on supplies of food or energy even as these shifts are happening in the background.

For governments we might want something similar: a more endogenous way of driving change. This is the promise of collective intelligence—opening up government to the ideas and creativity of people; constantly experimenting with new ideas that can then be spread, if they work well; opening up public finance so that newcomers can get the chance to try out their ideas. In other words, transformation without collapse.

What's suggested here is the conscious, deliberate, iterative, experimental design of a better world, fed by expansive imagination, informed by systemic analysis and put in practice through experiment. This could be a golden age for such an approach, given the data and technologies that governments today have at their disposal. Around the world there are many impressive attempts to mobilise collective intelligence—like Taiwan, which involves millions in decision-making; the widespread use of experiments in countries like Canada and Finland; the open-data movement; the evidence movement; and the creation of large-scale societal platforms and programmes like India's Aadhaar project.

In their different ways, each of these reinforces the idea that good government in the future will depend on the quantity and quality of feedback of all kinds. A more ideal government is open by default; attends to the various methods it needs for gathering intelligence, from observation to empathy to prediction; links these together in intelligence assemblies for all the tasks that matter most; and is led by officials and politicians with the skills to integrate data from complex systems and make sense of messages that come from a wide variety of ways of seeing and knowing.

13

IMAGINING A MORE ADVANCED
CONSCIOUSNESS AND A WISER SOCIETY

The most powerful way to conceptualise imagination is as a loop, so that we imagine a future society that is itself better able to imagine and then act on its best ideas. If, as I have argued, social imagination is an aspect of our freedom, then we should want to encourage a world that has more of that freedom, a world where imagination is endogenous rather than exogenous, rather as the economy has been refashioned in ways that make continuous innovation at least partly endogenous. Instead of offering a utopia, a mountain with a summit, this ideal suggests a perpetual movement upwards.

The difficulty lies in trying to glimpse a future consciousness that far transcends our own, one that is not just cleverer than us but wiser too. John Carey, editor of a good collection called *The Faber Book of Utopias*, wrote that the weakness of utopias is that they 'eliminate real people'. He argued, 'In a utopia real people cannot exist, for the very obvious reason that real people are what constitute the world that we know, and it is that world that every utopia is designed to replace.'[1]

Carey sees human nature as essentially unchanging, probably selfish, prone to doing wrong, and therefore bound to upset benign plans. But this view is as misleading as its mirror, which holds that human nature can be whatever we want it to be. A more realistic perspective sees humans as malleable, shaped by environments and certainly co-evolving with their environments. Contrary to the expectations of conservative thought, the vast majority of people have turned out to be able to contain violent impulses, to drive cars at high speed, to use their vote and to become good parents. Many societies have pushed racism, militarism and sexual harassment to the margins, disproving the claim that they are somehow part of our immutable nature.

Yet attempts to decree advances in human nature have not been an unalloyed success. Gene modification may in the foreseeable future do much to enhance our bodies and our minds, but the science behind it has advanced much more slowly than was expected a few decades ago, and it is fraught with ethical and political risks, whether driven by states or by wealthy parents.

Our challenge is to think of what equivalents might lie ahead without falling into the twin traps of believing in either rigid limits or no limits. In this chapter I try to grasp what it might mean to imagine a more advanced form of consciousness—how might we think about it, and what might a leap in collective intelligence, and ultimately in collective wisdom, look like?

How consciousness evolves

Let's start in the present, with an organisation that some see as an emblem of a superior future consciousness. Buurtzorg—meaning 'neighbourhood care'—provides care services in the Netherlands. Although it was founded as recently as the late 2000s, it now employs some 15,000 nurses. It has become famous all over the world, partly because of its obvious successes—high levels of client satisfaction and staff commitment and happiness, alongside strong financial results. But it has also attracted interest because its model of self-governing teams seems to embody a different kind of consciousness, more aware, empathic and intelligent than the norms of twentieth-century organisations, and much less hierarchical—a possible harbinger of a future world. Its example echoes some of those found on the economic frontiers—in high-tech manufacturing or software—that are organised around self-managing teams.

Examples like Buurtzorg matter because they point to different ways of being as well as different ways of doing. Looking back through history, radical social imagination has always entailed some kind of shift in consciousness, and some progress to more ethical, richer, deeper and broader ways of thinking and feeling. We can see in retrospect that the biggest changes were those that involved new ways of seeing the connections between things, or recognising different groups as ends rather than just means, worthy of dignity and respect. In the past, that led us to radically transform our views of violence and honour; of slavery and sexuality. It allowed us to empathise with strangers and to grasp the dynamics of complex ecosystems like the world's climate.

These shifts happen all the time. Often, they involve a change of perspective and scale—seeing our own lives in much wider contexts of history, geography and culture, part of a bigger 'now', and a bigger 'here'. They involve giving up older illusions and attachments, such as to the symbols of the tribe or the rituals of religions.

There is now plenty of evidence of the scale and depth of these changes. The World Values Survey is one source that has told a broadly optimistic story of how values are changing, as people move away from primary concerns over scarcity or survival towards valuing self-expression and freedom, and away from traditional values to rational-secular values. This deep, long-term

trend correlates closely with economic prosperity and the presence of a healthy democracy (it's less clear when incomes have
been stagnant, as in the US, or democracy has been in retreat, as
in Russia or Turkey).

Christian Welzel is one of the advocates of a long-term trend
towards emancipation, fed by the universal human desire to live
free from external restriction. According to his argument, when
the main existential constraints on life have been removed,
people become more interested in freedom and direct their
energies into social movements and the fight against discrimination of all kinds. He also suggests that some parts of the
world—those with relatively cold climates and seas, and low
incidence of infectious disease—have been able to move more
quickly in this direction than others, suggesting a rough geography of emancipatory imagination that's very different from the
geography of the first civilisations or states that grew up in
much hotter climates.

Welzel's views echo those of many others who have tried to
make sense of how consciousness evolves. In one view of the
future, consciousness will continue to evolve in a direction
beyond identification with the tribe or nation towards identification not just with humanity as a whole but with the whole bio-
sphere, so that we become part of a truly collective consciousness
and intelligence.

Yet these shifts are, by their nature, hard to pin down. We
may be able to glimpse what such a 'waking up' could mean for
the world—less deluded, more compassionate, more aware of our
smallness in the universe. But there are many equally plausible
views of what that would look like in practice. At a basic level,
would the billions of people on earth be more alike or more different? Would things be held more in common or in more radically decentralised ways? Would democracy be more global or
more local?

A MORE ADVANCED CONSCIOUSNESS

It's easy at the level of rhetoric to answer 'both' to all these questions, but not so easy when thinking through any specific example. Indeed, this may be the most difficult theoretical issue around social imagination. Societies shape ways of thinking and feeling, which in turn shape how societies function—whether through damage and violence or through habits of collaboration and tolerance. But there is no reliable theory which can tell us which shifts in the present may presage the future.[2] We may have to try to feel and sense them rather than deducing them. Indeed, the importance of consciousness—and spirit—to social progress is a crucial reason why overanalytical, incremental or evidence-based approaches may be less useful for understanding social imagination, since there can, almost by definition, be no hard evidence for an imminent change in consciousness.[3]

Some theories have suggested linear evolutions. These became fashionable in the nineteenth century, with Auguste Comte arguing that humanity moved through time in a series of ever more rational stages, an idea that Marx also incorporated into his theory of history. In the twentieth century, a parallel but distinct tradition followed with the influential work of Jean Gebser on human consciousness, leading to Clare Graves' work as a basis for Spiral Dynamics, as well as to Ken Wilber's integral theory. Frederic Laloux's book *Reinventing Organizations* spread these ideas to a wider audience, examining organisations like Buurtzorg as premonitions of a more advanced future society.

Their shared account describes a linear progression in human consciousness over thousands of years. The idea is that successive stages of consciousness (each summarised by a colour) become mainstream, one after another. So, 'red' consciousness is that of strong leaders, absolute authority, everyday violence and an obsession with loyalty. It is succeeded by an 'amber' consciousness of big organisations, like churches and armies, with rigid hierarchies. 'Orange' consciousness is more flexible but still very much a hierarchy—think of big multinational companies, with project teams and innovation labs. 'Green' consciousness organisations are a step beyond this, with an emphasis on empowerment of the frontline staff. 'Teal' is the ultimate stage, a living adaptive system with power distributed widely. In this view, older forms of consciousness—like the 'red' of organised crime or street gangs, or the 'amber' of organised religion and the state—persist rather than disappear, even though the direction of travel is towards greater self-organisation, and better integration of self and organisation.

There are many other such accounts of progression, one of the most interesting of which is Michael Commons' model of hierarchical complexity, which focuses on the complexity of the tasks handled by consciousness, rising through fifteen levels up to 'cross-paradigmatic'.

All these theories attempt to counter the crude dichotomy that suggests we can either have relatively small-scale and simple social organisation, with high levels of freedom, or complex, large-scale societies that trap us in an iron cage of restraints. Instead, they suggest that progress can mean more complexity and scale as well as more autonomy.

There is much that is attractive in these accounts, despite uneven evidence of there being fixed stages in human evolution. These ideas chime with many of the claims of wisdom studies, which has sought to understand what is seen as wise in many different societies and cultures. What they see as an historical progression is close to what past thinkers have seen as a progression in individual awareness, as well as finding echoes in mindfulness traditions that have encouraged the cultivation of habits that enable more intense awareness of self and others.

At their best, these theories encourage a version of what American sociologist C. Wright Mills called the sociological imagination:

the capacity to shift from one perspective to another—from the political to the psychological; from examination of a single family to the comparative assessment of the national budgets of the world; from the theological school to the military establishment; from considerations of an oil industry to studies of contemporary poetry.[4] In this way, the particularities of an individual's life are linked to the much larger social forces that shape it.

However, these models always risk generalising from the author's own values, which are taken to be the norm of the future. They ignore the fact that all real societies depend on multiple complementary cultures and moral syndromes, rather than a single one (if you want to be safe, you need your army to be vigilant and even paranoid, rather than compassionate, for example). Their ideas annoy people who come from backgrounds they deem backwards (which often includes most of the world), and they are at odds with at least some of the recent science of behaviour and beliefs.[5]

We are left in an uncomfortable position. These writers ask good questions and have some glimpses of new insight. Indeed, it's impossible to have a serious view of social imagination without some conception of the accompanying progression of consciousness. But the theories are not yet providing good enough answers. Ways of seeing and thinking evolve, and more complex, dense, knowledge-intensive societies have different values from more rural ones. Yet it is also obvious that any society will struggle to imagine a way of thinking that does not yet exist.[6] In the end, we have no reliable way of knowing which of today's values are the true harbingers of the future.

A wiser society

An alternative approach avoids trying to predict what will happen to consciousness and instead focuses on a narrower question:

what might a wiser society look like? This is potentially a more manageable field of inquiry and one that can lead to action in the present.

There is no shortage of forecasts of societies with more machine intelligence, usually signalled by attaching the epithet 'smart' to something else (cities, homes, governments). But these are strikingly lacking in frameworks for asking whether more data necessarily leads to better outcomes, despite recent experience repeatedly showing that it does not automatically result in greater wisdom. Here I explore the thought experiment of a wiser society in more detail. I look at what wisdom has meant in the past, how we can recognise it, what its elements might be, and how these elements could be cultivated. I then look to a possible future with wiser institutions and in which wisdom will be more embedded in technologies and things.

Past wisdom

For most of human history and prehistory, wisdom came from experience. Elders were valued for their accumulated knowledge and experience, revered and listened to when they were no longer strong enough to help with the hunt, gathering fruits or growing crops. Their knowledge helped the community when it was hit by shocks, such as a change in the weather, disappearing food sources, internal conflicts or external threats. Indeed, humans have evolved to stay alive long after they cease to be capable of reproduction, presumably because of the benefit their wisdom confers on others. Confucianism and other traditions later turned this perspective on wisdom into a comprehensive social and political philosophy, emphasising hierarchy, deference and respect for experience as essential to the natural and social order.[7] A vast 'wisdom literature' can be found all over the world that aimed to pass on the insights of the elders, thinkers and prophets.[8] In some societies, the more contextual, holistic wisdom of the elders continues to be revered,[9] and there is also considerable interest now in the wisdom of indigenous peoples less touched by modernity.

In more modern societies, by contrast, there has been much more ambivalence about wisdom and disagreement about who has it, what it means or how it can be recognised.[10] In fast-changing environments, old knowledge and past experience are as likely to be misleading as illuminating, leaving the old as often scorned as respected. This was the case in the China of the Cultural Revolution, when elderly professors and teachers were humiliated and mocked, and in the US and Europe at a similar time as the West experienced its own version of a cultural revolution in values and mores.

When values are changing rapidly, what looks like wisdom to one person can seem like inflexible orthodoxy or dogma to another. It can seem anti-ethical rather than the essence of ethics. What, after all, is wisdom in relation to gay marriage, driving a car or eating meat?

Since the Romantics, the modern world has also sought a rupture with the accumulated wisdom of the present. The ideal of self-transcendence implies that the richest and truest life is one in which we take big risks and embark on great adventures that almost by definition are *not* wise or prudent. And the beliefs of the past can easily come to seem very unwise. As Ralph Waldo Emerson put it in one of the most influential 'wisdom books' of the nineteenth century: 'As men's prayers are a disease of the will, so are their creeds a disease of the intellect.'[11]

So, the search for wisdom is not easy and often sits at odds with the claims of imagination. It may not be enough just to gather some grand elders and hope that they can offer insight into solving the problems of the world.[12] Yet wisdom clearly matters, and we can easily see its absence—whether in leaders who are the epitome of folly, institutions that make grave errors, dominant systems that degrade wisdom, or education systems lacking space for wise reflection. From the vantage point of the early twenty-first century, it's also hard not to be struck by the lack of progress in wisdom: philosophers from more than two millennia ago still appear wise in their insights and relevant today, while knowledge in so many other fields, from physics to psychology, has advanced dramatically in the same time.[13] This makes it all the more intriguing to think about what a wiser future society might look like.

What is wisdom?

We can start by trying to pin down what wisdom actually is. A burgeoning field of wisdom studies has attempted to make sense of the many meanings and uses of wisdom.[14] There are widely used frameworks and taxonomies, such as the Berlin Model,[15] the Three-Dimensional Wisdom Scale, the 'Balance Framework', the San Diego Wisdom Scale, and others. Researchers who have investigated wisdom have found some common patterns in the understanding of wisdom in very different cultures and civilisations across millennia,[16] usually identifying it with behavioural traits such as calm, detachment, avoidance of impulse, and an ability to see multiple perspectives.

Looking to the future, what might we imagine in a society that was often wise, and that had wisdom built into its ways of thinking and acting? We could imagine it as simply featuring higher levels of the traits captured by these various measures. But another way of grasping it is simpler, and perhaps more useful: to see wisdom itself as a kind of loop.

Wisdom as a loop

Wisdom is sometimes thought to be timeless and abstract. But the kinds of wisdom we need to make better decisions in our lives—around work or relationships—or as a society are very much matters of context. It is therefore more useful to think of wisdom as bringing together a set of ways of thinking—cleverness, knowledge and ethics—to guide decisions, but with an explicit loop to learn. In other words, we best cultivate wisdom by trying to predict what might happen, or what effect our actions might have, observing what actually happens and then adjusting our models and perspectives accordingly. A wiser society, then, is one where this habit is much more widespread, whether among individuals or within institutions.

A crucial implication of this analysis is that wisdom can be learned—albeit slowly—in relation to different domains, and that it is best learned, just like many other skills, through practice and reflection. In particular, it helps to mobilise arguments from different models, frameworks and theories and then to reflect consciously on past judgements and how well, or badly, they have fared.[17]

This must be part of the kind of 'examined life' that Socrates advocated, and there are many partial examples of how this is done well in institutions—in medicine, when doctors reflect together on patterns, surprises and new knowledge, or share evidence and experience of patient care through 'Schwartz Rounds' in hospitals; in teaching, such as through study circles; or in the military, with lessons learned through exercises. This kind of self-reflection can also happen a lot in coaching.

But these moments are relatively rare. Many roles and institutions that are meant to be wise—from judges to parliaments to boards—*literally* never have these moments of shared conscious reflection on the loops that connect thought, action and results. Yet, it's not far-fetched to hope that in the future, every profession or expert will do just this, with much more explicit predictions of what might happen and much more visible learning from what actually does happen.

Wisdom as argument

This kind of looped learning depends on more, not less, argument. To reach wiser answers, we learn to test and organise arguments inside our head—the more vigorously, the better. The many frameworks and models we have for thinking about a question have to be pitted against each other to discover which are most relevant and most coherent. 'He that wrestles with us strengthens our nerves and sharpens our skill. Our antagonist is our helper', as Edmund Burke put it.[18] This kind of shuffling between different modes of thought is easier in conditions of calm; exterior silence allows for internal cacophony and argument. Out of this competition of frames, models and ideas emerge patterns or winners, helped by our stances and our relationships to the people or issues at stake.[19] The same is true of institutions and systems—the better they mobilise and organise these arguments, the more likely they are to act wisely.

Wisdom as plurality

A common theme in many wisdom traditions encourages us to see things from many viewpoints and avoid the illusions that come from looking only through our own eyes. Buddhist practice can take this to extremes, adopting the perspectives not only of other people but also of animals, plants or physical objects, breaking down the distinction between us and the rest of the universe. More modest methods simply try to understand situations by grasping their many dimensions, rather than being trapped either in the perspective of the individual or that of a single discipline.

Wisdom as diversity

To guide good arguments and see things in a plural way, we also need diversity. Crowds can make better predictions than individuals. But research has also explored what kinds of groups show signs of wisdom in the sense of superior problem-solving, pointing to the importance of combining diversity, sophistication and integration.[20] Diversity in the sense of negatively correlated predictions produces better outcomes; in other words, the diversity has to be relevant, generating different viewpoints. Sophistication means that there needs to be some deep knowledge in the group, though without diversity this leads to errors. Integration means, as above, abilities to make sense of which model or knowledge to use for what task, but there is also interesting evidence that adding an element of randomness into group interactions improves their performance.[21] All of these factors matter much more than the size of the crowd.

Wisdom as collective as well as individual

Wisdom rarely occurs solo; most of what we know is learned from others, and groups are usually better at thinking than individuals. Mobilising group intelligence has become a major new area of activity—such as crowdsourcing ideas in business, or for agencies like NASA; crowd design and democratic decision-making, for example in Taiwan; and crowd observation and engagement in citizen science. An interesting example from fiction was an episode from the television series *Black Mirror* in which an individual and an online crowd advise someone on a date, giving them a larger menu of options and a much bigger pool of experience to draw from.

All of these examples are grappling with how the insights of a large group can lead to wiser decisions. However, what's surprising is how few of the methods that evidence suggests are most effective are used in those meetings that we most rely on to be wise, including around topics such as science policy or the generation of global consensus on complex challenges.

Wisdom as integration

Having gathered data and perspectives, we then have to integrate—seeking what Oliver Wendell Holmes Jr called the 'simplicity on the other side of complexity'.[22] This ability to integrate is clearly key to complex thought. It involves valuation—how we decide what matters, and which kinds of knowledge or heuristics to apply to which situation—followed by melding together different kinds of information and ideas into a judgement or decision. It always involves choosing what to ignore and disregard as well as what to take into account from a potentially infinite amount of relevant data; as William James put it, 'Wisdom is learning what to overlook.'

There exists no meta-theory to guide these decisions; no super-knowledge that sits on top of every other kind of knowledge. At a certain point, after much rational analysis, many people rely on intuition or gut instinct to guide their decisions. Even ethics has to be guided by what we learn from knowledge, and part of ethical fluency is knowing just how far to push any line of reasoning. If we picture in our minds a control room that rationally synthesises multiple elements, we're almost certainly being misled. There is no commander. Instead, wisdom emerges from the competition and collaboration of multiple parts of the brain. Judgements about what to value and attend to, and how to integrate diverse sources into a single conclusion, can only be made on the basis of experience; like any skill, this requires repetition and then feedback as to what ways of thinking and what resulting actions lead to desirable outcomes. In other words, wisdom is grown through loops of thought involving arguments within our heads, followed by integrative judgements, which are then improved through reflection on what actually happens, the feedback we get from the world.

These loops parallel the Bayesian inference that underpins much artificial intelligence and data science: first you decide on a 'prior' or estimated fact, along with an estimated probability; then you observe the true facts; then you adjust your model—and your estimate—accordingly.

Wisdom as dark matter

If these arguments are right, then a wiser society is one where such methods and habits are ubiquitous, rather than one ruled by a council of elders. They also point to a more fundamental observation—that what really makes societies tick, now and in the future, is not just the surface facts of GDP, institutions or law, though these are important. Instead, a subtler mix of norms, dispositions and cultures, in their widest sense, helps people and places to make sense of their world and how to solve their problems. These can be thought of as an equivalent to dark matter in physics. We see them through their effects on other things, rather than directly.

This dark matter is the everyday presence of the kinds of attributes listed above—cleverness, knowledge, ethics, compassion, taking the long view, and so on. It is this kind of everyday wisdom that stops conflicts from escalating, dampens hysteria, challenges false claims, and gives others the benefit of the doubt. And it can be widespread or scarce.

Where wisdom and people with wise capacities are widespread, the effect is to calm and balance.[23] There are more people around to contain impulsive, angry, hateful behaviour, as well as envy or greed. There are more people skilled in the kind of conflict resolution that leads to 'integrative harmony', both externally and internally.[24] As a result, unnecessary harm and suffering are reduced.

The implication is that we need a social imagination that amplifies and grows this dark matter, and that any desirable future society must be one where the contrary forces that promote illusion, distraction and deception are kept at bay. That will include a healthy scepticism of the necessary fictions that glue any society together—from money to laws—and an awareness that these are only fictions.

Wisdom in institutions

To help a society made up of higher numbers of wiser people, we would want institutions to be wiser too. Most societies have some specialised institutions that are designed to be wise. Sitting alongside parliaments, supreme courts or business boards, these institutions are often less powerful or rich but have the privilege of being partly protected from the everyday pressures of markets, votes or media.

Such organisations include the foundation and the trust; the research institute and the religious institution; and the core bodies of the key professions. All are meant to be guardians of wisdom and to influence more powerful institutions. They are expected to reason ethically, to understand multiple perspectives and to take a long view more often than mainstream institutions.

One part of our imaginary could be a stronger role for these institutions to act as a conscience or guardians of the long view. Similarly, one view of progress would be the proliferation of bodies of this kind with an explicit remit to observe and seek truth: independent central banks, scientific advisory bodies, statistical offices, offices for future generations, and so on. All can only do their jobs with a distance from everyday power.

For the more mainstream institutions, wisdom depends on how well the learning loops described earlier are made part of everyday life. Coaches, mentors, reverse mentors and 360-degree feedback all bring insights to the surface that are likely otherwise to be invisible. These all help to reinforce cultures that encourage peripheral vision, that can draw on a wide collective input of information, insights and ideas, and that ensure that cognition is distributed, open and shared. (A contrary system is visible in Iran, where the Supreme Ayatollah and the Guardian Council that he appoints tend to narrow the range of perspectives in government; or in countries like Thailand where a monarch plays a similar role.)

These internal institutional capabilities are then also influenced by external organisations and environments that either provide useful feedback or distorting feedback. Free and critical media committed to truth can make all institutions behave better, while media committed to sensation or ideology can have the opposite effect. Institutions of inspection, oversight and audit can reduce the space for careless, reckless or unethical behaviour (dependent in turn on the ethos of their professions). By contrast, opposite pressures come from powerful forces of organised crime, corruption or disinformation in the surrounding environment.

Institutional wisdom is therefore best understood in terms of the combination of ethos, leaders and the internal organisation of intelligence, alongside a wider division of labour that generates wisdom as an emergent property of their interaction.

Wisdom in systems and technologies

Looking further out, this analysis suggests that it is also meaningful to talk of wisdom at the level of a whole system. A wise system is one with a similar mix of features, including cleverness, knowledge, ethics, time horizons, multiple perspectives including empathy, and processes of looped reflection that feed back into its designs and decisions.

As a thought experiment, we could apply this framework to imagining a wiser energy or transport system. It would be able to access and deploy multiple kinds of knowledge—from the engineering challenges of supply, to market dynamics, to psychology, to usage patterns, to consumer needs, to potential alternatives. It would be able to think in multiple dimensions. It would be competent in ethical reasoning, and thus able to cope with the ethical dimension of its impacts on poverty, climate change or geopolitics. It would be able to situate itself in a temporal context, perhaps understanding how it might need to evolve to sharply cut carbon emissions or change behaviours.

Some systems do have reasonably good capabilities of this kind, distributed within major companies, campaign groups and regulators. Others have only a limited capacity for cognition and can only think in one or two dimensions. Some approaches, such as health collaboratives, system dynamics simulations and scenario planning exercises, are attempts to help large numbers of people within a system to take part in feedback processes of this kind, enhancing the system's capacity to be wise.

Some of the newer global institutions are also live experiments in how to organise wisdom, particularly in fields that involve scientific knowledge from many disciplines. The Intergovernmental Panel on Climate Change (IPCC)—founded in the 1980s—draws on vast inputs of data, sophisticated models and scientific argument to synthesise a shared global understanding of climate change. Since 2014, it has also recognised the need to include 'indigenous, local, and traditional knowledge systems and practices, including indigenous peoples' holistic view of community and environment', and its processes include argument, review, evaluation and reflection—all aspects of wisdom.

The Intergovernmental Science-Policy Platform on Biodiversity and Ecosystem Services (IPBES), set up in 2012, is another fascinating test case for the organisation of global wisdom. Established under the auspices of the UN, it exists to provide assessments on the current state and future of biodiversity and ecosystems in addition to policy support to help conservation and restoration, while also building capacity and knowledge. Its work focuses on topics like pollination, land degradation and how to value nature, drawing on a lot of voluntary input from scientists, as well as indigenous knowledge.

IPBES has arguably gone further than the IPCC in its attempt to be truly transdisciplinary and to cover multiple kinds of knowledge. But like the IPCC, its main job is analysis, rather than organising the learning loops that I have described. Both remain detached from the roles of decision and action, involving politicians, officials and businesses, and both tend to use very traditional meeting methods that don't make the most of collective intelligence.

Wisdom in artificial intelligence

Much has been written about the tension between artificial intelligence and wisdom. AI tends to be smart at particular types of tasks, including spotting patterns in large datasets, but is generally very poor and unhelpful for the kind of integrative thinking and wide peripheral vision described here. There have been many attempts to create alternatives to the logic models that computing has followed ever since Alan Turing, including Japan's attempts at creating 'wisdom computing'. So far, however, although these are generating interesting dialogues on how to create ecosystems that combine machines and people, they fall some way short of delivering useable results.

As I showed in my book *Big Mind*, AI *can* be used to systematise judgements of all kinds. It can help with labelling, selecting and sorting huge quantities of information, and it can guide and challenge human judgement, for example on a clinical diagnosis. Conversely, it is often useful to mobilise human judgement to oversee and challenge AI recommendations in turn—like, for example, Facebook's army of people who moderate content to block hate speech.

The rapidly advancing research on how best to combine artificial intelligence and collective intelligence is promising.[25] For example, it has demonstrated AI's ability to feed back to a group, shifting patterns of opinion in real time in order to facilitate consensus. Such a route that brings together AI and shared human intelligence looks likely to open up better insights into wisdom than the mainstream of AI research,[26] in which this has been a blind spot.[27]

I've also been fascinated for decades by the problems of knowledge management in organisations. How do they know what they know? Despite decades of investment and experiment, none of the systems used in business or government work very well. There are often strong disincentives to sharing knowledge, and it's always a challenge to get people to tag knowledge in coherent ways. Moreover, what is usually needed is a combination of explicit knowledge and tacit knowledge (which means finding a person who has worked on a similar problem in the past).[28]

There are many ways these systems could be improved, but one that is particularly relevant to this discussion is the reconfiguration of internal knowledge management platforms, including search engines of all kinds, to combine questions and answers. Google and other tools are designed to locate popular—and linked—answers to any question. But often, this quickly gets people to the wrong answer, or to an answer that only works in certain contexts. The model of information retrieval often works counter to the aim of wisdom.

There has been much discussion about adding truth dimensions to search engines, so that Google's search results would display how reliable or verifiable information is, rather than only reflecting how many times content is linked or clicked.[29] A different way of organising knowledge is always to combine the answer with a suggestion, steer or question. For example, a search might return the message, 'This idea or example may be the answer to your question, but if you haven't already mastered x, y and z, you risk misunderstanding it.' Or: 'This may be the answer, but before implementing it, ask yourself the following vital questions, which will help you know if it really solves your problem and is appropriate to your context.'

These combinations of answers and questions can then be curated through a mix of AI and human input—experimenting with different types of searches and then refining the answers that come back, rather than relying only on a single dimension for ranking results. Thus, alongside offering answers to 'frequently asked questions', 'frequently *needed* questions' would be posed to the reader too.

Wise things

So, wisdom could be part of how search engines or knowledge management systems are organised, and the means for achieving this would be to embed repeated loops of reflection and learning. We'll now see how wisdom can be embedded into things as well as systems. Recent research on thought of all kinds emphasises that it takes place in networks that involve non-human objects.[30] These help with observation, interpretation and decision-making, and they include a vast range of things, from road markings to measuring tools, computers to animals.

Much of the history of design has been focused on automating functions in order to free up brainpower for other things. Thus, our utility systems operate invisibly; we rely on highly complex food systems for our nutrition; and energy systems automatically adjust power sources, flows and loads, with ever less human intervention. Minimisation of friction is the usual goal.

I have already suggested how systems as a whole might be wiser: automated optimisation of energy flows could be matched with conscious human reflections on other, unautomated dimensions of a system's design and behaviour, such as its effects on economic location or ecology. Another approach, however, would deliberately promote things, or parts of a system's user interface and experience, that encourage wisdom. A well-designed car might help a driver to drive more wisely, for example, by directly preventing foolish actions that could lead to accidents while also giving feedback that develops safer habits. Food systems are increasingly educational as well as functional, providing information on contents and calories. Home energy systems can now be designed in ways that educate consumers to better understand how much energy their appliances use and how they might reduce usage and bills. We could imagine a school of engineering and design that more deliberately addressed the capabilities of its users.

This also takes us to the broader issue of mind-enhancing environments. While the trend for a century or more has been to make urban environments frictionless, a recent counter-trend has tried to slow things down, reintroducing pedestrianised areas, or making children's play areas slightly *less* safe so as to help them learn about risk. Going further, we could imagine environments that prompt wisdom, not just by providing quiet spaces for contemplation but also through organised stimulus. Alongside commercial advertising, there might be prompts and messages that encourage critical thought; online maps and augmented reality that enable easy access to history and experience as well as to future plans; or environments that prompt insight and empathy, or that respond to your movements or expressions in ways that make you feel more alive.

I hope this chapter has given you a flavour of a parallel social imaginary, very different from technological determinism.[31] A society that energetically cultivated its wisdom—from the dark matter of everyday wisdom in families and communities, to the design of technologies, to the workings of institutions—might be less likely to find itself stuck in pointless conflicts and illusions. Such a society might be a much happier place to live.

14

SITUATING IMAGINATION IN TIME

All imaginative ideas have a relationship to time because they seek, at some point, to become part of history as well as part of the biographical lives of millions of people. Yet it's never easy to judge when an idea might mature or when the world might be ready for it. In this chapter, I explore how we might think about the relationship between imagination and time.

The trouble with time

Let's start with how difficult it is to get the scales right. Hinduism proposed vast cycles of time, proclaiming that we are now in the last of four great eras, the Kali Yuga, an era of strife and discord that began some 5,000 years ago and has over 420,000 years to run. Modern astronomy has given us an equally extraordinary sense of the scale of time—the 13.8 billion years since the Big Bang and the 4.5 billion since the creation of Planet Earth.

In some of the literature of social imagination, the scales are just as wild and varied. While Edward Bellamy looked only to the year 2000 (at first he intended to set his utopia in the year 3000 but decided to be much more optimistic and, as it turned out, realistic about the speed of change), George Bernard Shaw wrote about what might be happening in the year 31920. H.G. Wells went even further to the year 802701, Richard Haldane to 17864151, while *Last and First Men* by Olaf Stapledon ranged hundreds of millions of years into the future, through an era when multiple species of humans succeed each other and in the end achieve asexual reproduction.

Such vast expanses of time tend to leave us a bit cold. Like vast expanses of space, they leave little option but to turn back to everyday life with a shrug. Bertrand Russell thought this a good thing: 'Optimism and pessimism, as cosmic philosophies, show the same naïve humanism ... All such philosophies spring from self-importance and are best corrected by a little astronomy.'[1] Unfortunately, astronomy is of little help if we want to get to understand social change—a feel for the pace of things or just how malleable they might be.

All things have their rhythms, some easier to grasp than others. In the virtual world of cyberspace, things can change in an instant. But in the physical world of buildings and infrastructures, change is much slower. We are surrounded by anachronisms, which survive anyway—five minutes' walk from where I am writing this, a church that has been in continuous use for a thousand years stands next to the remains of a large power station that has just been demolished but once looked equally permanent.

We have trouble grasping exponential trends, like economic growth (at growth rates of 3 per cent, economies or populations double in size every twenty-three years), and even more so if such trends are fast, like the spread of pandemics or digital platforms.[2] We struggle both intellectually and personally to know how to value the claims of the future and of the unborn, and to think about low-probability but high-impact threats that may be vivid in our minds (like the risk of Earth being hit by a meteorite).

Social science and history have no reliable methods for predicting the pace of change, despite many attempts. There are some common patterns, such as long-run economic growth rates, and many retrospective accounts of tipping points, but no reliable ways of predicting exactly what will change and how fast. The recently developed discipline of cliometrics is attempting to explain these patterns using large datasets, but it remains unclear whether it can predict well.[3]

Paces and rhythms

Yet many things we do in life have a pace and a rhythm—bringing up a child, evolving our relationships or trying to change the world. Sometimes the pace of change is obvious, like when growing plants in a garden. If you try to force the pace too much, your plants will die. Equally, if you are in the midst of a crisis, it's better to make fast but imperfect decisions than deeply considered ones.

But there is surprisingly little useful theory to guide us in most areas of life and to help us grasp latency, inertia or momentum in a situation. This became very apparent to me through working with governments. I soon learned that there are very different rhythms of change for different things, like the very long time horizons for transforming infrastructures, developing new drugs or changing the make-up of the armed forces. At the other extreme, there are the very short time horizons of news cycles and software development. In between are the rhythms of schools and hospitals, political programmes and the quite complex patterns of cultural and behavioural change.

I became convinced that often governments did slowly what they should have done fast (their internal processes were far more sluggish than they needed to be), but they also often tried to do fast things that had to be slow (particularly changes designed to shift attitudes and cultures). They, like the public, tended to overestimate how much could change in the short term while underestimating how much could change in the longer term.[4]

Some fields gravitate towards particular timescales for reasons of convenience more than logic. Most big foundations want their programmes to achieve impacts within a three-to-five-year time frame, mainly because this is the typical lifespan of boards and CEOs. Companies often develop strategies and change programmes with a similar timeline and for similar reasons.

Other fields shift their timescales out of necessity. Science now moves more slowly than in the past, with longer projects and more complex teams, simply because of the complexity of the tasks (though occasionally, with enough money, the pace can be dramatically accelerated, as in wars or with vaccine development during a pandemic). Conversely, the instant feedback of data means that marketing is even faster than in the past.

In the absence of any useful guides or much helpful insight from the social sciences, we can only learn about paces of change through our own experience, observation and reflection, as well as those of others.

Connecting past, present and future

I mentioned earlier the German idea of *Vergangenheitsbewältigung*— that you cannot have a healthy present or future if you have buried the shames of the past. I have suggested a mirror idea— that a healthy present also depends on a vigorous, positive and open argument about the possibilities and threats of the future. We need the potential routes ahead to be as visible, graspable and debated as our recent history is. We can benefit if those routes are mapped out, full of detailed diagrams and portraits of the possible, just as much as we need in our personal lives some sense of how our future might unfold, how our children might prosper or how our jobs might evolve.

The notion of a chain connecting past ancestors, present lives and future descendants is very vivid in pre-literate cultures and probably in humanity's shared prehistory. Edmund Burke used a similar idea to underpin a conservative scepticism of revolution but also of contract law, which he thought failed to account for past and future generations in its vision of justice. A related concept exists in Confucianism, even if the future is only imagined as a perfected version of the past.

Such ideas of a chain connecting past and future can also help us to make connections between our lives in biographical time, the larger sweep of historical time and the vastly greater sweeps of cosmic time. This can be aided by a more accurate understanding of our own position in time. The journalist Richard Fisher helpfully showed that some 100 billion people have lived since our species appeared. Nearly 8 billion are alive today, but these numbers are dwarfed by the 135 billion likely to be born in the next millennium, let alone the 6 or 7 trillion who might be born over the next 50,000 years.[5] Ignoring their lives and needs is a kind of violence and disrespect akin to colonialism. Philosopher Roman Krznaric describes it as treating the future as a 'tempus nullius', a blank slate with no inhabitants and no claims on the present, equivalent to the attitude of the colonists who declared Australia 'terra nullius', an empty land, and so justified ignoring any claims of the people who were already living there.[6]

Progress in time

For most of human history, it was assumed that time moved in cyclical ways, with good times being followed by bad ones, or involved inexorable decline, decay and entropy. Most of the modern social imaginary has by contrast assumed that history has a direction and a meaning and so brings with it a pattern of progress, albeit one that is sometimes obscured. The task of the imaginer is to divine what that direction is and, through extrapolating aspects of the present, to help us to accelerate our progress, or direct us to the better and not the worse routes. The assumption is that 'is' and 'ought', what will be and what should be, are closely aligned.

Capitalist economies oddly combine a disregard for the claims of the future with a profound bias towards hope. The use of discount rates means that any value more than a generation or two out is treated as zero. But capitalism also depends on the trick of turning the possible future into something sufficiently compelling and real to encourage risk, investment and invention in the present. In the intensified forms of venture capital, this becomes amplified—a promise of vast rewards for those who can divine the future best, and even greater ones for those who can also create the future they forecast. It requires a suspension of disbelief that is quite like fiction—with the business plan or prospectus aiming to strike a balance between hard evidence and numbers on the one hand, and hope and greed on the other.

In this way, economic and social imagination simultaneously seek to grasp deep patterns of change that are far bigger than us while also disrupting, disbelieving and ignoring some of those patterns. Doing this is exciting; it releases adrenaline just like for a gambler throwing dice to find out if fate is benignly disposed towards them. Getting it right then bestows the feeling of having resisted the likelihood of irrelevance, even of having resisted death.

Yet if we look deeper, our relationship to time is more complex. Now that we understand the Anthropocene better, and the logics of human-induced climate change, we realise that the industrial capitalist era was only possible because it could exploit the legacy of hydrocarbons that were locked in the ground hundreds of millions of years ago. In this way, this fertile hope in the future was—literally—fuelled by the distant past. The hope today is that a new kind of economy, fuelled by intangibles and, yes, imagination, can make up for this now-receding legacy. Where the Industrial Revolution promised one kind of all-encompassing transformation, we now hope for another—one towards a more sustainable, circular economy that becomes a perpetual motion machine, but in a different way (or perhaps a very different future where humans swarm across the solar system and beyond to find new planets and homes, having destroyed our first home).

Western culture has developed with a belief in the possibility of utter transformation, deeply influenced by the Jewish notion of a messiah and the Christian notion of the Second Coming. Early Christians assumed they were living at the end of time, while many later Christians also believed in an imminent rapture. This mystical belief was adopted by the Marxist revolutionaries and is echoed, too, in today's promise of an imminent singularity—the prediction of a moment when machine intelligence will grow beyond human control and supersede that of humans.

Other streams of social imagination promise a slower process of change, like the Whig view of history, dominant in Britain in the nineteenth century, which told of progress as cumulative and inexorable, with the occasional hiccup or step backwards, but driven forwards with a momentum that was unstoppable. It is a view that has similar equivalents today, often linked to faith in technology. It encourages a positive, expansive kind of imagination—a stately procession of new freedoms, rights and knowledge.

Tragedy

Yet it is just as easy to see history as remorselessly tragic. I remember as a child reading about how the arrival of agriculture worsened conditions for early farmers, who had shorter lives, smaller bodies, less nutrition, more war, more violence and worse teeth than their hunter-gatherer predecessors. That such a fundamental advance in human history could produce such ambiguous results made it hard ever to look at stories of apparent progress in the same way again. The story of the Industrial Revolution was not so different. Viewed through some lenses, it led to dramatic improvements in life, with more prosperity, health and education. But by the late twentieth century, it was also obvious that it had exacted a painful toll in terms of the atmosphere, pollution and species loss, all while leaving us in alienating concrete environments. The digital revolutions of the last few decades are just as ambiguous, offering boundless information at our fingertips but also destroying relationships, spreading lies as much as truth, and feeding self-destructive compulsive behaviours.

Humanity no longer looks at itself with quite as much unabashed admiration as it once did. Fewer people today believe that we are made in God's image or have any natural rights to dominion over the earth. We are aware of our capacity for self-destruction, whether at the hands of nuclear weapons or of crazed artificial intelligence. We know that as a species our domination may be temporary, possibly much shorter-lived than others, like the dinosaurs or sharks. In some ways, this sense of tragedy is the necessary complement to optimistic imagination, which it serves to temper.

The tragic sense also respects the role of contingency and chance in history. James Joyce plays with some of these ideas in *Ulysses*, imagining those histories which didn't happen, such as a timeline in which Caesar was not murdered. He remarks that the events which did happen, however unlikely, cannot be:

> thought away. Time has branded them and fettered they are lodged in the room of the infinite possibilities they have ousted. But can those have been possible seeing that they never were? Or was that only possible which came to pass?[7]

Joyce's answer is that imagination and poetry can defeat this dead hand of history and open up the room of infinite possibilities: 'It must be a movement then. A movement of the possible as possible.'

Imagination, in other words, is the ground on which we fight against determinism, fatalism, the dead hand of hindsight and the unavoidable tendency of our brains, always hungry to find meanings and patterns, to conclude that whatever did happen was the only thing that could have happened.

What might have been

This way of thinking takes us to a different kind of history. Instead of just being a chronicle of what happened, alternative histories fiddle with what might have happened. One example is the phenomenon of *uchronie*, or uchronia in English, which creates utopias of the past rather than of future possibilities—the imagined, wishful thinking of how events could have taken a different direction. A popular strand of uchronia in nineteenth-century France, for example, would start with Napoleon's victory at Waterloo and then imagine how things could have evolved differently. In opposition to what is seen as the determinism of the left, counterfactual history of this kind has mainly been the preserve of the political right, which has sought to show that history was more random, unpredictable and meaningless than we might think. Its virtue, when done well, is that it forces attention to the difficult, and ultimately unanswerable, question of how much autonomy anyone, or any nation, can really have.

It helps us to be humble about time, and not to hold too tightly to any simple stories, whether of inevitable progress, cycles or decline.

15

THE ROLE OF ART IN SOCIAL IMAGINATION

Poetry is not alone among the arts in helping us to see the world in fresh ways and to think by analogy and metaphor, revealing connections between things that are otherwise hidden. The arts should be ideal means for conjuring up dreams and visions of a better future, since the greatest art reaches into our minds, hearts and souls like nothing else.[1] Marshall McLuhan even suggested that art could 'anticipate future social and technological developments', providing what he called 'indispensable perceptual training'.[2]

Here I argue that the arts help us laterally, or tangentially, rather than directly. They are not well suited to describing or designing future societies. But whether in visual art, music or fiction, they help us to grasp new forms of dissonance and how they can be made sense of as consonance. By analogy, this helps us to grasp future societies that may be more complex, differentiated and diverse, and to understand their unity or integration at a higher level. As Samuel Beckett put it, 'To find a form that accommodates the mess, that is the task of the artist now.'[3] This is a profound—and profoundly important—role. But it is rather different from the story that artists often tell themselves.

ANOTHER WORLD IS POSSIBLE

In praise of imagination

Two centuries ago, the Romantics made the case for giving imagination a central role in the world, seeing it as the spark that makes us both more god-like and more fully human. John Keats famously wrote of the 'negative capability' of creativity: of being able to cope 'in uncertainties, mysteries, doubts, without any irritable reaching after fact and reason'.[4] Not long after, Samuel Taylor Coleridge, another great believer in the power of imagination, wrote that it 'dissolves, diffuses, dissipates, in order to recreate ... It is essentially vital, even as all objects (as objects) are essentially fixed and dead.'[5]

For the Romantics, imagination was everything, the key to being liberated from stultifying orthodoxies and cloying habits, a way of opening oneself to the true divinity that organised religion had long forgotten, and a challenge to being imprisoned by reason.[6] Their ideas are now deeply embedded in the worldview that many artists have inherited.

Today, however, the links between imaginative art and social imagination are not as clear as they might seem. Great artistic works have warned against or borne witness to terrible things, like Picasso's *Guernica*; others have celebrated grand revolutionary acts, like Beethoven's Eroica symphony, originally dedicated to Napoleon. Many revolutions have produced great pieces of art to glorify their achievements and make heroes of their actors, like Jacques-Louis David's paintings, Sergei Eisenstein's films, and the Mexican murals of Rivera, Orozco and Siqueiros. And arts of all kinds have often provided a backdrop and a soundtrack for political change, whether for Fidel Castro in Cuba or for the African National Congress in South Africa.

Joseph Beuys claimed that 'Only art is capable of dismantling the repressive effects of a senile social system that continues to totter along the deathline.'[7] But I don't think he had it quite right. The arts play a role in amplifying social imagination that is tangential rather than head on, opening up thought rather than offering visions of a future that then materialises. Indeed, this indirectness is an almost defining feature of recent art. Old art could be very straightforward and direct—in praise of a saint or a ruler, or portraying a familiar event like the crucifixion. But the nearer to the present we come, the more artists rush away from transparency, obviousness and meaning. Satire and caricature are too blunt, propaganda too servile, and artists feel uncomfortable that art should be in service of anything. Gerhard Richter summed up the late-twentieth-century ethic: 'Pictures which are interpretable, and which contain a meaning, are bad pictures.' A good picture, by contrast, 'takes away our certainty ... shows us the thing in all the manifold significance and infinite variety that preclude the emergence of any single meaning and view.'[8] The postmodern ethos, which has been so influential in the arts, encourages a playful, ironic scepticism of any absolutes or certainty, let alone any sense that history might have a meaning or direction.

Not all artists are quite so evasive, and the arts can sometimes play a vital role in preparing people for different ways of imagining the world. Olafur Eliasson's blocks of ice melting in city squares vividly make people think about climate change as a reality and not an abstraction. A similar effect is achieved by Andri Snær Magnason's plaque to commemorate a lost glacier in Iceland.[9] The flood of works playing with digital technologies prompt critical thinking, like Joaquín Fargas and Elia Gasparolo's Robotika, a machine 'nannybot' that uses facial recognition software to learn how to take care of a human baby. Natasha Marin's 'Black Imagination' exhibition in Seattle is another good example, combining fragments, stories, experiences and poetry of suffering and survival to bring to life a very different perspective to that of the arts mainstream.

A similar impulse lies behind the many artworks made of discarded rubber or other kinds of waste. Here the medium is the message, criticising the wastefulness of consumer capitalism and prompting a different way of seeing and a different aesthetic. But these works are stimuli rather than deep reflections, let alone accounts or proposals. Beyond the materiality of their creation, something additional is needed if they are to reveal something deeper.

Art can testify and bear witness to realities that are otherwise suppressed, which can be a precursor for imagination. An example from the same era as *Guernica* was *The Migration Series*, sixty panels painted by Jacob Lawrence in the early 1940s to depict the lives of African Americans who fled the American South in the Jim Crow era in search of a better life in the North. A more recent example is the work of street artist JR, whose extraordinary, huge pieces of what he calls 'pervasive art' have spread across Brazilian favelas, cities in Palestine and Israel, and Parisian housing estates. These initially illegal works of flyposting were meant to break down the barriers between spectators and participants—old and young alike were mobilised to play their part in the act of creation, their images made into vast displays that reclaimed space and turned the street into an art gallery.

At their best, artworks like these are moving and not just clever, opening up ways of seeing in the gut and heart as well as the head—the below-the-neck awareness that is such a vital complement to awareness above the neck. To the extent that they have a message, it's very simple. They are a spark. But someone else has to follow up with the hard work of translating that spark into ideas or politics.

Mockery is another healthy—and living—tradition, and many artists see their role as one of resisting or dismantling dominant ways of thought. Satire in the early 1960s opened the way for the counterculture movement, eroding respect for hierarchy. More recently, street artist Banksy made fun of the absurdity of the art market by shredding one of his works, *Love is in the Bin*, in an auction house just after selling it for nearly £1 million, an act that was clever and funny, even if it took on a pretty easy target.

Innumerable productions have mocked consumer capitalism, such as an image of the Burger King logo branded with the slogan 'eat the rich'. But ultimately, like Che Guevara t-shirts, they simply prove how easily capitalism can absorb its critics. Music is an artform particularly prone to this trap of making people feel rebellious and transgressive but without much success when it comes to actually drawing blood. Taking the example of Kurt Cobain and Nirvana's 'gestures of rebellion', Mark Fisher explained that 'even success meant failure, since to succeed would only mean that you were the new meat on which the system could feed'.[10] Musicians want audiences, but the more popular they are, the more they become enmeshed in the commercial system.

Artworks playing with artificial intelligence, surveillance and data have gone rather further and can be more sophisticated and interesting, perhaps because these so closely touch the heart of imagination and its ability to visualise, dream and create. The Art Center Nabi in South Korea has explored 'neotopias' of all kinds and commissioned works that explore the frontiers of how data might reinvent or dismantle our humanity. Lu Yang's brilliant *Delusional Mandala* investigated the brain, imagination and AI, connecting neuroscience and religious experience to our newfound powers to generate strange avatars. *3x3x6*, a multimedia installation by Taiwanese-American artist Shu Lea Cheang, is another good example. The title references the standard dimensions of modern prison cells, 3 metres by 3 metres, and their continuous monitoring by six cameras, an idea that the artist uses to raise questions about surveillance and the use of facial recognition technologies to judge a person's sexuality (including in parts of the world where it's illegal to be gay).

Each of these examples attempts to bring into view the often invisible new systems of power and decision-making that surround us, the hugely complex problems of ethical judgement that come with powerful artificial intelligence, and the role of error and imperfection in evolution and human progress. They tend to be more comfortable in the role of jeremiad—warning of lost humanity, warmth and wisdom—or playfully pulling apart the strange dynamics of networked relationships, rather than offering even a fuzzy route to a better future. But that is probably exactly what we should want and expect of art.

What can and can't be pictured

This pattern derives in part from the nature of imagination itself—it is visual, and this is inherent in the word's very etymology. By contrast, social arrangements are invisible, or at least their most important characteristics—power, relationships, feelings of safety or agency—are invisible. The result is that artists struggle to visualise society's future possibilities, and when they do, they risk descending into cliché, banality or propaganda. Art and music can be powerful as commentary on existing realities, as with the thousands of people who lay down on the ground in cities across the world for Black Lives Matter or Extinction Rebellion, brilliantly embodying a shared critique of what had gone badly wrong. But they are less able to create or suggest. You cannot dance, paint or sing a possible future constitution.

Another good reason for art's indirectness is its autonomy. Herbert Marcuse once commented that the unavoidable ambiguities of art reflect the nature of its practice. All art has its roots in the everyday world of social practices—getting paid and seeking audiences, finding time away from housework or looking after children. But it can quickly separate itself from its social roots and contexts in order to imagine freely and without constraint. Like our own imagination, art can wander off, seeking out the edges, the borderlands, the mysteries. Indeed, this autonomy is art's power and part of its emotional appeal. But this very ability to separate from everyday material life may also make art impotent in trying to shape the world from which it has escaped. At most it can be a nudge or a suggestion; in order to have real influence, it needs a translator or another means to be re-embedded in a form that connects to reality.

The political economy of the arts also plays a role. A century ago, in his famous essay on 'The Work of Art in the Age of Mechanical Reproduction', Walter Benjamin discussed the ways in which art had lost its aura and authenticity, as first photography and then recorded sound and film turned artworks into commodities. One response of the art world was retreat into the idea of art for art's sake, which Benjamin called 'a theology of art', with the aim of at least protecting itself from challenge. Another response was to attempt to create art that played a social role and appealed to both critics and the public, an approach particularly popular in film and television. Here we find a lot of art concerned with the future and exploring possible worlds, yet it is much better at evoking fear than hope, at building nightmares than dreams.

Indeed, there are no utopian films to match the reach and influence of the utopian novels of the nineteenth century. One reason may be that ideas on screen tend to be made literal, and a literal portrayal of a better tomorrow is unconvincing for the reasons I have suggested. Alternatively, when film and television become more abstract and suggestive, they often lose most of their audience and become preserves of an elite.

But I suspect another, and even more important, reason has to do with audiences and the nature of politics. The kind of dangers that can be portrayed in sci-fi films are unifying: humanity comes together against the threat of alien invasion, an asteroid heading for Earth, or feral artificial intelligence. By contrast, the promise of a better society, at least if it is specific, may be divisive, because it more obviously introduces politics, and with it divergent interests and narratives. A single exhibition or film cannot construct a new coalition of political interests; this comes instead from the slow processes of argument and thrashing out alternatives. Thus, art can form part of a movement—for disability rights, radical ecology or libertarian anti-statism—but it cannot lead it.

The implication is that art works better as a way of seeing than as a way of showing. The arts can document and sometimes pre-empt changes in how people view the world around them, pointing to multiple perspectives or clashes, deconstructing and reconstructing, taking people up to the cosmic or down to the microscopic. They can do this in compelling ways that reach large audiences. In this sense, the visual arts, film, music, literature and dance are ideally suited to the 'how' of seeing the future differently. But, as a rule, the arts become more mute and inarticulate when 'how' becomes 'what' and thought has to move from awareness to design. A portrait of the future school, neighbourhood or parliament risks being banal or bland. This is the catch-22 of all art that aspires to be part of a social imaginary—it can be socially significant only if it either portrays what's bad or sticks to the 'how' of perception. If it moves on to the 'what', it risks quickly becoming dull, an echo of corporate marketing or just propaganda.

This also seems to be true of architecture. Architecture has often been visionary—whether in the anarchist ideals of garden cities, the authoritarian dreams of Le Corbusier, or the logic of nineteenth-century Parisian boulevards designed to make revolution harder. It has also often been socially progressive, providing decent housing for the masses or vibrant public spaces.[11]

But again, the more specific these ideas are—as in the detailed prescriptions for living that Le Corbusier promoted and that were taken up with vigour by Soviet architects—the more oppressive they can be, leaving less space for people to make their own history or their own cities. A partial exception is the kind of architecture exemplified by Buckminster Fuller, whose 'Dymaxion houses'—round structures weighing only 3 tons (as opposed to the typical home's 100)—embodied the view that architecture should 'sublimate' itself, providing simple shelters that offer security from the weather rather than vaunting the architect.[12] But this anomaly proves the rule, and even architects lack the means to imagine socially, for the same reasons mentioned above: they deal with the visible while societies are made up of what's invisible.

One of the unique powers of art is to make the familiar seem other; 'estrangement' is vital for opening up space for imagination. Yet many of the social movements of our times are set up precisely to combat the 'othering' force of mainstream power, whether in relation to gender, race, sexuality, empire or disability. While the last thing a marginalised group needs is to be made even more other and strange, good artistic responses can flip things around and instead play with the strangeness of the established order.

A final reason for the uncomfortable link between art and social imagination may have to do with memory. Memory feeds imagination and vice versa.[13] We need the raw material of our own memories and experiences to construct plausible future scenes. But these memories have to be owned and internalised to be meaningful.

Over 2,000 years ago, Socrates warned about the dangers of writing, which he feared as the enemy of memory and thus of wisdom. He believed that true knowledge required internal memory (anamnesis), which was distinct from external memory of the kind provided by writing, as well as from any representation that by its nature was deficient or partial (hypomnesis) because it wasn't fully absorbed.[14] Perhaps, then, art that is merely consumed or contemplated is never quite as powerful as when we have ourselves worked on it, internalised it and absorbed it into ourselves.

What art—and only art—can do

It follows that for art to serve social imagination, it has to be organised in ways that allow time for it to be absorbed and adapted, so that it becomes an act of co-creation rather than just an act of consumption or an enjoyable way to pass the evening.[15] If it is only an object for the passing gaze, then it is, perhaps, bound to fail. Experiences that are shared and embodied affect us more.

This was the argument of Joseph Beuys and led to his concept of social sculpture. Beuys' favourite phrase, borrowed from Novalis, was that 'everyone is an artist'; his dream was to turn the whole of society into a work of art, with each individual involved in shaping the world around them, from the most everyday acts to public spaces.

Elements of this tradition can be seen today, such as in the projects of Umbrellium, who use technology to help people rethink aspects of how cities could be run, from air quality and road safety to directly controlling public digital sculptures through tablets. The company Collusion used big projections and social media to bring the people of a town—King's Lynn in the east of England—into a conversation about its future. My home town, Luton, marked the 2019 centenary of a riot that burnt down the town hall in a novel way. The perpetrators of the riot had been WWI veterans, bitter because of the lack of help they were getting from the town's elite, who were dining in the building that day. The aim of the commemoration was to use this half-forgotten memory to prompt a conversation about the town's past, present and future, with theatre, music, social media and video as the prompts. Promising experiments have also used technologies to generate immersive shared experiences and to play with the embodiment of different ideas of social organisation, notably Ghislaine Boddington's work in the 2016 *Collective Reality—Experiencing Togetherness* installation and The *Litmus Effect—Artist Links* project in 2003.

These are all pointers to a future fusion of technology, the arts, and community engagement in shaping cities, where our minds and bodies are activated in different kinds of experience, connection and imagination. They echo an earlier point about politics. If the tools of art can be used to construct possible future options for a society, to flush out competing feelings and interests, and then to help re-synthesise in a dialectical way, they can indeed help social imagination. But this requires the artist to be a facilitator more than a prophet.

The role of memory may also suggest a causal connection between an ever more ubiquitous digital world on the one hand and a defective collective imagination on the other. If we are stuck in an eternal present that bombards our brains with messages but never with enough time to absorb them and remake them as our own, then we might expect a stunted imagination to result. The same damaging effect can come from a loss of historical sense: an eternal present destroys any sense of the arcs and rhythms of processes working themselves out over long periods of time. The art world sometimes becomes part of the problem rather than the solution: a polished, brilliant and clever surface, blending into the world of fashion, which by its very nature struggles to go deep.

Fiction may be less susceptible to this trap. Narratives provide depth and take time, and the written word leaves our brains to fill out the pictures rather than only consuming someone else's creation. In a rather different way, television too may be better suited to grasping a multiple future. Over the last two decades, its storylines have become ever more complex, interwoven, ambiguous and drawn out, as audiences have become more sophisticated and better able to juggle multiple characters in motion at once. It's no longer necessary for everything to be explained, tied up, closed down. Here we see both a cause and an effect of the rising levels of conceptual reasoning that may make it easier to grasp a plural, multi-dimensional future. But TV cannot escape being literal, and its very literalness—showing every building, piece of clothing or means of transport—renders it less effective as a vehicle for imagination than the novel, which leaves much of this work to the reader.

My suggestion, then, is that art can help us see in new ways. It can help us to perceive our own perceptions, to be more conscious of our consciousness and aware of our awareness, in a loop that keeps reverberating afterwards on the boundaries and peripheries of knowledge and reason. In this way, it can open up metaphorical thought by a loosening process and can play the role suggested by Marshall McLuhan of perceptual training ahead of social change.

As we progress into a world of omnipresent smart technologies, this perceptual training could be vital in helping us to retain a critical view. It is precisely the kind of dialectical positioning that is so essential to social imagination—engaging rather than just rejecting; criticising but in order to guide; and avoiding the twin pitfalls of mindless acceptance and equally mindless avoidance.

But the arts are unable themselves to fill the space that's opened up—they cannot become, in Shelley's words, an 'unacknowledged legislator'. They can be ironic and playful, dismantling meaning and pomposity. They can warn and prophesy. They can harmonise with social movements, providing an appropriate soundtrack or a visual accompaniment. Their methods can even prefigure a future society—perhaps one with a shared consciousness and a deep feeling of connection to nature.

But what the arts can't do is design a plausible future. They cannot offer a truth about the future and indeed are dangerous when they think they can. Instead, art deals in other truths, bringing to the surface contradictions and tensions, in contrast to propaganda, which is still and dead. Art is at home with resistance, with speaking for freedom; but it cannot build.[16]

Perhaps what we need is art that is suggestive but not prescriptive, unashamedly mysterious, not didactic. Indeed, this is what art is uniquely able to do—seeking in places that reason and knowledge can't reach, beyond the sacred, beyond the descriptive and beyond the coded world of technology. Perhaps we need this role more than ever, these spaces which can only be explored artistically, at a tangent, not head on. They will keep us young, in the spirit of Andrea, who concludes Bertolt Brecht's *Life of Galileo* with the words: 'There are a lot of things we don't know yet, Giuseppe. We're really just at the beginning.'

16

WHAT TO DO?

The French psychologist Jean Piaget is reputed to have said that 'intelligence is knowing what to do when you don't know what to do', and this is precisely the kind of intelligence we need now. There are no manuals or blueprints for the century ahead. It's up to us to escape from the yoke of resigned fatalism, in which the most positive thing we can hope for is to preserve the best of the present.

All of us can use some of the methods described in this book to push the boundaries of our imagination, in our workplaces, our neighbourhoods or the organisations to which we belong. These approaches will not produce a single answer but rather a constellation of ideas that can be tried out; as the Chinese proverb says, it's a matter of crossing the river by feeling the stones beneath our feet. In reality, this is how progress has always happened. It's just that now we need it to happen faster and with fewer wrong turns.

It is up to each of us as individuals to decide what we have to do, whether to be bystanders or to act. Hamlet lamented, 'The time is out of joint. O cursèd spite, / That ever I was born to set it right!';[1] indeed, many feel an unavoidable sense of duty to act. But it's very hard to do this work alone. Most of us need collaborators, resources and time.[2] As Lola Olufemi puts it in her fascinating book on imagination, 'the otherwise', the 'firm embrace of the unknowable' and the wish to be 'engulfed by the horizon', have to be shared: 'How does a single person put a break in inevitability? Well, by finding others.'

Imagination is like a muscle that needs regular exercise. That's true for the older amongst us who have the benefit of experience—having seen how much can change for the better or worse, we should know that the world is less fixed than it appears. It's also true for the young, for whom there is so much at stake and who have the impatience to make a difference. If you don't try to shape the future world you will live in, you have less of a right to complain when it disappoints you.

But political and social imagination—like other kinds of imagination—depends on a few supports and structures. We need some specialists who will become truly proficient in designing the 'future possible', even perhaps adepts in what will become new artforms. Here I turn to what we need, and who can help to make it happen.

A creative ecosystem

To think about what social imagination needs, it's useful to start by picturing it as an artistic ecosystem, which at its best is both broad and deep.[3] In the last chapter, I described some of the limits of the arts when it comes to social imagination. But the ways in which art is organised are very useful pointers. They remind us that imagination flourishes best in a supportive milieu, as demonstrated brilliantly by Mihaly Csikszentmihalyi in his work on creativity, and by Peter Hall in his work on creative cities like Renaissance Florence, nineteenth-century Manchester or twentieth-century Memphis.

WHAT TO DO?

Csikszentmihalyi and Hall showed that it's not enough to have brilliant artists, academies and schools, or funders, or a critical mass of other creative types, or even enthusiastic audiences. Rather, it is when all of these factors coalesce that creative work becomes much more likely to be truly exceptional. It's the combination of these elements that leads to the fizz and the buzz, as people feed off each other, on the cusp of randomness and order, to generate new insights and ways of articulating them.

Social imagination requires a comparable mix to create, share and criticise designs for the future: imaginative individuals, funds, critics and audiences. Just as the arts thrive best with intensive feedback, so do we need an equivalent for social imagination that can judge new ideas by their plausibility, novelty and ambition.

Resources and places

Imagination, again just like the arts, needs to be supported with resources to provide individuals and teams with the time and space to explore and create. We need academies or training programmes to spread the methods described in Chapter 4, as is normal for the arts. These are the methods that help us to extend, graft or use metaphors to think in novel ways and flesh out what the future of anything from public libraries to childcare, parliaments to the United Nations, might be like. They are the methods that help us to sketch out possible futures, utopifying. It takes time to become proficient in any creative practice, but if many people gain fluency in these methods, social imagination will be greatly helped.

We also need physical places dedicated to imagination. Just as galleries provide an outlet for the arts, we need what might be called imaginariums—places, virtual and physical, that gather, curate and promote imaginative ideas, like museums of the future.[4] It has long struck me as odd that a typical city or town has many places dedicated to understanding the past—museums, galleries and great houses—but usually none dedicated to understanding the options for the future, what our future travel or learning or health might look like. There are hints of what these could be like in fields such as speculative design and science fiction. At their best they spark thought and argument, while also giving audiences a chance to experience how different futures could feel. To support this, we will need a new cadre of curators, good at making these options compelling and convincing, picturing potential utopias whether near at hand or far, just as the best museums and galleries work so well at making the distant past, or challenging art, engaging and full of meaning.

Of course, and again as in the arts, we need the pull of demand. As I showed in Chapters 7 and 8, ideas can take many paths to reality: top down through persuading a handful of leaders, bottom up pushed by social movements, or through the middle. The crucial point is that supply needs to be met by demand, and this is where engaging the potential users of ideas—political parties, governments, NGOs—in the life of the milieu can be so important.

Global webs of ideas

Thanks to the internet, we can now access information, shop or travel with greater ease than ever before. But the internet is far less well organised when it comes to ideas and imagination.

There have been thousands of attempts to create easily searchable repositories of ideas. Some took the form of books, like Nicholas Albery's many editions of *The Book of Visions: An Encyclopaedia of Social Innovations* back in the 1990s. Others used the web to create 'ideas banks' of many forms, with a few hundred or a few thousand ideas. Where Wikipedia gathered global collective intelligence about the past and present, these hoped to organise global collective intelligence about the future.

That dream remains relevant, indeed vital. There are now thousands of repositories of ideas, covering design, architecture or technology. But ironically, it remains surprisingly hard to find the right ones or the most relevant ones, particularly for more complex social needs. Indeed, the lesson of these many experiments is that this knowledge needs to be organised, and that doing this well is much harder than the pioneers assumed. Most of the big successes of the internet depend on standardisation—from platforms like Facebook and Instagram to Wikipedia—and on signposting. So, for ideas banks to be useful, they need labels and indexes, and to be categorised with more than keywords. There needs to be some ranking, whether by volunteers or by experts, and some interpretation alongside the ideas themselves. Ideally, there should be some reward or recognition if an idea is adopted, adapted or used.

This is a technical challenge, but not a difficult one. It's been largely ignored because there's no money in it. There will never be definitive ways to track how ideas mutate and evolve—and trying too hard leads to the pathologies that can be seen in the world of patents, where court cases over patent infringements drag on for years. Very few ideas are ever truly original; almost always, they are combinations of existing ideas.

My guess is that we will need new professionals who will become skilled at curating ideas in virtual spaces, just as curators in museums and galleries become skilled in handling objects, or librarians in the organisation of books.

Social sciences for the imagination

Social scientists might be expected to play a decisive role in articulating imaginative ideas about where our societies might be headed: pictures of possible futures that combine creativity and rigour, a grasp of how the world really is with the ability to see how it could become something more. Yet by the late twentieth century, social science had largely given up on trying to imagine. Its role had focused instead on how to analyse, theorise and explain the past and present, which are very worthwhile aims, but not the same. There are many reasons for this, including healthy trends of taking data and evidence more seriously. But the result has been to make it a bad career choice for an ambitious young social scientist to focus on the future.

The result has been an odd polarisation. On the one hand, people who have devoted their lives to understanding economies, societies and organisations are reluctant to think into the future or to propose designs and options. On the other hand, there are plenty of other people—usually outside universities—happy to speculate and invent, but often without the depth of knowledge needed to do this well, or in overly generic 'futures' fields that sacrifice depth for breadth.

As a result, the analysts and the dreamers have lived in separate worlds, and we lack even a name for people who straddle the two. The more practice-oriented disciplines of social science tend to be pulled into incremental work rather than radical imagination, and most prominent figures in the social sciences achieve fame through diagnosis more than prescription.

This matters because imagination can't float entirely free from evidence and knowledge. We need better fusions of deep knowledge and lively creativity. That is why I advocate a new approach to complement the work of mainstream social science: a growth of what I call 'exploratory social science' that deliberately works on potential designs for future societies. This shouldn't in any way constrain the best methods of the mainstream, but it should add to them. As in other fields, a strong grounding in a discipline makes it more likely that there will be imaginative, useful and creative new ideas (Howard Gardner observed that it takes at least ten years' immersion in an art or discipline to make genuinely creative breakthroughs).

Exploratory economics would combine the insights of the discipline with the use of creative tools to design possible ways of organising firms, sectors, trading and investment in the future. Exploratory sociology would look at new ways of organising care, friendship or families. Exploratory urban geography might look at how we could organise cities, everyday life in neighbourhoods or food systems. Speculative political science would imagine future ways of designing elections, legislatures and government structures. Exploratory genetics would think through the potential legal, ethical and practical implications of different kinds of human enhancement.

Even better would be centres and teams that worked on fields such as health or cities and were flexible in their use of different disciplines to solve problems. We could imagine 'Exploratory Social Science' degrees that would require students to show a grasp of their subject and its theory as well as an ability to create. The test for them would be competence in future-oriented designs that work in three dimensions: logic and coherence; use of evidence and existing knowledge; and creativity and imagination.

There is no direct way to confirm the usefulness of a work of social imagination—only history can do that. But ideas can be assessed in these three dimensions. For example, a project might look at how a world or sector without intellectual property rights could function; how firms could internalise different externalities; how new fields might be marketised. Or, imagine if financial credit ratings could be turned into ownership rights of a nation's banking system—earned equity. What would be the dynamics of that?

These new sub-disciplines of exploratory social science would use some of the methods described earlier: playing with scenarios, fiction and creativity tools such as extensions and inversions. Many of these would come alive with stories that paint a vivid picture of a possible future healthcare system or new ways of taxing inheritance. But they would also be helped by using formal models to work through how they might operate: simulations and games, as well as complex agent-based models, create a space for imagination to be exercised in a rigorous way, varying assumptions and feedback to discover surprising patterns.

The seventeenth-century Japanese thinker (and much else) Miyamoto Musashi once wrote, 'By knowing things that exist, you can know that which does not exist.' Exploratory social science is just one new way to act on that insight.

Universities for the future

What I have just set out suggests some of the important roles that universities could play in providing a home for new practices and sub-disciplines. In fact, they could go much further. The university is a public space as well as an ivory tower, and it can become a more organic part of the shared imagination of the place where it is based. I've long been convinced of the potential for more 'challenge-based' universities, which organise more of their output around unanswered questions rather than just bodies of knowledge, and which work with their home regions or cities on the cutting edge of science or social innovation. The spread of innovation labs, design teams and social science parks all point in the right direction: towards more imaginative and engaged ways of organising knowledge alongside the often tired formats of the lecture, the peer-reviewed journal and the PhD thesis. The more that universities become immersed in the life of cities in this way, the more it will also become obvious that they need to help their societies to think about the future, design alternative futures and explore their appeal or flaws.

WHAT TO DO?

There is an important place in any university for research that is purely speculative and doesn't aim to be useful. But there should also be space for research that is engaged. Indeed, universities could be good bases for some of the imaginariums described earlier—physical places which help communities to think through what the choices, threats and challenges might be for future generations. How could London end homelessness or the worst cases of loneliness? How could Copenhagen become self-sufficient in food? Could Shenzhen adapt its remarkable innovation ecosystem for technology into an equally effective innovation ecosystem for society? These generative questions can unlock energy, drawing on the depth of knowledge of many disciplines while also connecting to people's hopes and fears.

Philanthropy to fund the sparks

Imagination across many fields, such as film or the visual arts, rests on an ecosystem of funding—some philanthropic, some public and some commercial. We need an equivalent for the social field. The freest money in our society is philanthropic, the result of past or present extreme wealth. It has little accountability and no one to answer to, and so it has a unique ability to take risks.

Yet philanthropy has been largely absent from the story I have told so far. It did at times play a role in pioneering new kinds of research and some new ideas. But it has tended to be cautious; it is, by its nature, locked into powerful status-based networks and is therefore uncomfortable challenging power in anything more than a rhetorical way. Rob Reich's description of philanthropy as 'an exercise of power by the wealthy that is unaccountable, non-transparent, donor-directed, perpetual, and tax-subsidised' is hard to disagree with.[5]

A small minority of foundations are in fact interested in systems change, radical action on poverty and disadvantage, and programmes like the Omidyar Group's 'Imaginable Futures'.[6] But the big money steers well clear. The largest funds—Gates, Ford, Hewlett, Rockefeller, Lilly, Bloomberg, Getty, Wellcome, a roll-call of past and present tycoons—have a scale which pushes them towards conservatism. They tend to be attracted to a narrow problem-solving approach, using data and evidence to address specific issues which are seen as separate from the broader structural conditions of society. This is sometimes laudable, but it is different from radical imagination and in some respects inherently conservative, since there can, by definition, be no evidence for a radical new way of organising the world. Evidence tends to be thick in high-status, wealthy systems (such as hospitals) and relatively absent in lower-status ones (like homelessness).

The influence of commercial consultancies has reinforced this conservatism, promoting approaches to philanthropy that never question, let alone challenge, power structures or systems, seeking niche solutions rather than structural ones, and backing already proven ideas rather than opening out to new ones. The net effect of these big consultancies has been a blunting of imagination and radicalism at just the time they were needed, and when philanthropy could instead have offered some restitution for the unfairness of the systems that had made it possible to accumulate so much wealth, so far in excess of proportionate talent or worth. Although many of the new billionaires wanted to do good—and to burnish their reputations—perhaps it's not surprising that very few thought that a system that had rewarded them so handsomely might be flawed.

But there is plenty of room for smaller foundations to blaze trails where the larger ones cannot. They can pick from among the above-mentioned fields, such as care for the elderly, or generative ideas, such as new forms of commons, and then fund both thought and action, think-pieces and experiments, encouraging a hundred flowers to bloom, then seeing which ones catch the public imagination and deserve to be grown to larger scale.

Foundations can be more creative in how they use money and can apply this within broad fields of imagination, such as how to deal with mental health at the level of a national population. In my role at Nesta (a medium-sized foundation by global standards), we tried out many different ways of working with money, such as grants, crowdfunding, equity, loans and competitions. We encouraged grant recipients to adapt their ideas rather than insisting that they stick to their original proposals. We trialled work with open data, encouraging maximum transparency alongside many other funders. We also experimented by directly funding beneficiaries and social movements, or by having community groups report through public blogs rather than in written reports that would only be seen by funders.

We were in some ways reacting against a trend of technocratic philanthropy that had been encouraged by figures like Michael Porter. In the name of being strategic, they had encouraged very top-down, unimaginative ways of using money, hoping that pulling a few levers would achieve predictable results. The pendulum swung back against these ideas, which had tended to exaggerate both the power and the knowledge at the disposal of foundations.

The more open, humble methods have tended to fare better: backing many ideas and then seeing which ones work, rather than believing that the funder is capable of picking the winners (as Stalin is supposed to have said, quantity has a quality all its own). Similarly, focusing on the capabilities of recipients rather than their ability to comply with the demands of the funder tends to generate better results, even if these are harder to predict.

Politics hungry for imagination

Much social change at some point passes through politics and government. Ideas often need to become laws and programmes to achieve their impact. This was true of the abolition of slavery and in the case of equal rights for women, and it will just as well apply to building welfare states suited to precarious work or a rapid shift to net zero. Nothing is conceivable without the power of the state. Social imagination therefore needs its supply to be met with demand from politicians, and imaginative ideas need to be shaped in ways that can be fitted into manifestos, speeches and programmes, or turned into laws, experiments and pilots.

That demand has to come from politicians or officials who feel a sense of connection to the future and a hunger for better. This is far from guaranteed. A large swathe of political opinion now looks backwards to a better yesterday. But there are many interesting counter-examples, like the Wellbeing Economy Governments partnership,[7] or various global networks of mayors committed to carbon reduction. Many politicians and ministers appreciate the need to replace the zombie orthodoxies they see all around them, and they should be encouraged to see the benefit that can come from looking beyond the timescales of their terms to the needs of their societies a generation into the future.

This is not just about creating taskforces and commissioning ideas and research. It's also about encouraging a more hopeful, forward-looking culture. This is the mark of some of the most able and creative politicians, like Antanas Mockus, who became mayor of Bogota in 1995 at a low point in the city's history, when it was beset by an extraordinary murder rate and surrounded by civil war. Mockus saw his role as that of a teacher, provocateur and changer of cultures, and he earned these titles through deliberately surprising set-pieces: mooning at students, employing mime artists to mock bad drivers, asking men to stay at home to allow women out for an evening, gun amnesties, voluntary taxes and much more. The aim of all of these was to shift the culture so that citizens felt a shared responsibility for their city, while expanding their sense of what might be possible after a long period of depressed fatalism.

Alongside that of other leaders—like another equally creative Colombian mayor, Sergio Fajardo in Medellín, who put some of the city's central institutions in its poorest districts—Mockus' work helped the country to turn itself around, dramatically cutting murder rates. Few politicians have quite this level of fluency with images, ideas and practical change. The examples of Mockus and Fajardo are reminders that imagination often has to be embodied to be felt—it's not enough just to talk about it; it has to be seen to be believed.

Beyond committed individuals, there's an important role for political parties that are willing to engage with imagination to set up commissions, deliberations and explorations of the landscape ahead of them. Since parties remain our only institutions designed to create synthetic programmes that can win majority support, it's vital that they attend to this task, rather than worrying only about winning elections.

Unfortunately, it has now become acceptable to think of the job of politician as one of the few that requires no training and no expertise. Amateurs are put into positions of immense power with only a rudimentary grasp of how governments actually work, how economies move, or how science shapes the world. There are a few exceptions: China trains its mayors and ministers intensively; there is an embryonic new academy for politicians in Australia; and Michael Bloomberg has funded a city leadership programme at Harvard University. But oddly, even these rare programmes do not include imagination and future thinking in their curriculums. A modest and non-utopian proposal would be to greatly enhance the opportunities for politicians to learn about the past, present and future, helping them to be better vehicles for the imagination of their societies as well as to better address the problems of today.

Becoming authors of the future

Who, ultimately, needs social imagination? The answer is that we all do, and we need to become more engaged. John Dewey argued that every political project needs to create the public that can be its author.[8] In the same way, every utopia has to call into existence the public necessary for its creation, a public that can champion and own it.

The promise of doing this well is that more communities can, once again, become heroes of their own history. Too often today, the only narratives that matter are personal ones, and many have seen a widening gulf between their individual hopes and dreams and those of the world around them. Too often, as well, people feel like powerless observers of forces and trends they cannot control. The rekindling of social imagination is one aspect of taking back control—describing a future in which we can feel at home, and then using the power of that vision to catalyse action to help us get there. As the Chinese proverb goes, 'When the wind of change blows, some build walls, while others build windmills.'

If we try to picture a better future, most of us will think of more harmony, less conflict, perhaps even a return to oneness, whether the oneness of imagined primordial human communities or of our lives in the womb. In our attraction to better alignment, we mirror the natural world. As Ursula Le Guin described, two clock pendulums placed side by side on a wall will start to swing together. Any two objects that are close to each other and oscillate at around the same rate will move into a lockstep of this kind because it requires less energy. Le Guin wrote, 'Things are lazy. It takes less energy to pulse cooperatively than to pulse in opposition. Physicists call this beautiful, economical laziness mutual phase locking, or entrainment.'[9]

One version of human history sees it as a messy, hungry search for new avenues to align and cooperate in just this way, but at ever larger scale, punctuated with endless setbacks and disappointments. In this view, we are slowly breaking free from the inheritance of evolution and the many biases it imprinted on our brains that make us selfish, greedy, jealous, and over-attached to group and tribal identities. Progress means seeing these for what they are and learning more objectively what helps us thrive.

That hope provides some of the *pull* of a possible future. The promised land of milk and honey calls to us from over the horizon. But the urge to cooperate is also a *push* or movement forward from the fertile present—trying to improve things step by step, testing and experimenting with new ideas, often driven by frustration or anger as well as creativity.

These are two very different mindsets and approaches. Imaginative, speculative work involves ambiguity, uncertainty, spotting connections and creating compelling visions. The push from the present tends to be more organic and incremental, building on what already is, trying out through experiments and single steps rather than giant leaps. But the two can connect, feeding and complementing each other as broad-brush dreams are fleshed out with practical options. Together these help us to see beyond the particular to grasp the deeper unity not just of human beings but also of the living world and the cosmos of which we are part—that integration and insight at the heart of so much of the deepest thought throughout history.

Such imagination echoes the ways in which all of the great religions are organised around the dialectic between the transcendence of the divine and its immanence in the world. All deny divisions and assert our common humanity, unlike the religions that preceded them. We should hope for the same from the social imagination of the future: that it can recognise our need for belonging, at the modest scales of daily life, without losing sight of the bigger picture of unity.

Our lives are by their nature limited and constrained, bounded by death. Bur our imagination is limitless. At the conclusion of

Purgatory, Dante imagines himself transformed into a tree pointing to the stars: 'remade, as new trees are renewed when they bring forth new boughs, I was pure and prepared to climb unto the stars.'[10] That is a good metaphor for us—connecting the materiality of the tree, literally rooted in the soil around us, to our aspirations to transcend the limitations of our world.

APPENDIX 1

A ROUGH THEORY OF SOCIAL IMAGINATION

Here I summarise some conclusions about what social and political imagination is, and what it can and cannot do.

Society now and in the future depends on imagination

Any kind of social organisation depends on imagination; something has to be thought before it can become real. So, imagination is both the glue for any society and the only fuel for change. Present imagination helps societies cooperate and cohere. Future imagination helps to map out 'possibility spaces'—options for societies to consider and choose.

It does so through a double move. The first challenges the fixity or naturalness of the present, recognising how much of social life is governed by useful fictions: money, marriage, law and democracy. The second move is to shape alternatives to present arrangements, often starting with the 'adjacent possible', nearby options, but then ranging much further.

Every society has imaginaries of possible futures, sometimes in competition with each other. But societies founded on continuous change need these more, and they need an imaginary of the future as well as of the present, both to legitimate power and to encourage the necessary work of thinking ahead.

Imagination feeds off a shared unconscious

These imaginaries feed off underlying mental modules—ways in which we all think—including our physical, social and moral intuitions and heuristics, which help us make sense of societies that are far more complex than our brains can cope with. These include 'folk' economics, politics and psychology, ideas we pick up from family structures and ideas circulating in a collective unconscious that is constantly mutating.

Generative ideas

The most influential ideas tend to be quite simple: generative concepts that can spark multiple interpretations and adaptations. Fully formed plans and utopias tend to be less useful and less influential. But it is still valuable to think through possible futures in a rigorous and comprehensive way, to help clarify possible unintended consequences or connections. These produce prompts for thinking rather than detailed blueprints to be implemented.

Pioneers of ideas and pioneers of practice are complementary

Imaginers have to find collaborators—doers, organisers, regularisers—if their ideas are to be more than imaginary. The collaborators' job is to turn poetry into prose; theology and prophecy into ritual; compassion into organised generosity; mercy into justice. It involves testing and experimenting to find out what works—which always leads to answers that were unexpected. This process of translation is experienced as ambiguous, since ideas lose some of their freedom and limitlessness to become, literally, quotidian.

Imagination is part of evolution

The role of imagination can be understood in evolutionary terms: imagination allows a multiplication of options (this time through the organisation of cultures); selection; and then spread. The adaptive efficiency of any system depends on its ability to multiply, its capacity to select and the intelligence with which it organises adoption/spreading.

Imagination can be thick or thin

No one can imagine a future society in any detail. Instead, even the greatest see only through a dark glass, glimpsing fragments of what might become possible. The social world is far too complex for any mind to grasp.

But over time imaginaries can become more complex, evolving from thin to thick. The thin ones offer only a vague ethos or idea whereas the thick ones combine ethos and vision with generative ideas, domain applications and implementations. Thickening usually takes time, and some imaginaries lack key elements. However, real societies are hybrids, combinations of multiple, often contradictory elements; overly pure, logical and coherent utopias or imaginaries never work in practice.

Imagination can be progressive or reactionary

Imagination can focus on a better yesterday, promising a return to a lost golden age. Alternatively, it can focus on tomorrow. Progressive imaginaries point to futures that are simultaneously more differentiated and integrated, showing an underlying unity on a larger scale and a heightened awareness. They offer general-isable ideas, albeit ones that then need to be adapted to context. Reactionary imaginaries look backwards, reinforcing separation, and offer answers that only make sense in the context of a particular nation, place or religion.

From ideas to routines

Imagination is like thin air, cloud-like. Imagination only truly influences the world when it ceases to be imagination and mutates into repetitions, habits and cycles, becoming embedded in the rhythms of daily life, a part of people's jobs and routines. Societies are best understood as patterns of regularity of this kind—what Pierre Bourdieu described as 'habitus'. So, for imagination to change these, it has to be translated via shared frames for seeing and for thinking into an organised, repeatable form of action. Indeed, imagination becomes most powerful when it is no longer thought but becomes automatic.

Pioneers try to translate ideas into the form of regularities, which may mean a daily habit (eating vegan, living as transgender) or a formal organisation (a kindergarten, hospice or recycling centre). Once an idea becomes organised, it becomes exclusive (organisation is a way of selecting and deselecting—what we eat and don't eat; who gets supported or not; who has which rights and who does not). This implies a pattern of hot and cold, the heat of imagination that especially thrives in times of social turbulence and around revolutions becoming cool when translated into laws and institutions.

Imagined ideas mutate as they become practice

Imagination comes alive in its struggles with the reality of the material world and humans with their own purposes, characters and interests. Contrary to the assumption of the Romantics, this kind of imagination always mutates as it becomes actualised, transforming through its interaction with the world of reality, like a chemical forming new compounds as it comes into contact with oxygen. This living, dynamic and embodied imagination is what really changes the world.

Ideas become part of assemblies as they become embedded in the world

Very few social institutions are logical deductions from a single idea. Instead, they tend to be assemblies of multiple elements and multiple moral syndromes. This is true of schools, hospitals, parliaments, companies and even organised religions. In this sense social change mirrors technology, which depends on assemblies of diverse elements to create useful things like cars, computers or aircraft.

Only history (and evidence) can validate imagination

There is no way to validate imaginative ideas except through practice. Thus, the imaginer has few ways of knowing whether they are a deluded fantasist or a brilliant trailblazer. A few ideas may be untrue in the sense of being literally unworkable. But few can be disproven or verified with logic, beauty or even evidence, which by definition is from the past. So, we verify by implementing, testing and learning—through lived history and the accumulation of data and evidence.

Nor can imaginers easily judge over what timescales their ideas might become real. Working in this space therefore requires a degree of mental toughness to resist the demons of rational doubt and self-doubt.

ANOTHER WORLD IS POSSIBLE

Imagination depends on a material base

Imagination needs a material base: it rests on resources, time and techniques. In some periods, this was provided by inherited wealth and patronage of the kind that supported figures such as Saint-Simon or Marx. Today, while we have very developed infrastructures to support imagination in the arts, business and science, they are lacking in society. This is a task for social science and what I call 'exploratory social sciences'; it is a task in which philanthropy can play a vital role, resisting its tendencies towards conservatism; and it is a space in which we need politics to be an effective, hungry user of ideas, keeping open the pathways that can take ideas from being sparks to being large-scale realities.

Political imagination and structural change

Our world is shaped by dominant political imaginaries of which there are relatively few at any point in history. These offer a semi-coherent account of the world, of what is, what matters and what is possible. But in their practical application, these imaginaries tend to be impure and hybrid, often containing contradictions.

It is tempting to imagine wholly formed systems—complete alternatives to capitalism or nation states. These can be vital as thought experiments which confirm the arbitrariness of existing arrangements. But no real society can be deduced from a few principles. Instead, all existing and possible societies will be assemblies of multiple, often contradictory elements, just as contemporary capitalism depends, in reality, on large states, committed families, science organised as a commons and many other very non-capitalistic elements.

APPENDIX 1: THEORY OF SOCIAL IMAGINATION

Imagination is freedom

The world into which we are born was shaped by a capacity to generate the new through billions of years of evolution. Now, for us, a comparable capacity to imagine, together, is a vital aspect of what it means to be free and alive. Imagination liberates us from the illusion that the way the world is now is the only way it can be. In this sense, imagination is an energiser, a source of light and hope.

In a densely interdependent world, our imagination must be shared as well as individual, and it must reach out into the deep future, not just the immediate future. Freedom in the moment is not a true freedom. Without alternative options, we cannot plan or choose. We become slaves to the ideas of others.

APPENDIX 2

SOME PROMPTS FOR IMAGINATION

In this appendix, I build on Chapter 6 to briefly describe some of the other fields that will most demand creativity and imagination in the decades ahead. These are sketches and fragments of the landscapes of future possibility. My hope is that we will see much more work to flesh out good options in all of these fields over the next few years, with sufficient detail and clarity that they can be fully interrogated and assessed.

Care and relationships

Care for children and the family

What if the family fragmented into ever more complex forms, with more extended families, same-sex parents, communal parenting and so on? What if frozen eggs and related technological developments gave women far more control over the timing and organisation of childbirth? And what if governments took seriously the strong evidence about the importance of early years in child development and became more active and interventionist in relation to such things as diet, literacy and exercise?

Care for the elderly

At the other end of the age spectrum, the options are equally wide-ranging. In one scenario, future care might be largely industrialised, with robot companions, carers and cleaners. Care would become a technology- and capital-intensive industry, whether provided by markets or as a public service. Would such a future be worse—more callous—or in fact more caring, freeing people up to provide more genuine love alongside the machines that would do the hard labour? Alternatively, we could imagine care being re-embedded in communities, with neighbours rewarded for care provided, and new models of specialised housing alongside housing deliberately designed to mix up the generations.

Transparent communication

Navigating life in complex societies is often hard at the best of times, and particularly hard for anyone with cognitive impairments (which can include many groups, from the frail and elderly, to the illiterate, to small children). Some countries try to respond by making laws comprehensible and putting them in plain language, offering navigators to help people make sense of social security systems, or using pictograms and visual aids to make complex issues less opaque. These are all far from being the norm, whether in business, everyday law or pensions—think of the reams of contracts linked to buying a mobile phone or computer.

Disability

All of us are likely to experience disability at some stage of our life, certainly when we are young and very old, and often in between. We may already be seeing a shift in perceptions of what disability is, partly thanks to militant movements for disability rights. Their bigger impact on the world is to encourage us to see everything through multiple lenses. The accessibility of buildings and transport; entertainment and communication; and different jobs and skills can no longer be thought of in terms of what applies to a 'normal' majority, but rather in terms of a spectrum of different abilities.

Reconstructing the role of marriage

Marriage went through a period of decline in the late twentieth century and then experienced a revival in the twenty-first, partly thanks to worldwide moves to legalise same-sex marriage. There may be more momentum in this reconstruction of an ancient institution, with rethought rights and obligations as well as rituals. But in the future, there could also be ever more differentiation between the different roles of life partner, sex partner, companion, co-carer and co-parent (which was sometimes the norm for the wealthy in the past), but with different treatments of those roles in relation to inheritance or financial maintenance.

Welfare

Social contracts

Our inherited social contracts were mainly designed to cope with the risks of poverty in old age and unemployment. But are there now other important risks we cannot handle alone, such as isolation, disability and mental illness? What packages of financial support and services might be needed?

The household

Twentieth-century economics and social policy assumed that household work would happen automatically, mainly done by women. It was not measured in GDP statistics and was little analysed. But we know that work in the household is vital for everything else—bringing up children, caring for the elderly and everyday maintenance. So will this be measured? Will policy more deliberately reward household work, perhaps through more generous parental leave and payments linked to children?

New welfare models

I've mentioned how much support universal basic income (UBI) has achieved as a valid response to the precariousness of many people's livelihoods. There are variants that are very local (like the Mumbuca digital currency in Marica, Brazil as part of their UBI experiment), and others linked to national governments (like the short-lived pilot in Finland). There are also other parallel ideas, such as universal basic services (which give pre-scribed rights to a bundle of services), or universal basic rights to capital, mobilising central banks as sources of loans secured on lifetime earnings.

My guess is that the movement for UBI will mutate into a wide variety of options, few of which will be universal, reflecting the simple fact that people's needs are so varied (depending on whether they have children, have a disability and so on). These could include universal basic incomes for particular groups most at risk of poverty; minimum income guarantees with some conditions; time-limited UBI (for example, for a set number of years during one's lifetime); and many others.

Democracy

Deeper democratic decision-making

Most forms of democracy (parliaments, parties, regular elections) are essentially nineteenth-century in their origins, but a lot of work and experimentation has been done to reimagine how democracy could be organised to allow something closer to genuine collective intelligence, tapping into the expertise across society and involving millions in shaping and making decisions. Citizens' assemblies, deliberative experiments and digital agora are happening in cities, in nations and even at a global level. Perhaps we may also see an extension of the jury (like in Nick Harkaway's science-fiction novel *Gnomon*, in which many decisions are taken by randomly selected juries of 200 people).

Quadratic voting and quadratic finance models

'One person, one vote' may no longer look such an ideal way to organise democratic decisions. Many others are now being explored, such as quadratic voting, which allows you to show how strongly you feel about options as well as which ones you prefer, for example offering a number of votes which can be allocated between different options. An offshoot is the idea of quadratic funding, which uses quadratic voting to decide on funding allocations for public goods. Or what about dual voting systems, where you have one vote for yourself as well as a second vote that you can allocate to someone else whom you trust to use it wisely?

Economy

The firm

Will the classic joint-stock company become a thing of the past, superseded by new organisational models like the B Corp certification system for companies (there are now some 2,500 B Corp organisations in sixty countries) which require multiple goals to be embedded in the company's DNA, including social and environmental goals? Or will we see a proliferation of corporate forms in place of the current dominant model of the listed public company, with more private companies, mutuals, co-ops and others too?

Investment

We live in a capitalist world, which means that the detailed design of capital markets has a huge impact on how people live. There have been many moves to help capital markets better reflect 'externalities', whether social or ecological, with carbon prices and social impact investment and reporting. In India and South Africa, companies are required by law to spend 2 per cent of their profits on corporate social responsibility. Beyond these now maturing approaches, others are just coming into view. For example, might it be possible to design asset classes whose value is directly linked to physical facts such as levels of carbon, deforestation or air quality in buildings, or where there would be more automated instructions for buying and selling linked not to price but rather to ecological or social factors?

Taxation

How will tax evolve to meet the needs of the twenty-first century? In recent decades, tax has weighed more heavily on smaller businesses and the less mobile while the very rich as well as the biggest digital companies have found ways to avoid it. Governments have started fighting back, with moves on digital taxes and a possible return to land taxes and wealth taxes, reviving the ideas of Henry George. In Norway, for example, about 500,000 people pay a 0.85 per cent charge on their assets above the value of about $150,000. The 2021 global minimum corporate tax rate could be a first step towards radically different ways of organising tax of all kinds.

APPENDIX 2: PROMPTS FOR IMAGINATION

Deconstructing property rights

Imagine rethinking the ownership of something like a building or a firm as a stack of rights and responsibilities rather than as straightforward ownership. Instead of ownership being absolute, the deed of ownership would set out various obligations—for example, to share energy and water, and to manage waste, noise and emissions—but also some rights to take part in shared decision-making for the neighbourhood. The same might apply to farmland or even gardens.

The spread of commons for land, housing, energy or data

The last two decades have seen growing interest in the revival of commons models of ownership. These are an alternative to ownership by individuals or the state and involve various kinds of collective ownership. The models can be applied to land in cities and rural areas, as well as to fields like energy (for example, with shared ownership of solar panels) and data (with shared ownership, for example, of data recording energy use).[1] But how should these best be organised? Do they require new democratic forms for organising their governance (such as triggered contestability models, where boards can renew themselves unless a percentage of their users decide they want a change)?

True sharing economies

Digital platforms have been used for many areas of the economy, from shopping to travel to renting rooms and taxis. At one point there were high hopes that a true sharing economy might arise. But instead, what took shape were traditional capitalist ownership models. Alternatives, some using platform cooperative ideas, are being experimented with on a small scale—for example, minicab drivers organised as cooperatives, rather than under private firms like Uber. But could these become much larger? What would they look like? How might they be taxed?

Addressing pay inequalities

Growing pay inequality between privileged knowledge workers and manual workers has become a stark issue in many countries. It was brought into even sharper relief during the COVID-19 pandemic when it turned out that most of the truly essential workers were amongst the lowest paid (nurses, care workers, delivery workers and retail workers). There have been some steps to address these inequalities, including the generous tax credits introduced in countries like the US and the UK in the 2000s, as well as higher minimum wages. Governments can also directly influence at least some of these labour markets through the pay levels they set, and in the longer term through the introduction of stricter qualification requirements. Pay inequality is often presented as a fact of nature (and this is how it's taught in economics courses). But the truth is that pay is highly socially determined.

Ecology

Wars on waste

Imagine if our societies became much less tolerant of waste of all kinds. This might extend from policies to encourage recycling to a shift in norms, perhaps penalising people who own properties and cars they rarely use or who throw away food. One of the effects of the Fourth Industrial Revolution will be to make this far more visible, counterposing a broad view of efficiency to the current narrow market view of efficiency (in which it can still be efficient for an expensive inner-city apartment to be left empty 95 per cent of the time or a car to be unused 99 per cent of the time).

APPENDIX 2: PROMPTS FOR IMAGINATION

A cleaner world

Half a century after the book *Silent Spring* and the birth of the modern environmental movement, many countries still have high death rates from pollution: the Central African Republic, Niger, Guinea-Bissau, Lesotho, Afghanistan and Georgia all have death rates of over 2,000 per 100,000.[2] For such countries, the priority is to achieve both prosperity and the right regulations and laws to ensure clean air, clean water and safe food. For others, the question is whether a further leap in cleanliness is possible to radically cleaner air, cleaner water and less noise pollution.

Relocalisation

Another common theme is relocalisation, reversing decades of globalisation. This can involve moving more food production to the area or neighbourhood, for example transforming public land into productive spaces as well as housing. Relocalisation of production may also be encouraged with hyper-local manufacturing, maker spaces and 3D printing. Face-to-face services and local retail can be encouraged with local currencies or tax advantages. Big cities like Paris are meanwhile promising a return to the 15-minute city, where everything you need can be found within 15 minutes of the home.

Technology

Data and machine intelligence

We've become used to a digital environment dominated by a handful of companies, but there are strong movements now pushing for more civic control over data. What if data were owned and curated by data trusts, and made publicly accountable? What if the algorithms of machine intelligence were not proprietary? What if many AI applications were simply banned (as both the EU and China now propose)? A host of new issues are already becoming apparent, ranging from issues of liability with artificial intelligence to cross-border flows of data.

Automated decision-making tools

We are bound to see more use of automated decision-making tools, supported by artificial intelligence, in the near future. Many are already in use, like automatic fines for speeding or automated decisions on social security. How can these best be made accountable even if they can't easily be explained? How could their decisions be challenged? And could they be adapted to other uses, for example to speed up neighbourhood planning decisions while ensuring that everyone has a chance to have their voice heard or to help licensing decisions?

Buffers and temperance

The years ahead are likely to bring ever more powerful technologies that can exploit our ways of thinking, fuelling addictive and compulsive behaviour. The world has lots of experience of trying to handle or at least contain potentially destructive addictive behaviours. Will these prompt new temperance movements, focused now on digital behaviours (like the anti-alcohol movements that became vast in the nineteenth century)? Will they prompt prohibitions (like the nationwide US ban on producing, importing, transporting and selling alcoholic drinks from 1920 to 1933)? New voluntary organisations modelled on Alcoholics Anonymous? How will we learn the right diets, the ability to resist temptations and distractions?

Energy systems

Much of our society and economy reflects its energy sources, yet the next half-century is likely to see a big move away from oil and gas, with great implications for how infrastructures are organised. A shift to hydrogen as an energy source might imply radical decentralisation and localisation—and perhaps a growth in community-owned energy trusts. Equally, energy production might be ever more integrated into building design, for example through solar roof tiles.

Media

For many years, there have been predictions of a further shift towards personalisation in media, where everyone gets a distinct view of the world, increasingly enhanced by virtual and augmented reality. But it's also possible we'll see a reaction: a revival of a local public sphere (local news and video channels providing curated material on what's happening in schools, sports, the arts or crime), and a recognition that independent, accurate media are essential for democracy. That might lead to more public funding for truthful news and investigation, as well as moves to recycle money from online advertising into content (similar moves were made in the twentieth century for film and TV in the UK and magazines in France).

Fallback designs

An interesting new trend is the attention to sustaining low-technology alternatives to high-technology systems for when the latter might collapse: traditional radio networks, off-grid power, local food, etc. Sometimes these older, more frugal alternatives also look good in their own right.

Humans and non-humans

Human enhancement

As more advanced genetic treatments and prosthetics become available, offering enhancements to our strength, beauty or intelligence, these will become a political battleground as arguments rage over whether access should be governed by ability to pay or by rights. Should there be rights to bodily or brain enhancement, initially perhaps for the most disadvantaged but over time spreading to everyone?

Animals and nature

A big theme of recent decades has involved radically different views of nature, giving animals, nature and ecosystems the equivalent of rights and legal claims, and dealing with the many unhealthy interactions between humans and wildlife. These usually concern negative rights—the right not to be confined, eaten or killed for pleasure. What if these went further, perhaps building on New Zealand's innovation in giving nature rights of legal personhood? And will we see a further move to rethink humans' relationships with animals, making meat-eating taboo and recreating wildernesses protected from human interference?

Experiment and imagination

Society as laboratory

We increasingly have the capacity to turn the whole of our society into a living laboratory in which to test new ideas of different kinds. There are thousands of local labs or testbeds worldwide, covering topics as varied as drones and care for the elderly. This idea—of taking innovation out of the classic laboratory and into society—could have big implications for fields like public health, policing and education. But how should risk be managed? How should the results of experiments be organised? Imagine, for example, if every teacher regularly ran their own experiments to test out different teaching models.[3]

APPENDIX 2: PROMPTS FOR IMAGINATION

Museums of the future

Should every city or nation have physical spaces dedicated to exploring the future, combining experiences (using virtual reality), visualisations, games and 'objects of the future'? We could imagine a new cadre of curators and orchestrators who become skilled in helping people to explore possible future worlds.

These are just a few fragments of possible future imagination. They are shared as prompts, to encourage you to think about what's wrong with them, what's missing or what could be improved.

NOTES

INTRODUCTION

1. In the Chinese context, there are obvious reasons for people to block and self-censor. In stifling authoritarian environments, there is little space for speculation or imagination. Ideas are dangerous. Better to play safe and stick with how hardware might develop, or just talk about how the future might bring more of what there already is in the present.
2. Then, for all the energy of the early phases of the Biden administration, it soon became clear that all he was really offering was for the United States to become a bit more like northern Europe. This is not a bad aspiration, but it is very different from trying to be a beacon for the world.
3. Hallam, Roger, 'Advice to young people as you face annihilation': https://www.gwern.net/docs/sociology/2019-hallam.pdf, accessed 11 January 2022.
4. 43 per cent of the UK's electricity came from renewable sources in 2020. Rayner, Tristan, 'UK power generation in 2020: Renewables up to 43%', *pv magazine*, 29 July 2021, https://www.pv-magazine.com/2021/07/29/uk-power-generation-in-2020-renewables-up-to-43, accessed 8 February 2022; Statista, 'Greenhouse gas emissions in the United Kingdom (UK) from 1990 to 2020', https://www.statista.com/statistics/326902/greenhouse-gas-emissions-in-the-united-kingdom-uk, accessed 8 February 2022.
5. Beuys, Joseph, 'I Am Searching for Field Character', first published in

English in Tisdall, Caroline, *Art into Society, Society into Art*, London: ICA, 1974, p. 48.

6. Graeber, David, *The Utopia of Rules: On Technology, Stupidity, and the Secret Joys of Bureaucracy*, New York, NY: Melville House Publishing, 2015.

7. Le Guin, Ursula K., *The Language of the Night: Essays on Fantasy and Science Fiction*, Susan Wood (ed.), New York, NY: Ultramarine Publishing, 1980, p. 58.

1. THE PRESENT: IMAGINATION STALLED

1. 33 per cent of Generation Z and 32 per cent of millennials feel this way, compared with 22 per cent of Generation X and 19 per cent of baby boomers, according to the survey in Duffy, Bobby, *Generations: Does When You're Born Shape Who You Are?*, London: Atlantic Books, 2021.

2. China now has a lively field that questions technological determinism and the power of algorithms, part of a broader global shift to better shape technology: Ding, Jeffrey, 'ChinAI #157: Resistance in an Algorithmic Society', *ChinAI Newsletter*, 27 September 2021, https://chinai.substack.com/p/chinai-157-resistance-in-an-algorithmic, accessed 2 February 2022.

3. Bollen, Johan, Marijn Ten Thij, Fritz Breithaupt, Alexander T.J. Barron, Lauren A. Rutter, Lorenzo Lorenzo-Luaces, and Marten Scheffer, 'Historical language records reveal a surge of cognitive distortions in recent decades', *Proceedings of the National Academy of Sciences* 118(30), 2021.

4. However, back in the 1930s, French poet Paul Valéry also commented that the future wasn't what it used to be: '*L'avenir est comme le reste: il n'est plus ce qu'il était*'. Valéry, Paul, 'Notre Destin et Les Lettres' (1937), in *Regards sur le monde actuel & autres essais*, Paris: Gallimard, 1945.

5. Another writer, Franco Berardi, claimed that 'the future', as thought of by science-fiction writers, futurists and modernists, had peaked in 1968, and was essentially dead by 1977 (and, although he might have been confusing his own life with that of the world, there was still a grain of truth in his comment). Berardi, Franco, *After the Future*, Gary Genosko and Nicholas Thoburn (eds), Arianna Bove et al. (trans.), Oakland: AK Press, 2011.

6. Orlik, Tom and Bjorn Van Roye, 'An Economist's Guide to the World in 2050', *Bloomberg Businessweek*, 12 November 2020, https://www.bloomberg.com/graphics/2020-global-economic-forecast-2050, accessed 2 February 2022.

7. I'm thinking particularly of the Reaganites and Thatcherites, and figures like Newt Gingrich. These trends were much less visible in other parts of the world.

8. Reckwitz, Andreas, *The End of Illusions: Politics, Economics and Culture in Late Modernity*, Cambridge: Polity, 2021.

9. Most blockbuster science-fiction films reaching big audiences present essentially pre-modern social and political worlds, with empires and kings, barons and great families, warrior states and Roman-style senates. A remarkably high proportion of popular science-fiction literature is just as reactionary. Isaac Asimov's *Foundation* series pictured a future in which women occupied no positions of significant power. Frank Herbert's novel *Dune* describes empires, baronies and kingdoms but no sense that social or political organisation might advance in the next 8,000 years.

10. Kim, Kyung Hee, 'The creativity crisis: The decrease in creative thinking scores on the Torrance Tests of Creative Thinking', *Creativity Research Journal* 23(4), 2011, pp. 285–295.

11. These trends may also reflect recent educational policies that have tended to focus much more on exams and on teaching to the test.

12. However, there is controversy over just how much the echo chamber is real, or whether perhaps it is a more extreme phenomenon in some countries, such as the US and India, than in others. See, for example, Dubois, Elizabeth and Grant Blank, 'The myth of the echo chamber', *Oxford Internet Institute*, 9 March 2018, https://www.oii.ox.ac.uk/blog/the-myth-of-the-echo-chamber, accessed 2 February 2022.

13. Clancy, Matt, 'Are Ideas Getting Harder to Find Because of the Burden of Knowledge?', *What's New Under the Sun*, 11 June 2020, https://mattsclancy.substack.com/p/are-ideas-getting-harder-to-find, accessed 2 February 2020.

14. Bloom, Nicholas, Charles I. Jones, John Van Reenen, and Michael Webb, 'Are ideas getting harder to find?', *American Economic Review* 110(4), 2020, pp. 1104–1144.

15. Jones, Benjamin, 'Age and Great Invention', *The Review of Economics and Statistics* 92(1), 2010, pp. 1–14; Jones, Benjamin, 'The Burden of Knowledge and the "Death of the Renaissance Man": Is Innovation Getting Harder?', *The Review of Economic Studies* 76(1), 2009, pp. 283–317.

16. Brendel, Jan and Sascha Schweitzer, 'The Burden of Knowledge in Mathematics', *Open Economics* 2(1), 2019, pp. 139–149; Schweitzer, Sascha and Jan Brendel, 'A burden of knowledge creation in academic research: evidence from publication data', *Industry and Innovation* 28(3), 2021, pp. 283–306.

17. It's hard to know for sure. Tyler Cowen, for example, is a popular commentator who has swung from believing that we are experiencing a great stagnation to having faith in a new wave of technological innovation.

18. This piece gives a good explanation of why this might be happening: Thompson, Derek, 'America Is Running on Fumes', *The Atlantic*, 1 December 2021, https://www.theatlantic.com/ideas/archive/2021/12/america-innovation-film-science-business/620858, accessed 2 February 2022.

19. Big data at first glance makes it easier to spot everything from tumours to domestic violence, and it seems obvious that precisely targeted interventions using data should be better than blunt ones. This has become widely accepted in medicine and social policy. But experience has been much more mixed, partly because of flaws in data and partly because of the complexity of the phenomena. Together this means that there are often too many false positives in attempts to use data to predict and pre-empt problems. It continues to be the case that it is often more efficient to work at the level of whole populations.

20. A recent paper commented: 'Distributed-ledger experiments have produced a uniquely creative barrage of exploration around voting systems, dispute resolution, collective resource management, and other processes that can advance democratic traditions.' Schneider, Nathan, 'Cryptoeconomics as a Limitation on Governance', University of Colorado Boulder, 2021.

21. I avoid using any particular definition of the 'social' here; the standard definition 'relating to society and its organisation' is pretty capacious,

and it encompasses many aspects of technology, though without any precise boundary.

22. Judith Butler distinguished this general precariousness from what she called the 'precarity' of particular groups.

23. See, for example, McCray, W. Patrick, *The Visioneers: How a Group of Elite Scientists Pursued Space Colonies, Nanotechnologies, and a Limitless Future*, Princeton, NJ: Princeton University Press, 2012.

24. The problem is misleadingly interpreted by the wealthy of the region as the result of restrictive planning laws; these do indeed play a role in homelessness, but experience elsewhere shows that the solutions to street homelessness are as much about issues of mental health, drugs, alcohol and jobs as they are about housing supply.

25. Bill Gates was co-author of *The Road Ahead*, a book promising a glorious future based on the new 'information superhighway'. Gates, Bill, Nathan Myhrvold, and Peter Rinearson, *The Road Ahead*, London: Viking, 1995.

26. A partial exception was the creation of centres like the Berkman Klein Center for Internet & Society at Harvard University in the late 1990s, the Oxford Internet Institute in 2001, and others.

27. An excellent recent article on 'cognitive complexity' summarises the point: 'Regulating the balance between exploration and exploitation in search is fundamental to adaptive success. This trade-off arises in many fields, often under a different name. In organizational research, exploration encompasses things such as search, variation, risk-taking, flexibility, experimentation, discovery and innovation. Exploitation includes aspects such as refinement, choice, production, efficiency, selection and implementation. In foraging, the contrast is between extensive versus intensive search; in artificial intelligence, breadth versus depth-first search; in time, long- versus short-term; in visual attention, diffuse versus focused; in memory, global versus local. This disparity in terminology has made it harder for specialists in different areas to recognize these varied facets as part of the same underlying pattern.' Taylor, Helen, Brice Fernandes, and Sarah Wraight, 'The evolution of complementary cognition: humans cooperatively adapt and evolve through a system of collective cognitive search', *Cambridge Archaeological Journal* 32(1), 2022.

28. It must matter that seriously organised social imagination is so monopolised by the already rich and powerful (such as think tanks in California funded by, and reflecting the narrow worldview of, male billionaires), and so little is being done to shape a world in line with the interests and values of the great majority.

29. Frankl, Viktor, *Man's Search for Meaning*, New York, NY: Washington Square Press, Pocket Books, 1985 [1946], translation first published by Beacon Press, 1959.

30. More recently, the Australian psychologist Ken Nunn described hope as 'a pervasive and significant correlate of health and disorder' in a study of the psycho-social impact of the earthquake that struck Newcastle, New South Wales, in 1989. He and his colleagues found that people's hopefulness was as important in explaining post-earthquake illness as their level of exposure to disruption and threat. The American psychiatrist Jerome Frank wrote in a similar vein that: 'a unique feature of human consciousness is its inclusion of the future. Expectations strongly affect all aspects of human functioning ... Hope inspires a feeling of wellbeing and is a spur to action. Hopelessness, the inability to imagine a tolerable future, is a powerful motive for suicide.' Nunn, Kenneth, 'Personal Hopefulness: A Conceptual Review of the Relevance of the Perceived Future to Psychiatry', *British Journal of Medical Psychology* 69, 1996, pp. 227–245. Frank, Jerome, 'The Role of Hope in Psychotherapy', *International Journal of Psychotherapy* 5, 1968, pp. 383–395.

31. Macy, Joanna, *Despair and Personal Power in the Nuclear Age*, Philadelphia, PA: New Society Publishers, 1983.

32. In his great book on the future, Fred Polak asserted that 'the rise and fall of images of the future precedes or accompanies the rise and fall of cultures.' This may not be quite accurate. Widely held beliefs in decay and endings often better reflect threats to particular social groups or milieux that then generalise their own position. But societies that cannot generate plausible and desirable shared pictures of the future do indeed risk atrophy, as people turn to private life as the only source of meaning and lose the hope that fuels striving and ambition. They also risk alienation. Polak, Fred, *The Image of the Future*, translated and abridged by Elise Boulding, London & Amsterdam: Elsevier, 1973.

2. WHAT IS IMAGINATION?

1. Neuroscience research on the connection of memory and imagination suggests that impairment of one impairs the other—see the PhD thesis by DeepMind founder Demis Hassabis, 'Neural processes underpinning episodic memory', University College London, 2009: https://discovery.ucl.ac.uk/id/eprint/16126, accessed 2 February 2022.

2. Not all philosophers agreed. For Hegel, the very representation of art and imagination made them in some ways backward compared to pure thought. This is explored in O'Connor, Kieron and Frederick Aardema, 'The Imagination: Cognitive, Pre-cognitive, and Meta-cognitive Aspects,' *Consciousness and Cognition* 14, 2005, pp. 233–256.

3. Pelaprat, Etienne and Michael Cole, '"Minding the gap": Imagination, creativity and human cognition', *Integrative Psychological and Behavioral Science* 45(4), 2011, pp. 397–418.

4. McGilchrist, Ian, *The Master and his Emissary*, New Haven, CT: Yale University Press, 2009, p. 107.

5. Hawkins, Jeff, *The Thousand Brains: A New Theory of Intelligence*, New York, NY: Basic Books, 2021.

6. The cleverest people are, perhaps surprisingly, often the most fixed on a familiar way of seeing the world.

7. Searle, John, *Making the Social World*, Oxford: Oxford University Press, 2010, p. 121.

8. There are equivalent concepts to 'possibility space' in the arts. For example, someone working within a craft tradition will generally be tightly constrained as to what they can do, and even what they can think. Nineteenth-, twentieth- and twenty-first-century arts have by contrast exploded the range of options open to any artist, particularly now thanks to the availability of AI and augmented and virtual reality. In the arts, the very lack of constraints means that artists often impose their own, using limitations of materials and forms to spark greater creativity.

9. For an interesting overview of eighteenth-century discussions of slavery, see Dabydeen, David, 'Commerce and slavery in eighteenth century literature', *Kunapipi* 5(2), 1983, p. 4.

10. Du Bois, W.E.B., *The Souls of Black Folk*, Chicago, IL: A.C. McClurg, 1903, p. 3.

11. A striking contemporary example is the project by Henry Hargreaves documenting and recreating the last meals of prisoners about to be executed in the US. It's hard to think of a less sympathetic group of people. The project showed the huge bowl of mint ice-cream for Timothy McVeigh (convicted of 168 murders), the fried chicken and comfort food requested by most of the murderers, and the single olive requested by Victor Feguer, convicted of kidnap and murder. It was a simple device to help humanise even the most evil monsters and so stretch our capacity for imaginative empathy. See 'No Seconds' at https://henryhargreaves.com, accessed 2 February 2022.

12. A deeper sense of this capability was captured well by the philosopher Emmanuel Levinas, who—after years of captivity under the Nazis— concluded that it's only in the encounter with 'the other', with people and forces radically different to us, that our true consciousness of our self and our freedom arises. To recognise the other is to recognise a hunger, and vulnerability, in ourselves.

13. Escobar, Arturo, *Pluriversal Politics: The Real and the Possible*, Durham, NC: Duke University Press, 2020.

14. See George Orwell's 1946 essay 'The Prevention of Literature', in *All Art is Propaganda: Critical Essays*, George Packer (ed.), Orlando, FL: Harcourt, 2008.

15. This was the role of *orgia* in the ancient world—carnivals and Mayday celebrations, with modern equivalents like Burning Man—with dancing, drugs, sex and ecstasy not only revealing individual truths but also reminding us of a deeper union and communion that is hidden by the petty roles and competition of daily life.

3. THE PAST: HOW IMAGINATION SHAPED OUR WORLD

1. See Dudok, G., *Sir Thomas More and his Utopia*, Amsterdam: A.H. Kruyt, 1923, pp. 45 et seq., for a discussion of folk songs as forerunners of utopias.

2. This recent way of thinking also allows us to see the present as surrounded by an infinite array of parallel possible worlds—pathways we could have taken, imagined futures that could have materialised—just as we can look out to a future which has myriad possible routes forward, none of which are pre-ordained.

3. Wilde, Oscar, 'The Soul of Man Under Socialism', *Fortnightly Review*, February 1891.

4. Otto, Eric C., *Green Speculations: Science Fiction and Transformative Environmentalism*, Columbus, OH: The Ohio State University Press, 2012.

5. Engels, Frederick, 'Socialism: Utopian and Scientific', 1880, in Karl Marx and Frederick Engels, *Selected Works*, vol. 2, Moscow: Foreign Languages Publishing House, 1962.

6. My book *Social Innovation: How Societies Find the Power to Change* (Bristol: Policy Press, 2019) provides much more detail on the routes that social entrepreneurship, enterprises and innovations can take.

7. Hall, Peter, *Cities of Tomorrow: An Intellectual History of Urban Planning and Design Since 1880*, Chichester, UK: Wiley, 2014.

8. Ibid.

9. Geddes, Patrick, *Cities in Evolution*, London: Williams & Norgate, 1949, p. vii.

10. The US even has a Federation of Egalitarian Communities to link up many hundreds of idealistic communes.

11. Elmhirst, Sophie, 'The disastrous voyage of Satoshi, the world's first cryptocurrency cruise ship', *The Guardian*, 7 September 2021, https://www.theguardian.com/news/2021/sep/07/disastrous-voyage-satoshi-cryptocurrency-cruise-ship-seassteading, accessed 2 February 2022.

12. Mwai, Peter, 'Did Ethiopia plant four billion trees this year?', BBC News, 20 December 2019, https://www.bbc.co.uk/news/world-africa-50813726, accessed 2 February.

13. Such as ImagineLancaster at Lancaster University: https://www.lancaster.ac.uk/lica/research/imaginationlancaster, accessed 2 February 2022.

14. A good example is the work of the duo who write under the pseudonym 'Hanzi Freinacht'. Their ideas on the future 'listening society' are an attempt at a synthetic view of social progress (which, in the last century, has meant that 'the games of everyday life become milder, more sensitive, fair and forgiving'), primarily through the lens of psychological growth.

15. Dunne & Raby, http://dunneandraby.co.uk/content/bydandr/36/0, accessed 30 January 2022.

16. Kolehmainen, Isa, 'Speculative design: A design niche or a new tool for government innovation?', Nesta blog, 5 April 2016, https://www.nesta.org.uk/blog/speculative-design-a-design-niche-or-a-new-tool-for-government-innovation, accessed 30 January 2022.

17. Smyth, Jonathan, *Robespierre and the Festival of the Supreme Being: The Search for a Republican Morality*, Manchester: Manchester University Press, 2017.

18. In his classic book on the philosophy of science, *Against Method* (London: Verso, 1975), Paul Feyerabend wrote that 'we need a dream-world to discover the features of the real world we think we inhabit'.

19. Library of Congress, 'Born in Slavery: Slave Narratives from the Federal Writers' Project, 1936 to 1938', https://www.loc.gov/collections/slave-narratives-from-the-federal-writers-project-1936-to-1938/articles-and-essays/introduction-to-the-wpa-slave-narratives, accessed 2 February 2022.

4. PATTERNS: MAKING SENSE OF IMAGINATION

1. The idea was floated by then Environment Minister David Miliband and followed up with a series of government studies in 2008.

2. This database came to be called Contactpoint and was first proposed in a report I oversaw titled 'Privacy and Data Sharing: The Way Forward for Public Services', by the Performance and Innovation Unit in 2002 (I was then its director). The idea was later recommended by the Laming inquiry into child deaths. At its peak, the database was used by over 300,000 people working with children. It was shut down by the newly elected Conservative–Liberal Democrat coalition government in 2010.

3. Nostradamus wrote in elliptical quatrains that could be interpreted in many ways. One of his most famous predictions was of the imminent death of France's King Henry II. But even this prediction—itself ambiguous—predicted the king's death in battle, rather than in the friendly joust that transpired. A more recent example is Ray Kurzweil, famous for predicting the imminent 'singularity' when computation will supersede human intelligence: he forecast that by 2020 $1,000 would buy computer power equal to a single human brain and by 2045 the singularity would occur, with $1,000 buying one billion times more power

than all human brains combined today. Although predictions of exponential improvements in computation have proven broadly correct since the 1960s, predictions as to what they could achieve have been much less reliable.

4. For a more detailed account of these options, see my paper with Vincent Straub, 'The new ecosystem of trust', Nesta blog, 21 February 2019, https://www.nesta.org.uk/blog/new-ecosystem-trust, accessed 20 January 2022.

5. This is Engels' famous definition for his dialectics of materialism.

6. Hegel—who wrote more about dialectics than any other philosopher—described it not as a method but rather as the nature of the world; if you follow things as they actually are, you will tend to think dialectically.

7. I've written about this in many places, including the chapter on Mary Douglas in my recent book *Social Innovation* (Bristol: Policy Press, 2019).

8. Varela, Francisco J., *Ethical Know-How: Action, Wisdom, and Cognition*, Stanford, CA: Stanford University Press, 1992, p. 31. The lectures in this book were meant to be an elaboration of Varela's theory of 'enaction', which argues for a science that is more attuned to lived experience, initially developed in Varela, Francisco J., Evan Thompson, and Eleanor Rosch, *The Embodied Mind: Cognitive Science and the Human Experience*, Cambridge, MA: MIT Press, 1991.

9. Recent research shows that networks composed of differentiated specialised elements adapt better to changing environments—as goals and priorities change, they can rearrange themselves. In other words, they can reassemble themselves to combine the explorers and the people who follow up. See Kashtan, Nadav and Uri Alon, 'Spontaneous evolution of modularity and network motifs', *Proceedings of the National Academy of Sciences* 102(3), 2005, pp. 13773–13778.

10. 'For any type of entity, the appropriate level of variation will eventually emerge from the system. Moreover, that level will tend to track the rate at which the system churns.' Page, Scott, *Diversity and Complexity*, Princeton, NJ: Princeton University Press, 2011.

11. Jablonka, Eva and Marion J. Lamb, *Evolution in Four Dimensions:*

Genetic, Epigenetic, Behavioral, and Symbolic Variation in the History of Life, Cambridge, MA: MIT Press, 2005. The other mechanisms are genetic inheritance and epigenetic inheritance (changes in gene expression rather than gene frequency). Many accept the ideas of Dual Inheritance Theory, that there are two main streams of inheritance in humans, one cultural and the other genetic, and that these co-evolve, although far less is understood about how exactly the co-evolution with genetic inheritance happens, whether at the individual or the group level.

12. Taylor, Helen, Brice Fernandes, and Sarah Wraight, 'The evolution of complementary cognition: humans cooperatively adapt and evolve through a system of collective cognitive search', *Cambridge Archaeological Journal* 32(1), 2022.

13. McGilchrist, Ian, *The Master and His Emissary*, New Haven, CT: Yale University Press, 2009, p. 127.

5. THE FUTURE: HOW TO RE-ENERGISE OUR COLLECTIVE IMAGINATION

1. I'm a great admirer of the many organisations that do work in this, albeit often with very thin resources, such as Dark Matter Labs, Atlas of the Future, Doughnut Economics Action Lab, Constellations and others.

2. One of the most famous frameworks for creativity was developed by Graham Wallas in the 1920s. He divided the creative process into four stages: a stage of preparation (gathering materials and data); a stage of incubation (working on a problem and sometimes leaving it for a while); a stage of illumination (a sudden spark of insight); and finally, a stage of verification. This frame has worked quite well for some fields, particularly direct problem-solving in maths and science or the arts. But it has been less useful in fields where both the problems and the solutions are less specified and where the work of creating is collective. Wallas, Graham, *The Art of Thought*, New York, NY: Harcourt Brace, 1926.

3. George Dyson, quoted in Rhodes, Richard, *Visions of Technology*, New York, NY: Simon and Schuster, 2000, p. 180.

4. Meyvis, Tom and Heeyoung Yoon, 'Adding is favoured over subtracting

in problem solving', *Nature*, 7 April 2021, https://www.nature.com/
articles/d41586-021-00592-0, accessed 20 January 2022.

5. Henri Poincaré, the French mathematician, made a striking comment:
'Could anyone think that they have always marched forward, one step
after another, without having any clear idea of the goal they were trying to reach? It was necessary for them to guess at the proper route to
get them there, and to do so they needed a guide. This guide is primarily analogy.' Henri Poincare, quoted in Hofstadter, Douglas and
Emmanuel Sander, *Surfaces and Essences: Analogy as the Fuel and Fire of
Thinking*, New York, NY: Basic Books, 2013, p. 438.

6. Design tools can also help open up new spaces; the world of design
prides itself on its ability to imagine and enable non-linear leaps in thinking, or to embody ideas in objects as tools for thinking. I've already
mentioned some of the speculative design approaches that try to imagine how, for example, data-driven healthcare could evolve, producing
objects, images and videos to crystallise the choices that might arise.

There are many collections of tools that can help with this kind of
work, often drawn from consultancies working with multinational companies. They include companies like IDEO and the work of John Seely
Brown and Ann Pendleton-Jullian, who gathered some of these in their
collection 'Design Unbound', encouraging a playful approach to emergence, ambiguity and environments of rapid change. These are full of
useful vignettes; they encourage rapid prototyping, testing and visual-
isation of ideas, rather than overreliance on prose. They can be useful
as prompts and sparks, though a common weakness of designers is to
ignore deep knowledge, whether from social sciences or experience,
which often limits the usefulness of their ideas.

Very different design traditions argue that these methods risk an
overgeneralised view of the future. They prefer to emphasise the particularities of place and context, or prioritise the ideas and views of the
people who use goods and services, particularly those excluded by the
mainstream. Involving people with disabilities in design, for example,
often throws up radically different solutions to problems. Sandford,
Richard, 'Located futures: Recognising place and belonging in narratives of the future', *International Journal of Educational Research* 61,
2013, pp. 116–125.

7. Snow, Chet, *Mass Dreams of the Future*, Crest Park, CA: Deep Forest Press, 1989.

8. I was first introduced to this idea by Stephen Huddart at Wasan Island in Canada. See 'What is the Seventh Generation Principle?', Indigenous Corporate Training Inc. blog, 30 May 2020, https://www.ictinc.ca/blog/seventh-generation-principle, accessed 2 February 2020.

9. See, for example, the work of body>data>space: http://www.bodydataspace.net/2019/03/the-weave-co-creation-collaboration-process-the-incredible-beauty-of-interauthored-outputs, accessed 1 February 2022.

10. Blackwell, Alan F. and Sally Fincher, 'PUX: Patterns of User Experience', *Interactions* 17(2), 2010, pp. 27–31.

11. There have also been some attempts to adapt the pattern language idea to social design. But these attempts are more interesting as failures than as successes. Again, any particular society can be described through a set of dominant patterns—ways of organising families, firms, care or friendship. Describing the common patterns and modules can be useful for a task like setting up a new organisation. But these patterns are not universal, and they evolve over time. Indeed, much of the work of social imagination is valuable precisely because it helps with the design of new patterns that might become common: new ways of looking after children or organising extended families; new interpretations of the roles of coach, mentor, teacher or carer; new rights of decision or choice; or new types of ownership.

12. Alexander, Christopher, *The Timeless Way of Building*, New York, NY: Oxford University Press, 1979, p. 10.

13. Coleridge was borrowing from Friedrich Schelling's concept of '*Einbildungskraft*', which formed part of a grand theory of imagination. Coleridge liked to contrast fancy with imagination, fancy being decorative and incremental, whereas imagination was a true act of creation. Lachman, Gary, *Lost Knowledge of the Imagination*, Edinburgh: Floris Books, 2017.

14. Dewey, John, *Later Works of John Dewey, 1925–1953*, Jo Ann Boydston (ed.), vol. 10, Carbondale, IL: Southern Illinois University Press, 2008, p. 271.

15. Kant, Immanuel, *Critique of Pure Reason*, New York, NY: Collier, 1900.

16. Charles Peirce called this mix of recombination and exploration by analogy 'abduction', a non-deductive inference which he used to describe 'all the operations by which theories and conceptions are engendered'. Peirce, Charles S., 'Lowell Lectures on Some Topics of Logic Bearing on Questions Now Vexed', Eighth Lecture, 'Abduction', 1903, MS [R] 475.

17. For a longer paper on synthesis and its methods, see Mulgan, Geoff, 'The Synthesis Gap: reducing the imbalance between advice and absorption in handling big challenges, from pandemics to net zero', The International Public Policy Observatory blog, 1 December 2021, https://covidandsociety.com/synthesis-gap-reducing-imbalance-advice-absorption-handling-big-challenges-pandemics-net-zero, accessed 20 January 2022.

18. Demand from firms and investors keen for a crystal ball means that there are many methods in contention. They include 'Futures Literacy', the family of methods proposed by UNESCO's Riel Miller to promote stronger capabilities to imagine, which has helped grow a network of futures researchers from around the world: UNESCO Global Futures Literacy Network, https://en.unesco.org/futuresliteracy/network, accessed 20 January 2022.

19. International Futures Forum, 'Three Horizons', https://www.internationalfuturesforum.com/three-horizons, accessed 20 January 2022.

20. See, for example, Swart, Chené, *Reauthoring the World: The Narrative Lens and Practices for Organisations, Communities and Individuals*, Randburg, South Africa: Knowres Publishing, 2013.

21. This, of course, is why narrative also so easily becomes exclusionary or xenophobic.

22. In their interesting report 'This Too Shall Pass', Alex Evans, Casper ter Kuile and Ivor Williams suggested three types of myths that helped our ancestors to cope with crises and that are also relevant to contemporary dilemmas. These were apocalypse myths—stories in which something is *revealed*; restoration myths—stories in which something is *healed*; and emergence myths—stories in which something is being *born*. Many of the most compelling social programmes have some elements of at least two of these. Evans, Alex, Casper ter Kuile, and Ivor

Williams, 'This Too Shall Pass: Mourning collective loss in the time of Covid-19', The Collective Psychology Project, https://larger.us/wp-content/uploads/2021/01/This-Too-Shall-Pass.pdf, accessed 20 January 2022.

23. The communist arguments—which stripped away the more moderate, incrementalist thinking of the social democrats—echoed an idea that comes from graphic design: the concept of white space, i.e. that creating space around a message makes the message clearer. Uncluttering is itself part of the creative process.

24. Within the social sciences, narratives have played a vital role in making ideas acceptable. Deirdre McCloskey has been one of the pioneers of the study of these stories, showing how many theories spread and stuck because of their narrative shape as much as their evidence.

25. We now have a burgeoning literature on the Anthropocene, with stories of trouble, destruction and spoliation. See Haraway, Donna J., *Staying with the Trouble: Making Kin in the Chthulucene*, Durham, NC: Duke University Press, 2016.

26. USC School of Cinematic Arts, World Building Media Lab, http://worldbuilding.usc.edu, accessed 20 January 2022.

27. Project Hieroglyph, for example, tried to reignite a more positive and optimistic strand of science fiction: https://hieroglyph.asu.edu, accessed 20 January 2022. Various communities of sci-fi writers share methods and insights, such as the London Science Fiction Research Community: http://www.lsfrc.co.uk, accessed 20 January 2022.

28. Future Generations Commissioner for Wales, 'Well-Being of Future Generations (Wales) Act 2015', http://futuregenerations.wales/about-us/future-generations-act, accessed 20 January 2022.

29. Oroschakoff, Kalina, 'Top German court rules the country's climate law is partly "unconstitutional"', *Politico*, 29 April 2021, https://www.politico.eu/article/germany-climate-change-law-court-rules-partly-unconstitutional, accessed 20 January 2022.

30. By 2020, the UK was the world leader in offshore wind, with more installed capacity than any other country, powering the equivalent of 4.5 million homes annually and generating over 10 per cent of the UK's electricity. UK Research and Innovation, 'Harnessing offshore wind',

https://www.ukri.org/our-work/responding-to-climate-change/topical-stories/harnessing-offshore-wind, accessed 8 February 2022.

31. Halpern, David, Clive Bates, Geoff Mulgan, and Stephen Aldridge, with Greg Beales and Adam Heathfield, 'Personal responsibility and changing behaviour: the state of knowledge and its implications for public policy,' Prime Minister's Strategy Unit, 2004. This was circulated within government in 2002 and published in early 2004: https://webarchive.nationalarchives.gov.uk/ukgwa/+/http:/www.cabinetoffice.gov.uk/media/cabinetoffice/strategy/assets/pr2.pdf, accessed 20 January 2022.

32. I've written elsewhere about the science of meetings and how to run better ones. See the chapter on meetings in my book *Big Mind* (Princeton, NJ: Princeton University Press, 2017).

33. Magnetic South, https://www.iftf.org/our-work/people-technology/games/magnetic-south, accessed 20 January 2022.

34. Lyn Gardner, 'Early Days (of a Better Nation) review—your country and this play need you', *The Guardian*, 18 November 2014, https://www.theguardian.com/stage/2014/nov/18/early-days-of-a-better-nation-review-coney, accessed 20 January 2022.

35. Finsbury Park's 2019 Citizen Sci-Fi Programme, 'Time Portals': https://www.artrabbit.com/events/2019-citizen-scifi-programme-time-portals, accessed 20 January 2022.

36. In a similar spirit, other techniques have used digital technologies to engage people in scanning, exploring and forecasting the future, such as FutureCoast: https://onca.org.uk/event/futurecoast-launch-help-us-hear-our-futures, accessed 20 January 2022.

37. Unfortunately, however, less thought had been given to what to do with this outpouring of thoughtful reflection, and within a few months, the financial crisis had sharply refocused attention back onto immediate difficulties (which, perhaps thanks to skilled leadership, Australia handled better than almost any other country).

38. The Emerging Futures Fund, https://www.tnlcommunityfund.org.uk/funding/programmes/emerging-futures-fund, accessed 20 January 2022.

39. My friend and collaborator François Taddei at the Center for Research

and Interdisciplinarity in Paris is one of the world's great pioneers of reconnecting education and imagination.

40. Literature offers plenty of prompts, many very accessible to children. Montesquieu's *Persian Letters* were a good example. They imagined a visitor from Persia seeing France through fresh eyes, recognising the strangeness and arbitrariness of the arrangements that were taken for granted, and so helping to liberate people from overestimating the stability of the world. Today we might imagine a visitor from Mars. Antoine de Saint-Exupéry's great book *The Little Prince* plays a similar role, imagining the hero travelling from planet to planet, each quite distinct. But it's possible to go further and imagine whole worlds. How would they eat? How would they live together? What would it be like to live on this planet? Who would thrive; who might not? Would it crash or grow? What would the neighbours do—would they invade if they were jealous?

6. FROM IDEAS TO ACTION: POSSIBILITIES FOR THE DECADES AHEAD

1. Friedman, Milton, *Capitalism and Freedom*, Chicago, IL: University of Chicago Press, 1962.
2. Gramsci, Antonio, *Selections from the Prison Notebooks*, 'Wave of Materialism' and 'Crisis of Authority', New York, NY: International Publishers, 1971, pp. 275–276.
3. Here I offer parts and fragments, in the spirit of my broader argument that real social programmes are assemblies of multiple elements. I don't, for example, offer a complete alternative to capitalism, though a previous book of mine did try exactly this, covering everything from culture to relationships, manufacturing to banking. Mulgan, Geoff, *The Locust and the Bee: Predators and Creators in Capitalism's Future*, Princeton, NJ: Princeton University Press, 2013.
4. Wilde, Oscar, 'The Soul of Man Under Socialism', *Fortnightly Review*, February 1891.
5. Other factors include globalisation, 24-hour social media and perhaps more highly educated people competing for jobs. But even if these factors weren't in play, my guess is that working hours at the top might still be rising.

6. Keynes, John Maynard, 'Economic Possibilities for Our Grandchildren', *Essays in Persuasion*, New York, NY: W.W. Norton & Co., 1963, pp. 358–373.

7. More recently, I was fascinated by the similar analysis of artificial intelligence by Kate Crawford, which again anatomised its uses of materials and energy, and the true patterns hidden beneath the surface of the market economy and never taught in economics textbooks. These were truly new ways of seeing and thinking as well as new ways of doing, and although they are now much more mainstream, they are still the exceptions, not the rule.

8. I set out some of these ideas in a comprehensive analysis of the UK's needs in the late 2000s, working with Claus Moser and Rushanara Ali. We advocated a shift in focus towards issues such as mental health and isolation. Unfortunately, the work coincided with the financial crisis and the start of a decade of retreat and austerity in social policy. However, in the 2020s, interest has returned to these issues, in part because of the very visible mental health effects of the COVID-19 pandemic. The Young Foundation, https://www.youngfoundation.org/publications/sinking-and-swimming, accessed 24 January 2022.

9. Wellcome, 'Wellcome Global Monitor 2020: Mental health', 20 October 2021, https://wellcome.org/reports/wellcome-global-monitor-mental-health/2020, accessed 24 January 2022.

10. Solnit, Rebecca, *Orwell's Roses*, London: Granta, 2021.

7. SOURCES: WHERE DO IDEAS COME FROM?

1. See the work of linguist Leonard Talmy, in particular, *Toward a Cognitive Semantics, Volume 1: Concept Structuring Systems*, and *Volume 2: Typology and Process in Concept Structuring*, Cambridge, MA: MIT Press, 2000/2002.

2. Todd, Emmanuel, *The Explanation of Ideology*, Oxford: Blackwell, 1985.

3. However, they also acknowledge that a viable synthesis of psychology and economics at both the individual and the collective level remains distant. Akerlof, George and Robert J. Shiller, *Animal Spirits: How Human Psychology Drives the Economy and Why It Matters for Global Capitalism*, Princeton, NJ: Princeton University Press, 2009.

4. Anderson, Benedict, *Imagined Communities*, London: Verso, 1983; Taylor, Charles, *Modern Social Imaginaries*, Durham, NC: Duke University Press, 2003. Cornelius Castoriadis' *L'Institution imaginaire de la société* (translated into English by Kathleen Blamey in 1987 as *The Imaginary Institution of Society*, Cambridge, MA: MIT Press) took a similar stance. Another angle on this is Jens Beckert's *Imagined Futures: Fictional Expectations and Capitalist Dynamics* (Cambridge, MA: Harvard University Press, 2016), which examines how, when imagined futures fail to materialise, dynamics of alienation are produced.

5. Jameson, Fredric, *Archaeologies of the Future: The Desire Called Utopia and Other Science Fictions*, London: Verso, 2005, p. 283.

6. Wars and civil wars are also uncomfortable crucibles of imagination, though there are exceptions—like Gerrard Winstanley and the Levellers, who flourished during the vicious English Civil War, part of a vivid subculture of pamphleteering and radical thought depicted in Christopher Hill's classic *The World Turned Upside Down*, London: Temple Smith, 1972.

7. Nietzsche, Friedrich, 'Zarathustra's Prologue', in *Thus Spoke Zarathustra*, Walter Kaufmann (trans.), New York, NY: Penguin, 1978.

8. Mumford, Lewis, *The City in History: Its Origins, Its Transformations, and Its Prospects*, New York, NY: Harcourt, Brace & World, 1961.

9. Taylor, Helen, Brice Fernandes, and Sarah Wraight, 'The evolution of complementary cognition: humans cooperatively adapt and evolve through a system of collective cognitive search', *Cambridge Archaeological Journal* 32(1), 2022.

10. Shakespeare, William, *A Midsummer Night's Dream*, Act 5, Scene 1.

11. To use the phrase suggested by Flores, Fernando, Hubert L. Dreyfus, and Charles Spinosa, *Disclosing New Worlds: Entrepreneurship, Democratic Action, and the Cultivation of Solidarity*, Cambridge, MA: MIT Press, 1997.

12. Elster, Jon, *Explaining Social Behaviour: More Nuts and Bolts for the Social Sciences*, Cambridge, UK & New York, NY: Cambridge University Press, 2007, p. 379.

13. Rittel and Webber contrasted these with tame, soluble problems or ones where there was a single answer. They thought problems could be wicked either because there was no chance of a consensus about

what the societal good should be or because the nature of the problem made it difficult to experiment or test alternatives. This postulation meant that many of the most important problems were essentially insoluble, fuelling a profound pessimism about the possibility of social progress or planning. Rittel, Horst W.J. and Melvin M. Webber, 'Dilemmas in a general theory of planning', *Policy Sciences* 4(2), 1973, pp. 155–169.

14. Examining perturbations in dynamic systems, biologist Ilya Prigogine developed interesting theoretical perspectives on this idea in his co-written book with Isabelle Stengers, *Order Out of Chaos: Man's New Dialogue with Nature*, London: Verso, 1984.

8. PATHWAYS: WHERE DO IDEAS GO?

1. Blake, William, 'The Marriage of Heaven and Hell', in John Sampson (ed.), *The Poetical Works of William Blake*, London: Oxford University Press, 1925, p. 251.

2. Beckert, Jens, *Imagined Futures: Fictional Expectations and Capitalist Dynamics*, Cambridge, MA: Harvard University Press, 2016, p. 85.

3. Tocqueville, Alexis de, *Democracy in America*, New York, NY: G. Dearborn & Co., 1838.

4. Granovetter, Mark S., 'The Strength of Weak Ties', *American Journal of Sociology* 78(6), 1973, pp. 1360–1380.

5. Centola, Damon, *How Behaviour Spreads: The Science of Complex Contagions*, Princeton, NJ: Princeton University Press, 2018, pp. 32–33.

6. Milkoreit, Manjana, Anne R. Kapuscinski, Kim Locke, and Alastair Iles, 'Imaginary politics: Climate change and making the future', *Elementa: Science of the Anthropocene* 5, 2017, p. 62.

7. Mao Zedong, quoted in Dittmer, Lowell, *Liu Shaoqi and the Chinese Cultural Revolution*, Abingdon, UK & New York, NY: Routledge, 2015 (rev. ed.), p. 109.

8. Cialdini, Robert, *Influence: The Psychology of Persuasion*, New York, NY: Morrow, 1993.

9. THE LIMITS OF IMAGINATION

1. Sapolsky, Robert, in 'Human Nature talk with Robert Sapolsky, Gabor

Mate, James Gilligan, Richard Wilkinson' (29:26), YouTube, 28 December 2011, https://www.youtube.com/watch?v=o-brqskIoBw, accessed 27 January 2022.

2. David Graeber and David Wengrow's *The Dawn of Everything: A New History of Humanity* (London: Allen Lane, 2021) is an interesting recent overview (though much criticised for its detailed claims).

3. Marx, Karl, *The Poverty of Philosophy*, Moscow: Progress Publishers, 1955 [1847].

10. DANGEROUS IMAGINATION

1. Arendt, Hannah, *Totalitarianism: Part Three of The Origins of Totalitarianism*, New York, NY: Harcourt, 1968, p. 51.

2. Brecht, Bertolt, 'Hollywood Elegies', Adam Kirsch (trans.), in *Poetry* 198(3), 2011, p. 247.

3. Harry Frankfurt, in his famous book *On Bullshit* (Princeton, NJ: Princeton University Press, 2005), wrote: 'Bullshit is unavoidable whenever circumstances require someone to talk without knowing what he is talking about. Thus the production of bullshit is stimulated whenever a person's obligations or opportunities to speak about some topic are more excessive than his knowledge of the facts that are relevant to that topic ... The lack of any significant connection between a person's opinions and his apprehension of reality will be even more severe, needless to say, for someone who believes it his responsibility, as a conscientious moral agent, to evaluate events and conditions in all parts of the world.'

4. Le Guin, Ursula K., 'The Creatures on My Mind', in *Unlocking the Air and Other Stories*, New York, NY: HarperCollins, 1996, p. 65.

5. Sinclair, Upton, *I, Candidate for Governor*, New York, NY: Farrar & Rinehart, 1935.

6. Diehl, Paul F. and Gary Goertz, *War and Peace in International Rivalry*, Ann Arbor, MI: University of Michigan Press, 2001.

7. Enzensberger, Hans Magnus, *Dreamers of the Absolute*, London: Radius, 1988.

8. Ibid., p. 192.

11. COMPETING POLITICAL IMAGINARIES

1. Orwell, George, *Nineteen Eighty-Four: A Novel*, London: Secker & Warburg, 1949.

2. Lenin was interested in a comment by Dmitry Pisarev: 'The rift between dreams and reality causes no harm if only the person dreaming believes seriously in his dream, if he attentively observes life, compares his observations with his castles in the air and if, generally speaking, he works conscientiously for the achievement of his fantasies. If there is some connection between dreams and life then all is well.' Lenin adds: 'Of this kind of dreaming there is unfortunately too little in our movement' (*What Is to Be Done?*, S.V. Utechin (ed.), S.V. Utechin and Patricia Utechin (trans.), Oxford: Clarendon Press, 1963, p. 211). Ernst Bloch wrote, 'The point of contact between dreams and life, without which dreams only yield abstract utopia, life only triviality, is given in the utopian capacity which is set on its feet and connected to the Real-Possible' (*The Principle of Hope*, Oxford, UK: Blackwell, 1986, pp. 145–146).

3. A recent publication put it like this: 'At the end of the twentieth century and the beginning of the twenty-first, stimulated and encouraged by theories of "new empire" from Europe and America and with the "rise of a great nation" as its political background, the Chinese intellectual arena witnessed an attempt to formulate a program to substitute a reinterpreted ancient Chinese tianxia or "All Under Heaven" for the current world order.' Wang, David Der-wei, Angela Ki Che Leung, and Zhang Yinde (eds), *Utopia and Utopianism in the Contemporary Chinese Context: Texts, Ideas, Spaces*, Hong Kong: Hong Kong University Press, 2020, p. 32. Some Chinese scholars argue that the ancient Chinese concept of 'All Under Heaven' can be transformed into a new form of 'Sinocentrism' to reshape the contemporary world order, leading the world from the age of chaos through the age of order and into the age of great peace, following the ancient theory of the three stages of history. They suggest ancient China had already designed a world system with no distinctions between big and small nations, or civilised and backward peoples.

4. Ibid.

5. Wang Huning, *America Against America*, 1991, English translation available at: https://dokumen.pub/america-against-america.html, accessed 28 January 2022.

6. Bicchieri, Cristina, *The Grammar of Society: The Nature and Dynamics of Social Norms*, Cambridge: Cambridge University Press, 2006.

7. We can never easily judge just how worried to be. For as long as I can remember, we have been told by some that the world has no time left, that this is our last chance to save the environment, and indeed there are good reasons for campaigners to want to shock and frighten their audiences. For all the detailed modelling by the Intergovernmental Panel on Climate Change and others, there is a huge amount that isn't known about the potential feedback effects of a climate undergoing transformations. But the worst-case scenarios, which are often picked up by the media because of their dramatic interest, can encourage fatalism as well as action. This recent article provides a thoughtful articulation of a more sceptical position: Chivers, Tom, 'The great climate change fallacy', *Unherd*, 2 November 2021, https://unherd.com/2021/11/the-great-climate-change-fallacy, accessed 28 January 2022.

8. This was and is the promise of the study of emergence, complexity and the self-organising characteristics of systems, which show the deep roots of cooperation, and the many ways that inert matter becomes life. Theories of complexity have shown that there can be hierarchies without dominance and that order isn't always oppression. Indeed, the crucial insight of systems thinking was that wholes cannot be explained by their parts. You can describe a molecule by mapping its atoms, but you can't meaningfully explain it or predict its behaviour. You can describe the chemistry of the brain, but, again, that helps you explain very little. Similarly, you can describe the individuals who make up a community, but that will prove of little use in predicting the dynamics of that community. Each higher level of organisation transcends the ones below it, while still being dependent on them. This is even more true of the world of knowledge, consciousness and thought, which depends on a material base and the energy-hungry brain, but also transcends it.

9. Excellent gatherings of these ideas can be found in books by Kate Raworth and Rutger Bregman, amongst others.

10. I've argued elsewhere why these mongrel patterns are universal—why all societies and organisations are assemblies of hierarchy, individualism and egalitarianism, with their diverse cultures complementing each other. See Mulgan, Geoff, *Social Innovation*, Bristol: Policy Press, 2019, Chapter 10.

12. IMAGINING GOVERNMENT IN NEW WAYS

1. For example: Gray, Pat and Paul 't Hart, *Public Policy Disasters in Western Europe*, London: Routledge, 1998; King, Anthony and Ivor Crewe, *The Blunders of our Governments*, London: Oneworld, 2014; Jennings, Will, Martin Lodge, and Matt Ryan, 'Comparing blunders in government', *European Journal of Political Research* 57(1), 2018, pp. 238–258; Oppermann, Kai and Alexander Spencer, 'Telling stories of failure: narrative constructions of foreign policy fiascos,' *Journal of European Public Policy* 23(5), 2016, pp. 685–701; Bach, Tobias and Kai Wegrich, *The Blind Spots of Public Bureaucracy and the Politics of Non-Coordination*, Basingstoke, Hampshire: Palgrave Macmillan, 2018; Bovens, Mark and Paul 't Hart, *Understanding Policy Fiascos*, New Brunswick, NJ: Transaction Publishers, 1998; and Light, Paul C., 'A Cascade of Failures: Why Government Fails, and How to Stop It', Brookings Institution, 14 July 2014: https://wagner.nyu.edu/files/faculty/publications/Light_Cascade_of_Failures_Why_Govt_Fails.pdf, accessed 29 January 2022.

2. Diamond, Jared, *Collapse: How Societies Choose to Fail or Survive*, London: Allen Lane, 2005; Levitsky, Steven and Daniel Ziblatt, *This Is How Democracies Die: What History Reveals About Our Future*, London: Penguin, 2018.

3. Weber, Max, *The Protestant Ethic and the Spirit of Capitalism*, London & Boston, MA: Unwin Hyman, 1930.

4. James Scott's book *Against the Grain: A Deep History of the Earliest States* (New Haven: Yale University Press, 2017) is an eloquent explanation of how, for many people, the arrival of the state, as well as the separate arrival of agriculture, marked a decline in well-being and freedom.

5. Rees, Martin, 'If I ruled the world: Martin Rees', *Prospect*, 21 August 2014, https://www.prospectmagazine.co.uk/magazine/if-i-ruled-the-world-martin-rees, accessed 29 January 2022.

6. Heilmann, Sebastian, 'From Local Experiments to National Policy: The Origins of China's Distinctive Policy Process', *The China Journal* 59, 2008, pp. 1–30.

7. A recent Nesta report that I helped to write provided an overview of the many methods available to governments: Hopkins, Anna and Jonathan Breckon, 'The Experimenter's Inventory', Nesta, 21 January 2020, https://www.nesta.org.uk/report/experimenters-inventory, accessed 30 January 2022.

13. IMAGINING A MORE ADVANCED CONSCIOUSNESS AND A WISER SOCIETY

1. Carey, John, 'Introduction', in Carey, John (ed.), *The Faber Book of Utopias*, London: Faber & Faber, 2000.

2. Perhaps this is why literature emphasises leaps of faith. One character in Ursula Le Guin's *The Dispossessed* (New York, NY: Harper & Row, 1974) delivers a key speech which sums up some similar sentiments: 'We have no law but the single principle of mutual aid between individuals. We have no government but the single principle of free association. We have no states, no nations, no presidents, no premiers, no chiefs, no generals, no bosses, no bankers, no landlords, no wages, no charity, no police, no soldiers, no wars. Nor do we have much else. We are sharers, not owners. We are not prosperous. None of us is rich. None of us is powerful. ... if it is the future you seek, then I tell you that you must come to it with empty hands. You must come to it alone, and naked, as the child comes into the world, into his future, without any past, without any property, wholly dependent on other people for his life. You cannot take what you have not given, and you must give yourself. You cannot buy the Revolution. You cannot make the Revolution. You can only be the Revolution. It is in your spirit, or it is nowhere.'

3. Rousseau, who attempted to understand these shifts of consciousness, and arguably was one of the greatest contributors to them, suggested that they require 'a superior intelligence, capable of contemplating all human passions without feeling any of them'. See *Oeuvres complètes*, Bernard Gagnebin and Marcel Raymond (eds and trans.), Paris: Gallimard, 1959–1995, p. 381.

4. Mills, Charles Wright, *The Sociological Imagination*, New York, NY: Oxford University Press, 1959, p. 7.

5. For a well-informed recent book, see, for example, Mark Moffett's *Human Swarm* (London: Head of Zeus, 2019).

6. There are many flaws in arguments claiming a linear progression of consciousness in definable phases, including a general lack of hard evidence and lots of contradictions—some of which I set out in the final chapter of my book *Big Mind* (Princeton, NJ: Princeton University Press, 2017) and others of which are laid out in a punchy review by Zaid Hassan: 'Is Teal The New Black? Probably Not', Social Labs Blog 2.0, 13 July 2015, https://social-labs.org/is-teal-the-new-black, accessed 30 January 2022.

7. Confucius, whose life was full of disappointments, himself said: 'By three methods we may learn wisdom: First, by reflection, which is noblest; second, by imitation, which is easiest; and third by experience, which is the bitterest.'

8. Harold Bloom's *Where Shall Wisdom Be Found?* is one good overview of some of this literature (New York, NY: Riverhead Books, 2004).

9. See, for example, the writings of Tyson Yunkaporta, which include a critique of Plato for crushing contextual, linked thinking in favour of separating out concepts, ideas and knowledge.

10. Clayton, V.P., 'Wisdom and intelligence: the nature and function of knowledge in the later years', *International Journal of Aging and Human Development* 15, 1982, pp. 315–321.

11. Emerson, Ralph Waldo, *Self-Reliance*, White Plains, NY: Peter Pauper Press, 1967 [1841].

12. The group called 'The Elders'—part-founded by Nelson Mandela—was an interesting example of this approach while also showing its limitations: https://www.theelders.org, accessed 2 February 2022.

13. This was the topic of a *Daedalus* issue edited by Benjamin Schwartz, 'Wisdom, Revelation and Doubt: perspectives on the first millennium BC', 104(2), 1975. I also cover this question in my essay in Christie, Ian and Lindsay Nash (eds), *The Good Life*, London: Demos, 1999: https://www.demos.co.uk/files/thegoodlife.pdf, accessed 2 February 2022.

14. See https://evidencebasedwisdom.com, accessed 30 January 2022; Hall, Stephen, *Wisdom: From Philosophy to Neuroscience*, New York, NY: Alfred A. Knopf, 2010; and Jeste, Dili et al., 'The New Science of Practical Wisdom', *Perspectives in Biology and Medicine* 62(2), pp. 216–236.

15. The Berlin Wisdom Study under Paul Baltes came up with a definition of wisdom; they found that it was scarce and that it peaks at around the age of sixty. Baltes, Paul, and Ursula Staudinger, 'Wisdom: A meta-heuristic (pragmatic) to orchestrate mind and virtue toward excellence', *American Psychologist* 55, 2000, pp. 122–136.

16. I cover this in my book *Big Mind* (Princeton, NJ: Princeton University Press, 2017).

17. Much writing on wisdom implies that the writer is wise and offers insights from a uniquely advanced standpoint. I make no such claim; indeed, I've found it most useful to address this field through reflecting on the many times when I have *not* acted wisely.

18. Burke, Edmund, *Reflections on the Revolution in France*, Pall Mall, London: James Dodsley, 1790.

19. William Whewell, in his book *The Philosophy of the Inductive Sciences* (London: John W. Parker, 1840), coined the word 'consilience' to describe what happens 'when an induction, obtained from one class of facts, coincides with an induction, obtained from another class. This Consilience is a test of the truth of the Theory in which it occurs'. Quoted in Wilson, E.O., *Consilience: The Unity of Knowledge*, London: Abacus, 1998, p. 7.

20. This is addressed well in the work of Scott Page, including in *The Model Thinker: What You Need to Know to Make Data Work for You*, New York, NY: Basic Books, 2018.

21. Shirado, H. and N.A. Christakis, 'Locally Noisy Autonomous Agents Improve Global Human Coordination in Network Experiments', *Nature* 545, 2017, pp. 370–374.

22. As Oliver Wendell Holmes Jr put it: 'I would not give a fig for the simplicity this side of complexity, but I would give my life for the simplicity on the other side of complexity.'

23. It is perhaps not so far from the idea of *Bildung*, the self-cultivation

of character, which is credited with giving some nations their success and is also nurtured in the everyday practice of the great religions at their best, though it has fewer obvious homes in modern secular societies. A useful current example of a think tank focused on *Bildung* is https://nordicbildung.org, accessed 30 January 2022.

24. To use the language of conflict resolution, such as in Shapiro, Daniel, *Negotiating the Nonnegotiable: How to Resolve Your Most Emotionally Charged Conflicts*, New York, NY: Penguin Books, 2017.

25. For a very useful survey of research combining artificial intelligence and collective intelligence, see Berditchevskaia, Aleks and Konstantinos Stathoulopoulos, 'Is AI causing collective intelligence research to become less diverse?', Nesta, 16 June 2020, https://www.nesta.org.uk/project-updates/ai-ci-researchmapping, accessed 30 January 2022.

26. Berditchevskaia, Aleks and Peter Baeck, 'AI and Collective Intelligence: case studies', Nesta, https://www.nesta.org.uk/feature/ai-and-collective-intelligence-case-studies, accessed 30 January 2022.

27. This work can also draw on interesting mathematical approaches such as 'distributed Thompson sampling', which is designed to choose from actions with unknown results in ways that combine exploitation and exploration, and which can be adapted to combine sampling of views from a group. Granmo, Ole-Christoffer and Sondre Glimsdal, 'Accelerated Bayesian learning for decentralized two-armed bandit based decision making with applications to the Goore game', *Applied Intelligence* 38(4), 2013, pp. 479–488. Generative, evolutionary and distributed AI or even recommender systems could help us to extend cognitive boundaries to achieve more awareness of perspectives and contexts, enabling the training of wisdom.

28. In the early 2000s, I helped to design a knowledge management system for the UK government that was never implemented (I was head of the government's Strategy Unit at the time). I'm sure it would have paid for itself many times over. Consultancies tend to do this best— partly because they have the authority to impose rules, such as requiring people to share knowledge; partly because individual consultants and partners become curators of fields of knowledge; and partly because they have the resources to invest heavily in technical systems.

29. I tried to persuade various people at Google of this in the early 2000s, but with no success. I co-wrote a parallel proposal for the BBC—to improve standards of truth in cyberspace—but this too failed to win an audience. Mulgan, Geoff, Tom Steinberg, and Omar Salem, *Wide Open: Open Source Methods and Their Future Potential*, London: Demos, 2005.

30. This is the claim of the Actor–Network Theory movement, founded by Bruno Latour.

31. A fuller version of this material on wisdom can be found in my 2021 paper for Demos Helsinki, 'Loops for Wisdom': https://demoshel-sinki.fi/julkaisut/loops-for-wisdom-cultivate-wisdom-in-society, accessed 30 January 2022.

14. SITUATING IMAGINATION IN TIME

1. Russell, Bertrand, *What I Believe*, London: Kegan Paul, Trench, Trubner & Co., 1925.

2. The word 'exponential' is often misunderstood as meaning fast. In fact, exponential trends can be quite slow—but remorseless.

3. Diebolt, Claude and Michael Diebolt (eds), *Handbook of Cliometrics*, 2nd ed., Berlin, Heidelberg: Springer, 2019; Turchin, Peter, *Ultrasociety: How 10,000 Years of War Made Humans the Greatest Cooperators on Earth*, Chaplin, CT: Beresta Books, 2016.

4. The Scottish philosopher David Hume argued that 'The origin of civil government is that men are not able radically to cure, either in themselves or others, that narrowness of soul, which makes them prefer the present to the remote.' In other words, government is in part a collective device for thinking ahead, and part of what we might seek from future states is a better ability to do this. But there is no guarantee that they will fulfil this responsibility.

5. Fisher, Richard, 'The perils of short-termism: Civilisation's greatest threat', BBC Future, 10 January 2019, https://www.bbc.com/future/article/20190109-the-perils-of-short-termism-civilisations-greatest-threat, accessed 30 January 2022.

6. Krznaric, Roman, 'Future generations deserve good ancestors. Will you be one?', Psyche, 21 July 2020, https://psyche.co/ideas/future-genera-

tions-deserve-good-ancestors-will-you-be-one, accessed 30 January 2022.

7. Joyce, James, *Ulysses*, Part II, Paris: Shakespeare and Company, 1922.

15. THE ROLE OF ART IN SOCIAL IMAGINATION

1. A much fuller version of this chapter will be published as the book *Prophets at a Tangent*, Cambridge: Cambridge University Press, 2022.

2. McLuhan, Marshall, 'Introduction to the Second Edition', in *Understanding Media: The Extensions of Man*, 2nd ed., New York: McGraw-Hill, 1964.

3. Samuel Beckett, quoted in Driver, Tom F., 'Beckett by the Madeleine', *Columbia University Forum* 4(3), Summer 1961, pp. 21–25.

4. Keats, John, *The Complete Poetical Works and Letters of John Keats*, Cambridge Edition, Boston & New York: Houghton, Mifflin and Company, 1899, p. 277.

5. Coleridge, Samuel Taylor, *Biographia Literaria*, Oxford: Clarendon Press, 1907.

6. They were in turn influenced by philosophical shifts that transformed how imagination was conceived of, through works by Aristotle, Kant, Schelling, Hegel, Heidegger and many others. This is a long, complex and winding story, but it has taken imagination from being part of how we know the world to a means for knowing what does not yet exist; from being something primarily individual to something collective; from being transcendent to being located within history; and from connecting us to a single absolute truth to a recognition that the great power of imagination is to open up a multitude of possible truths.

7. Beuys, Joseph, 'I Am Searching for Field Character', first published in English in Tisdall, Caroline, *Art into Society, Society into Art*, London: ICA, 1974, p. 48.

8. Gerhard Richter in a note to himself (1964–1965), in Elger, Dietmar and Hans Ulrich Obrist (eds), *Text: Writings, Interviews and Letters 1961–2007*, London: Thames & Hudson, 2009, pp. 32–33.

9. Magnason, Andri Snær, 'The glaciers of Iceland seemed eternal. Now a country mourns their loss', *The Guardian*, 14 August 2019, https://www.theguardian.com/commentisfree/2019/aug/14/glaciers-iceland-country-loss-plaque-climate-crisis, accessed 31 January 2022.

10. Fisher, Mark, *Capitalist Realism: Is There No Alternative?*, Winchester: Zero Books, 2009.

11. Architecture has also, for that matter, critiqued the bland conformism of buildings and their functional soullessness, as in the work of the Italian group Archizoom. Sarkis, Hashim, Roi Salgueiro Barrio, and Gabriel Kozlowski (eds), *The World as an Architectural Project*, Cambridge, MA: MIT Press, 2020.

12. Watlington, Emily, 'A History of Architects Mistaking Design for Politics', *Art in America*, 7 June 2020, https://www.artnews.com/art-in-america/aia-reviews/world-architectural-project-mit-press-hashim-sarkis-architecture-politics-1202690156, accessed 31 January 2022.

13. Schacter, Daniel L., Donna Rose Addis, Demis Hassabis, Victoria C. Martin, R. Nathan Spreng, and Karl K. Szpunar, 'The Future of Memory: Remembering, Imagining, and the Bsrain', *Neuron* 76(4), 2012, pp. 677–694.

14. An intriguing (if sometimes confusing) discussion of these issues can be found here: http://arsindustrialis.org/anamnesis-and-hypomnesis, accessed 31 January 2022.

15. Gilbert Simondon's ideas about being with technologies and machines; learning to overcome our alienation from machines; and machines as open and rich in potential are also relevant here. See the introduction of his book *Du mode d'existence des objets techniques*, Paris: Éditions Aubier-Montaigne, 1958.

16. Bourriaud, Nicolas, *Relational Aesthetics [Esthetique relationnelle]*, Simon Pleasance, Fronza Woods, and Mathieu Copeland (trans.), Dijon: Les Presses du Réel, 2002.

16. WHAT TO DO?

1. Shakespeare, William, *Hamlet*, Act 1, Scene 5.

2. Olufemi, Lola, *Experiments in Imagining Otherwise*, London: Hajar Press, 2021, p. 135.

3. In an ideal world, we might be able to measure social imagination, i.e. the quantity and quality of plans and options for the future; and how well these represent the true aspirations of the people. For now, there is no such metric and a degree of risk in trying to create one. As Daniel

Yankelovich put it: 'The first step is to measure whatever can be easily measured. The second step is to disregard that which can't be easily measured ... The third step is to presume that what can't be measured easily really isn't important ... The fourth step is to say that what can't be easily measured really doesn't exist.' *Corporate Priorities: A Continuing Study of the New Demands of Business*, Stanford, CT: Yankelovich Inc., 1972.

4. There are many prototypes of these. A generation ago, the Institute for Social Inventions played this role, and current ones include whatisemerging.com or the gatherings of projects like Atlas of the Future

5. Reich, Rob, *Just Giving: Why Philanthropy Is Failing Democracy and How It Can Do Better*, Princeton, NJ: Princeton University Press, 2018

6. Imaginable Futures, https://www.imaginablefutures.com, accessed 1 February 2022.

7. Wellbeing Economy Governments, https://wellbeingeconomy.or wego, accessed 1 February 2022.

8. Dewey, John, *The Public and Its Problems*, New York: Henry H 1927.

9. Le Guin, Ursula K., 'Telling Is Listening', *The Wave in the Mind: T and Essays on the Writer, the Reader, and the Imagination*, Boston, N Shambhala, 2004.

10. Dante Alighieri, *The Divine Comedy: Purgatory*, Canto 33, 143–1

APPENDIX 2: SOME PROMPTS FOR IMAGINATION

1. See, for example, the many materials gathered at the Com Transition Platform: https://commonstransition.org, accessed 1 Feb 2022.

2. According to the site pollution.org.

3. At Nesta, for example, I helped commission a simple online tool t teachers in designing and running randomised control trials teaching methods, a small example of how, in principle, every f become a generator as well as a user of knowledge.

Yankelovich put it: 'The first step is to measure whatever can be easily measured. The second step is to disregard that which can't be easily measured ... The third step is to presume that what can't be measured easily really isn't important ... The fourth step is to say that what can't be easily measured really doesn't exist.' *Corporate Priorities: A Continuing Study of the New Demands of Business*, Stanford, CT: Yankelovich Inc., 1972.

4. There are many prototypes of these. A generation ago, the Institute for Social Inventions played this role, and current ones include whatisemerging.com or the gatherings of projects like Atlas of the Future.

5. Reich, Rob, *Just Giving: Why Philanthropy Is Failing Democracy and How It Can Do Better*, Princeton, NJ: Princeton University Press, 2018.

6. Imaginable Futures, https://www.imaginablefutures.com, accessed 1 February 2022.

7. Wellbeing Economy Governments, https://wellbeingeconomy.org/wego, accessed 1 February 2022.

8. Dewey, John, *The Public and Its Problems*, New York: Henry Holt, 1927.

9. Le Guin, Ursula K., 'Telling Is Listening', *The Wave in the Mind: Talks and Essays on the Writer, the Reader, and the Imagination*, Boston, MA: Shambhala, 2004.

10. Dante Alighieri, *The Divine Comedy: Purgatory*, Canto 33, 143–145.

APPENDIX 2: SOME PROMPTS FOR IMAGINATION

1. See, for example, the many materials gathered at the Commons Transition Platform: https://commonstransition.org, accessed 1 February 2022.

2. According to the site pollution.org.

3. At Nesta, for example, I helped commission a simple online tool to assist teachers in designing and running randomised control trials of new teaching methods, a small example of how, in principle, every field can become a generator as well as a user of knowledge.

ACKNOWLEDGEMENTS

I am hugely grateful to the many people I've talked to about the ideas in this book, only a few of whom there is space to thank here. In particular, Juha Leppanen and his colleagues at Demos Helsinki gave me a platform to publish a first set of ideas, 'The Imaginary Crisis', which then fed into the Untitled Festivals, a collaborative project of dozens of organisations across the world. I've also shared some of these ideas at online events from Brazil and Australia to Singapore and Canada, which encouraged me to flesh out my arguments.

Oliver Marsh helped with editing; Samantha Harvey guided me on some of the literature on imagination; Toby Mundy helped shape the book; Karina Dobrotvorskaya gave me many steers on both content and form; Roberto Mangabeira Unger was a constant companion for stimulating dialogues (and I was much influenced by his philosophical perspective). Wilhelm Krull and Georg Diez at the New Institute in Hamburg gave me the opportunity to develop much more detailed ideas on how universities and the social sciences could take things forward (published in the report on 'Exploratory Social Sciences'). Jo Chataway and other colleagues at UCL STEaPP provided feedback and ideas on the relationship between imagination, science and evidence. Cassie Robinson echoed some of the book's ideas in a very imaginative funding programme (Emerging Futures) at the National Lottery Community Fund. Others who have given me invaluable inputs include Rufus Pollock, Gemma Mortensen, Anab Jain and Joshua Ramo.

Imagination itself and writing about imagination are very much collective tasks. Dozens of others can probably see some of their influence in the text. My thanks to all of them; of course, all responsibility for any errors of judgement or fact lies with me alone.

INDEX

INDEX

INDEX

INDEX

INDEX

INDEX

INDEX

INDEX

INDEX

INDEX

INDEX

INDEX

INDEX

INDEX

INDEX

INDEX

INDEX

INDEX

INDEX

INDEX

INDEX

INDEX

INDEX